THE JEWISH SOURCES OF THE SERMON ON THE MOUNT

THE LIBRARY

OF

BIBLICAL STUDIES

Edited by

Harry M. Orlinsky

THE JEWISH SOURCES
OF THE SERMON ON
THE MOUNT

11540

By

GERALD FRIEDLANDER

Prolegomenon By
SOLOMON ZEITLIN

KTAV PUBLISHING HOUSE, INC.

NEW YORK

1969

FIRST PUBLISHED 1911

NEW MATTER
© COPYRIGHT 1969
KTAV PUBLISHING HOUSE, INC.

Library of Congress Catalog Card Number: 67-11897
Manufactured in the United States of America

TO THE MEMORY OF MY REVERED TEACHER

Dr. MICHAEL FRIEDLÄNDER

December 13, 1910; *Kislev* 13, 5671.

CONTENTS

PROLEGOMENON

The Gospel according to Matthew, chapters 5-7, gives a collection of the teachings of Jesus. The evangelist states (5. 1-2) that Jesus "went up on the mountain, and when he sat down his disciples came to him. And he opened his mouth and taught them." These teachings are usually referred to as the Sermon on the Mount. Luke 6.20-49 also records the teachings which Jesus delivered to his disciples. However, he said that Jesus went down from a mountain to a plain where he delivered his sermon (6.17ff.). The collection of the teachings of Jesus in Luke is shorter than that given in Matthew. Many of the sayings of Jesus given in Matthew are not found in Luke. Some of the sayings of Jesus, such as the Lord's Prayer, which are included by Matthew in the Sermon on the Mount, are found in a different chapter in Luke and in another connection. There are many sayings of Jesus in the Sermon on the Mount as given in Matthew that are found in different chapters in Mark.

Many scholars are of the opinion that Matthew utilized Luke and added many sayings. Others are of the opinion that Luke utilized Matthew and deleted or abridged many of the sayings of Jesus. The problem confronting us is that if Luke had before him Matthew, why did he place the Lord's Prayer as given by Matthew in the Sermon on the Mount in a different chapter? Views have been propounded by scholars that Matthew used Mark and, in addition, oral

or written collections of sayings of Jesus which derived
from the Church at Jerusalem.

The Sermon on the Mount was held to be the manifesto
to the Christians. It was also said to be the charter of the
Church. It is the heart of Christianity's ethical and religious
message to mankind. It is held to be a magnificent collection of ethical sayings and a great spiritual message given
to mankind. Many of the sayings are traceable to the Hebrew Bible and the Rabbinic Literature. Some Christian
theologians maintain that the ethical teachings in the Sermon on the Mount are superior to any of the teachings
of Judaism expressed in the Hebrew Bible and in the Rabbinic Literature.

At the end of the nineteenth century some Jewish theologians, particularly in Germany, took issue with Christian
theologians with regard to the ethical values of the Sermon
on the Mount and its relation to Judaism; to mention only
a few: Josef Eschelbacher, Israel Goldschmidt, Moritz
Güdemann, and Judah Bergmann. In England, Claude G.
Montefiore published in 1909 a book on *The Synoptic
Gospels* in which he dealt with the Sermon on the Mount,
and in 1911 Gerald Friedlander published *The Jewish
Sources of the Sermon on the Mount.** Friedlander divided
the Sermon on the Mount into three parts: one is based on
the Hebrew Bible and the Rabbinic Literature; another part
stands in opposition to Jewish teachings; and the third part
is anti-Pharisaic. In his book Friedlander took particular
issue with the statements which Montefiore made in *The
Synoptic Gospels.* However, Montefiore revised his book
and published the new edition in 1927. Thus a number of
statements challenged by Friedlander are not found in the
revised edition.

In the preface of his book, Friedlander took up other
problems in connection with the beginnings of Christianity.
Toward the end of the nineteenth century, Christian intellectuals were shocked by the works of J. M. Robertson,
Pagan Christs, and Arthur C. H. Drews, *The Christ-Myth,*

in which the authors maintained that Jesus was not an historical person but a myth. In his book, *Von Reimarus zu Wrede* (1906), which has been translated into English as *The Quest of the Historical Jesus,* Albert Schweitzer made the following assertion (1948; p. 398): "There is nothing more negative than the result of the critical study of the Life of Jesus. The Jesus of Nazareth who came forward publicly as the Messiah, who preached the ethic of the Kingdom of God, who founded the Kingdom of Heaven upon earth, and died to give His work its final consecration, never had any existence. He is a figure designed by rationalism, endowed with life by liberalism, and clothed by modern theology in an historical garb." Schweitzer's book made a profound impression upon the intellectuals in the English-speaking countries. Friedlander, apprehensive that he might be suspected of being in sympathy with the skeptics, wrote (p. xvii), ". . . I hold no brief for Drews, whose book contains many statements and theories, which I am not prepared to accept." And in another passage (p. xviii) he asserted that he is not prepared to go as far as Drews and Robertson in denying the possibility of the existence of Jesus.

Ever since Scaliger in the sixteenth century, the genuineness of the Christ passage in Josephus has been questioned. Friedlander, in following Niese, whom he regarded as the greatest authority on Josephus, considered this passage to be spurious. I fully share his opinion. In my article on "The Christ Passage in Josephus," *JQR,* 18(1927-28), 231-255, and in Appendix IV in *The Rise and Fall of the Judaean State,* Vol. II, I endeavored to prove that the Christ passage in Josephus was interpolated by the Church Father Eusebius.

Friedlander asks (pp. xii-xiii), ". . . can we accept the New Testament account of the trial of Jesus? Was Jesus sentenced to death by the Sanhedrin in which the Rabbis and Scribes deliberated?" In answering this question, Friedlander accepts the theory propounded by A. Büchler, "who maintains (p. 200) that, in all passages in the Gospels, the word [archiereis] does not mean 'chief priest,' but it should be translated 'temple authorities.' " Friedlander says, "Dr. Büchler argues that in Jerusalem there were two bodies, each called Sanhedrin, but exercising different functions (p. 38). One Sanhedrin had exclusive jurisdiction, as far as the Temple was concerned. It had to decide on the purity of the priests and other matters connected with the Temple (pp. 33ff.). This Sanhedrin was the governing body of the Sanctuary. The High Priest was naturally a member of this body. Dr. Büchler holds that if Jesus was seized, it was by the order of this Temple Sanhedrin, which dealt with his case." Friedlander concludes, "If this be so, Jesus did not appear at all before the other Sanhedrin, which is known to us from the Mishna (Synhedrin, xi, 4). In this body the Scribes and Rabbis deliberated under the presidency of the Nasi."

I rejected Dr. Büchler's theory for several reasons. During the Second Commonwealth the court was designated by the term Bet Din, never by the word Sanhedrin. The word Sanhedrin as applied to the Jewish court came into vogue only after the destruction of the Temple. Furthermore, Jesus was not seized by the order of the Jews but by the order of the Roman authorities. It is true that there was a court called Bet Din Shel Kohanim, the priestly court. This court dealt only with matters which affected the priests. One of its special concerns was the examination of the genealogy of the claimants to the priesthood, to ascertain whether they were bona fide, of priestly stock. It held its sessions in the lishkat ha-gazit, in the Chamber of Hewn Stone.[1] This court did not hold sessions in the house of the High Priest. The Bet Din Shel Kohanim, the priestly court, was never designated by the term Sanhedrin. I advanced the theory that after the establishment of the Second Commonwealth there were two courts in Judaea. One was the Bet Din, later known as Sanhedrin. The Bet Din was a permanent institution which tried religious offenders. Its members were scholars. There was another institution which tried political

offenders. It was not a court in the full sense of the term
but a privy council, and its name was *synedroin*. It was
invoked by the rulers of the state for advice and consultation when the need arose. In this sense it was used by the
Greek historians. When Judaea became a province of
Rome, the High Priests were responsible for the tranquillity
of the country. In dealing with matters concerning the civil
and political life of the people, the High Priests summoned
a council, *synedrion*, where cases were presented. Jesus was
brought before this *synedrion* which was assembled in the
house of the High Priest. I have substantiated this theory
in my book *Who Crucified Jesus?* and also in Appendix X
in the second edition of *The Rise and Fall of the Judaean
State*, Vol. II.

Friedlander raised a vexed question: What should the
Jewish attitude be today toward the teaching of Jesus? He
said (pp. 11-13), "In the past the Jews looked askance
at the Gospels and the other books of the New Testament.
They instinctively avoided all contact with this literature.
The reason for this is to be found in the attitude of the
Church towards the Jews. It was believed that the first duty
of the Church was to convert the Jews. In the Middle Ages
the persecuted Jews were forced to attend church and to
listen to the stories of the Gospels. Again, the Rabbis were
compelled to engage in disputations with renegade Jews
or with learned Christian divines. . . . This frequent experience naturally estranged the Jews from the Church and
her sacred scriptures recorded in the New Testament. . . .
The circumstances in England, both political and intellectual, are different today, and again we ask: What is the
modern Jewish attitude towards the teaching of Jesus?
Christian scholars and apologists are naturally concerned
to demonstrate the superiority of Christian teaching. They
claim that the last word in religion and ethics has been
taught by Jesus. They invite Jews and others to learn
the 'higher morality' revealed in the New Testament. . . .
We are today confronted by honest and well-meaning men,

who ask us to be candid, and to acknowledge that the
moral teaching of Jesus is higher and better than that of
any other teacher. Can we afford to imitate the old Jewish
attitude (which was quite right in the dark days of persecution) and shall we still refuse to read the Gospels or to
discuss their contents? . . . To remain Jews and to refuse
to defend the Jewish religion, or wilfully to ignore the
claims made by Christian teachers, when asserting the absolute superiority of their religion, is a cowardly and irreligious attitude."

The Gospels are acrimonious in their charges against the
Pharisees, whom they called hypocrites. Friedlander made
the following statement (p. 200), "The modern Jew, liberal
or orthodox, is a lineal descendant of the Pharisees of New
Testament times, and their honour and reputation are not
to be lightly attacked."

His book, *The Jewish Sources of the Sermon on the
Mount,* is polemical and apologetic. He argued against the
Christian theologians in defense of Judaism, and he insisted
(pp. IX-X) that ". . . we must compare the teaching of the
Sermon not only with the Old Testament and its Rabbinic
glosses preserved in the Mishna, Tosephta, Gemara, Midrashim and Targumim, but we must refer likewise to the
invaluable Jewish Hellenic literature, which includes the
Septuagint, the Apocrypha, Philo and the Apocalyptic
writings. Without this literature the New Testament could
never have been written."

After the author collated an array of citations, he con-
cluded (p. 266) that "Four-fifths of the Sermon on the
Mount is exclusively Jewish," and declared that "In our
opinion this Pharisaic teaching is infinitely superior to that
of the Gospel" (p. 214).

Friedlander,* in citing the numerous passages from the
Rabbinic Literature, did not apply critical, historical anal-
ysis. He quotes from tannaitic literature, amoraic litera-
ture, and from works composed during the Middle Ages.
He cites statements from *Tanna debe Eliyyahu, Derek Eres
Zuṭa,* and the *Yalkutim,* which were composed during the

Middle Ages. The author's quotations lack historical discipline, and are on a par with the work of H. L. Strack-P.
Billerbeck, *Kommentar zum Neuen Testament aus Talmud
und Midrasch* (1922-26). This work also is an array of
citations from the Talmud and the Midrash but lacking in
critical analysis of the passages which are quoted. The authors disregarded the historical background of the citations.

In his utilization of the tannaitic literature, Friedlander
did not carefully scrutinize the passages to determine whether they really came from the sages said to have uttered
them. There are many statements in the Talmud attributed
to certain sages which were never uttered by them. Thus
the Talmud states that Rabban Jochanan ben Zakkai had
disputations with the Sadducees regarding the Festival of
Weeks and the question of inheritance. But I have recently
pointed out that Jochanan ben Zakkai never had a controversy with the Sadducees on these matters.[1a] Again, an
halakhic statement is recorded in the Talmud in the name
of Samuel which he never could have made.[2] Similarly,
with regard to the Apochryphal and Apocalyptic literature,
the author followed the stereotype view without making a
critical analysis.

The critical historical method which we have to apply
to the Rabbinic Literature must also be applied to the
Sermon on the Mount. The Sermon on the Mount must be
placed in its historical perspective. It is axiomatic that the
sayings of Jesus on the Mount as reported by Matthew
were not put into writing by the disciples at the time that
he spoke. Jesus' disciples had different traditions of his
sayings, and these were not collected until generations after
his death. The Sermon, as given by Matthew, is an agglom-
eration of tradition. It cannot be regarded as a unit; it
must be treated as a collection of sayings drawn from di-
verse times and happenings. Many of the sayings were not
uttered by Jesus, but are the product of the time of the
compilations. Various sayings were incorporated in the
Sermon, so that we find repetitions and contradictions in
the Gospels. Hence in dealing critically with the Sermon on

the Mount, one must take cognizance of the historical background of the sayings.

This is not the place to deal with all the sayings in the Sermon on the Mount. I may have the opportunity to do so in the future. However, I shall deal with certain sayings attributed to Jesus, and cite parallels from the tannaitic literature of the time of the compilation.

THE SERMON ON THE MOUNT

Matt. 5.1-2

¹Seeing the crowds, he went up on the mountain, and when he sat down his disciples came to him. ²And he opened his mouth and taught them, saying,

Luke 6.12-20

¹²In those days he went out into the hills to pray: and all night he continued in prayer to God. ¹³And when it was day, he called his disciples, and chose from them twelve, whom he named apostles . . . ¹⁷And he came down with them and stood on a level place, with a great crowd of his disciples and a great multitude of people. . . . ²⁰And he lifted up his eyes on his disciples, and said,

THE BEATITUDES

Matt. 5.3 ff.

³Happy are the poor in spirit, for theirs is the kingdom of heaven.
⁴Happy are those who mourn, for they shall be comforted.
⁵Happy are the meek, for they shall inherit the earth.
⁶Happy are those who hunger and thirst for righteousness, for they shall be satisfied.

Luke 6.20 ff.

²⁰Happy are the poor, for yours is the kingdom of God.
²¹Happy are you that hunger now, for you shall be satisfied.

The Sermon on the Mount opens with an array of Beatitudes. The English translations begin with the word "Blessed . . ." The Greek word is *makários*. The Septuagint uses this term to render the Hebrew word *ashre*, which means "happy." It is well known that the authors of the Gospels followed the Septuagint version of the Hebrew Bible. Thus the Beatitudes should be rendered: *"Happy are the poor in spirit,"* and the like.

THE TORAH AND THE PROPHETS

In Matt. 5.17-19 the following sayings of Jesus are recorded: "Think not that I have come to abolish the law and the prophets; I have come not to abolish them but to fulfil them. For truly, I say to you, till heaven and earth pass away, not an iota, not a dot, will pass from the law until all is accomplished. Whoever then relaxes one of the least of these commandments and teaches men so, shall be called least in the kingdom of heaven; but he who does them and teaches them shall be called great in the kingdom of heaven." In Luke 16.16-17 it is stated that Jesus said, "The law and the prophets were until John; since then the good news of the kingdom of God is preached, and every one enters it violently. But it is easier for heaven and earth to pass away, than for one dot of the law to become void." In Luke, Jesus said that the Torah and the prophets were until John; and then the gospel of the kingdom of God is to be preached. In Mark 13.31, Luke 21.33, and Matthew 24.35 Jesus said, "Heaven and earth will pass away, but my words will not pass away." Here Jesus said that his words are for all eternity, without mention of the Torah and the prophets.

There is a discrepancy between the sayings of Jesus as given in the Sermon and other sayings of Jesus as recorded in other passages in the Gospels. In the Sermon, Jesus said that the Torah and the prophets are immutable, whereas in other passages Jesus said that his words are immutable, and the Torah and the prophets were until the coming of John. Jesus' words in the Sermon were actually a rebuke to Paul, or rather a rebuke to the followers of Paul. There was a conflict between the disciples of Jesus

and those of Paul. Acts records that when Paul came to
Jerusalem and met with James and the elders, they said to
him (21.20-21) ". . . You see, brother, how many
thousands there are among the Jews of those who have
believed; they are all zealous for the law, and they have
been told about you that you teach all the Jews who are
among the Gentiles to forsake Moses, telling them not to
circumcise their children or ·observe the customs." James
and the apostles wanted to carry on the laws as given in
the Torah and in the prophets. Paul wanted to discard the
laws of the Torah. He particularly opposed circumcision
and the Sabbath. The admonition of Jesus in the Sermon
on the Mount that the laws of the Torah are immutable,
"Whoever then relaxes one of the least of these commandments and teaches men so, shall be called least in the kingdom of heaven," was put in the mouth of Jesus by those
who were anti-Pauline. It was later interpolated by the
early Palestinian Church whose members observed the
Mosaic laws and regarded themselves as Judaeans.

ON MURDER

"You have heard that it was said to the men of old,
'You shall not kill; and whoever kills shall be liable to
judgement.' But I say to you that every one who is angry
with his brother shall be liable to judgment; whoever shall
say to his brother 'RAKA' shall be liable to the synedrion,
and whoever says 'You fool!' shall be liable to Gehenna of
fire." The word *Raka* is Hebrew *req,* "empty, worthless,"
a worthless man (cf. also II Samuel 6.20).[3]

The word Gehenna as a· place for punishment of the
wicked does not occur in any of the literature before the
destruction of the Second Temple. In the book of Enoch
(cf. 63.10) the word sheol has the connotation of a place
beneath the earth where the wicked are punished. The
word sheol occurs in the Bible, having the meaning of
grave, where the dead are placed.[4] In the Bible there is no
mention of punishment after death. The word Gehenna as

a place of punishment for the wicked is first mentioned in IV Ezra 7.36, "And then . . . the furnace of Gehenna shall be made manifest,' " and in the Apocalypse of Baruch 59.10 (cf. 85.13), *"et os gehennae, et statum vindictae, et regionem fidei, et locum spei."*[5] Thus we must assume that the word Gehenna in the Sermon on the Mount, as well as in other passages in the Gospels, could not have been used by Jesus. The term Gehenna, as a place of punishment for the wicked after death, came into vogue after the destruction of the Second Temple.

ON ADULTERY

"You have heard that it was said, 'You shall not commit adultery.' But I say to you that everyone who looks at a woman lustfully has already committed adultery with her in his heart. If your right eye causes you to sin, pluck it out and throw it away; it is better that you lose one of your members than that your whole body be thrown into Gehenna. And if your right hand causes you to sin, cut it off and throw it away; it is better that you lose one of your members than that your whole body go into Gehenna" (Matt. 5. 27-30). The Pentateuch has an injunction against the coveting of any married woman. Philo and II Maccabees relate that maidens were kept indoors so as not to be seen in public. Philo, in his book *The Special Laws, III,* 169-171 (Loeb Classical Library), wrote, "The women are best suited to the indoor life which never strays from the house, within which the middle door is taken by the maidens as their boundary, and the outer door by those who have reached full womanhood. . . . A woman . . . should not shew herself off like a vagrant in the streets before the eyes of other men. . . ." The author of II Maccabees also refers to "the maidens who were kept indoors."[6] Job prided himself by saying, "I made a covenant with my eyes; how then could I look upon a maid?"[7] The author of the Testament of Benjamin said, "He that hath a pure mind in love, looketh not after a woman with a view to fornication."[8] Before the time of Jesus, looking at a woman lustfully was considered a moral sin. Thus the admonition ascribed to Jesus, "One who looks at a woman lustfully has already committed adultery with her in his heart," is not new. According to the Sermon, to remove this moral sin a person had to pluck out his eye. This is not realistic; this is contrary to the nature of mankind. No man who has looked lustfully at a woman would maim himself by plucking out his eye, but would continue to live in moral sin. Judaism recognized the weakness of human nature. The sages made it possible for a man who committed a moral sin to live a righteous life. They introduced the principle of *teshuba,* returning to God, repentance. When a man repented, his moral sin was forgiven; God, being merciful, accepted the repentant. *Teshuba* became a tenet of the Pharisees. Friedlander is right when he said that Judaism is not only a religion, it is a way of life. The sages had a deeper understanding of human psychology than the author of the sayings in the Sermon on the Mount. They were realistic.

DIVORCE

"It was also said, 'Whoever divorces his wife, let him give her a bill of divorce.' But I say to you that every one who divorces his wife, except on the ground of unchastity, makes her an adultress; and whoever marries a divorced woman commits adultery" (Matt. 5.31-32).

There was a controversy between the schools of Shammai and Hillel on the question of divorce.[9] The former maintained that no man may divorce his wife save on account of adultery. The original plan of marriage was symbolized in the Pentateuch by the term "one flesh" (Gen. 2.24). If a wife commits adultery, this makes it evident that they are no longer one flesh, and the husband has to give her a bill of divorce. The Hillelites granted that by marriage, husband and wife are to be "one flesh"; but they maintained that where the husband no longer cares for his wife, the original plan of "one flesh" is not carried out, and hence it is better that they separate—thus permitting the husband to divorce his wife. In the matter of divorce, the author of the Sermon on the Mount followed the conservative school of Shammai. The moralists and the conservatives sometimes meet.

ON SWEARING

"Again you have heard that it was said to the men of old, 'You shall not swear falsely, but shall perform to the Lord what you have sworn.' But I say to you, Do not swear at all, either by heaven, for it is the throne of God, or by the earth, for it is His footstool, or by Jerusalem, for it is the city of the great King. And do not swear by your head, for you cannot make one hair white or black. Let what you say be simply 'Yes' or 'No'; anything more than this comes from evil" (Matt. 5.33-37).

From Josephus we learn that the Essenes did not swear[10]; they gave their word yes or no. Further we learn from Josephus that when Herod forced the Judaeans to take an oath of allegiance to him and to Caesar, he exempted the Essenes because they never swore and he trusted their word.[11]

Philo, in his treatise *The Decalogue,*[12] wrote, "To swear not at all is the best course and most profitable to life, well suited to a rational nature which has been taught to speak the truth so well on each occasion that its words are regarded as oaths. . . . But if necessity be too strong for him, he must consider in no careless fashion all that an oath involves, for that is no small thing, though custom makes light of it."

The early Tannaim interpreted the third commandment, "You shall not take the name of Yahweh, your God, in vain," i.e., to no purpose. The Targum according to Onkelos rendered the word לשוא by למגנא , "to no purpose." Josephus interpreted the Third Decalogue as not to swear *phaulos* lightly (*Ant.* 3. 5. 5[91]). Thus the admonition in the Sermon on the Mount not to swear at all was widespread among the sages. There was among them a certain fear and horror of all oaths.

LEX TALIONIS

"You have heard that it was said, 'An eye for an eye and a tooth for a tooth.' But I say to you, Do not resist one who is evil, But if any one strikes you on the right cheek turn to him the other also; and if any one would sue you and take your coat, let him have your cloak as well" (Matt. 5.38-40).

To comprehend the Biblical law "An eye for an eye," one must bear in mind that the ancients had a conception of the nature of crime and wrongdoing that was different from that of the moderns. Many wrongs which are today considered crimes against the state, and for which the state is empowered to impose punishment, were not so regarded in ancient times. Injury and bodily mutilation were considered private wrongs. The sufferer had the right to fix the punishment, and if he lost an eye or a tooth, he possessed the right to take out the eye or the tooth of the offender.[13]

The law of *talio,* as described in the Bible, was not for the state to enforce, since the action was not considered a crime against society, and the state was not empowered to punish the offender. It was a case between the person who inflicted the injury and the man who was injured. The man who suffered the injury could entirely absolve from punishment the man who caused the injury, or he could demand any satisfaction he desired, even to taking out the eye of the man who caused the loss of his eye. *Talio* was the ultimate and extreme satisfaction which the plaintiff could exact. However, he might take his satisfaction in the form of money. He was the sole judge. Josephus interprets the law of *talio* in the Pentateuch as follows: "He that maimeth any one, let him undergo the like himself, and be deprived of the same member of which he hath deprived the other, unless he that is maimed will accept of money instead of it; for the law makes the sufferer the judge of the value of what he hath suffered, and permits him to estimate it, unless he will be more severe."[14]

During the Second Commonwealth the Pharisees abolished the *lex talionis*. This was done by a legal fiction which limited the right of the man who suffered the loss of an eye to take out an eye that was exactly like his own in size and color. Since it was impossible for two men to have precisely the same organs in every respect, the injured could not make use of the law of *talio*. Thus, by this legal fiction, the law of *talio* was in reality abolished. The injured person had the right to demand only money satisfaction for the loss of his eye, for the pain, for medical care, for disability, and for humiliation. The law of *talio* was in reality replaced by a law of monetary compensation.[15]

Jesus, in the Sermon on the Mount, speaks as a utopian moralist when he says, "Do not resist one who is evil." He asks not only to refrain from demanding satisfaction, *talio,* but not to resist evil at all. Jesus approached the problems of his day purely as an ethical teacher. He disregarded state and society in his preaching, and addressed himself to the individual and his needs. He made ethical appeals, seeking the reconstruction of innate human nature. The sages, on the other hand, sought ethical goals by means of the social controls provided by the law and its interpretation.

LOVE YOUR ENEMIES

"You have heard that it was said, 'You shall love your neighbor and hate your enemy.' But I say unto you, Love your enemies and pray for those who persecute you, so that you may be sons of your Father who is in heaven; for

he makes his sun rise on the evil and the good, and sends
rain on the just and on the unjust. For if you love those
who love you, what reward have you? Do not even the tax
collectors do the same? And if you salute only your brethren, what more are you doing than others? Do not even
the Gentiles do the same?" (Matt. 5.43-48).

The saying "Love your enemies" is generally considered
the apogee of the Sermon on the Mount. In the Pentateuch
(Lev. 19.18) we read "You shall love your neighbor as
yourself." There is no assertion in the Bible that one should
hate his enemy. On the contrary, the book of Proverbs says,
"If your enemy is hungry, give him bread to eat; and if
he is thirsty, give him water to drink."[16] A man should
have compassion for his enemy. If the enemy is in distress
he should help him. The Bible does not say that a man
should love his enemy. The idea that a man should pray
for his enemy and repay good for evil is expressed in the
Testament of Joseph: "And if any one seeketh to do evil
unto you, do well unto him, and pray for him, and ye
shall be redeemed of the Lord from all evil."[17]

Jesus preached love and said, "If any one strikes you on
the right cheek, turn to him the other also." Yet Jesus
bitterly upbraided the people of the cities who rejected his
teachings. He was especially incensed against the people
of Capernaum and said, "But I tell you that it shall be
more tolerable in the day of judgment for the land of Sod-
om than for you (Capernaum)."[18] These words of Jesus
are inconsistent with the sayings in the Sermon on the
Mount, "Love your enemies and pray for those who persecute you." Nor does the saying of Jesus quoted by Matthew,
"Do not think that I have come to bring peace on earth;
I have not come to bring peace, but a sword,"[19] tally with
the sayings in the Sermon on the Mount. In the Rabbinic
literature it is related that when the sages noted contradictory passages in one of the books of the Hebrew Bible,
they boldly stated that the one who wrote the one passage
did not write the other.[20] I deem that this principle could
likewise be applied to the New Testament.

It is related in the Talmud that a heathen once came to Hillel and asked to be converted. Hillel welcomed him and said, "What is hateful to you, do not do to your fellow-man. This is the entire Torah, and the rest is commentary."[21] The story of the conversion may be a legend, but the fact is that Hillel laid down the Golden Rule: "What is hateful to you, do not do to your fellowman." Hillel's negative principle is more realistic than the admonition, "Love your enemies," given in the Sermon on the Mount. It is conceivable that a man who was wronged should be enjoined not to hate the person who may have committed the crime unintentionally. A person may forgive and tolerate one who has injured him or a member of his family; but how can one expect a person to love an enemy who has harmed him or killed a member of his family? This is humanly impossible. The Pentateuchal precept to love your neighbor as yourself is also unrealistic. It is not in the nature of a human being to love another as he does himself.

Hillel's Golden Rule may not be superior to the saying of Jesus, but it is more in accord with the realities of human nature. Jesus (if the saying "Love your enemies" was uttered by him) either did not fully comprehend the nature of human beings or else wanted his teachings to be a utopian standard which mankind should strive to achieve. Judging human nature by the history of the last two millennia, it may be said that it is possible for a man to love his neighbor, that it may even be possible not to despise his enemy, but it is impossible for a man to love his enemy. Men are not only not ready for the millennium, but bitter and deep hatred exists in the hearts of men, even among Jesus' followers. Utopian ethics can be practiced only in a utopian world.

Rabbi Akiba was of the opinion that the command "You shall love your neighbor (friend) as yourself," is the main principle of the Torah. Ben Azzai, a contemporary of Rabbi Akiba, held that the main principle of the Torah was to be found in the words of Genesis (5.1), "This is the book of the generations of Adam " (Sifra, Kdosh. 45).

By this, Ben Azzai meant to lay stress upon the principle that all men were the descendants of Adam, and that all were equal since they were the creatures of God. According to Ben Azzai, the main principle of the Torah is that men were born equal. After almost two millennia this principle has not been realized. Races and nations hold that they are superior to others. Individuals hold themselves to be superior to others not because of their intellect and culture but because they are members of different classes of society.

Hillel, a realist who knew human nature, said that a person should not injure his fellowman since he himself did not want to be injured by any one else. Human beings can be educated to accord with this principle. Hillel did not originate his Golden Rule;[22] many sages among different peoples have preached this, but Hillel emphasized it as a Judaean tenet.

ON PRAYER

"And when you pray, you must not be like the hypocrites; for they love to stand and pray in the synagogues and at the street corners, that they may be seen by men. Amen, I say to you, they have their reward. But when you pray, go into your room and shut the door and pray to your Father in secret; and your Father who sees in secret will reward you. And in praying do not heap up empty phrases as the Gentiles do; for they think that they will be heard for their many words. Do not be like them, for your Father knows what you need before you ask him" (Matt. 6.5-8).

In his admonition to his followers, Jesus said that they should not be like the hypocrites who pray in the synagogues. During the Second Commonwealth there were no synagogues as houses of prayer in Judaea.[23] The word synagogue does not occur in connection with prayers in the literature of that period. The synagogue, "gathering, assembly," came into being as an institution where the Pentateuch was read particularly on the Sabbath. Later the sages took advantage of the opportunities offered by the synagogue to propound their ideas by interpreting the Pentateuchal passages. In the course of time, the reading of the Prophetic Books was introduced.

The Synoptic Gospels refer many times to the synagogue as a house of instruction, of study, but not as a house of prayer. Mark wrote that Jesus went to the synagogue on different occasions. In 1.21, he states that Jesus and his disciples "went in to Capernaum; and immediately on the Sabbath he entered the synagogue and taught." In 6.1-2, Mark wrote, "He . . . came to his country; and his disciples followed him. And on the Sabbath he began to teach in the synagogue . . ." In Luke 4.14-16 it is stated, "Jesus returned . . . into Galilee . . . And he taught in their synagogues, being glorified of all. And he came to Nazareth, where he had been brought up; and he went to the synagogue, as his custom was, on the Sabbath day. And he stood up to read; and there was given to him the book of the prophet Isaiah. . . ." Again in 6.6 it is stated that Jesus "On another Sabbath . . . entered the synagogue and taught." Matthew (9.35) tells us that "Jesus went about all the cities and villages, teaching in their synagogues . . ." In the Synoptic Gospels many references are made to Jesus praying. He prayed on the mountains, and at other places in the open; but it is never mentioned that Jesus went into a synagogue to pray.

The only place where the synagogue is referred to as a house of prayer is in the Sermon on the Mount as given by Matthew. It is not mentioned in the Sermon on the Plain recorded by Luke. Hence we must conclude that the section "On Prayer" in the Sermon on the Mount belongs to a later period, after the destruction of the Temple, when the synagogue became a house of prayer.

In the section "On Prayer," Jesus said, "Amen, I say to you." The word *amen* has the connotation "truly" and also denotes an oath.[24] Placed at the end of benedictions and

at the close of admonitions, the people respond with *amen*
i.e., truly, indicating acceptance. However, when the word
amen comes at the beginning of a discourse or declaration,
it denotes an oath. Thus we may rightly assume that when
Jesus said "Amen, I say to you," he uttered an oath. This
is in contradiction to a previous saying of Jesus, "Do not
swear at all." Apparently the editor of the Sermon on the
Mount did not see the contradiction. It is to be noted
that the section "On Swearing" is not given by Luke in the
Sermon on the Plain.

Jesus said to his disciples that prayers should be rendered in secret. In ancient times prayers were rendered
aloud, sometimes accompanied by weeping. They were addressed by people in distress to God to whom they turned
for help. It is quite understandable that such prayers ex-
pressing great intensity of emotions would be voiced aloud.

We find the expression, "And they cried out to the Lord"
in every part of the Bible.[25] The author of Judith relates
that Judith in praying "cried out to the Lord with a loud
voice."[26] The author of I Maccabees relates that Judah
the Makkabee and his followers "cried out in prayer."[27]
The author of I Samuel relates that when Hannah came
to Shiloh to pray, and moved only her lips without using
her voice, Eli the priest thought that she was intoxicated,
because she did not pray with a loud voice.[28]

After the destruction of the Temple, when prayers were
codified and the prayer of *Shemoneh Esreh* was instituted,
it was maintained that these prayers should be recited
silently, and hence the term *Tephillah be-lachash*.

It is to be noted that Mark relates (15.34) that when
Jesus was crucified he "cried with a loud voice, 'Eloi, Eloi,
lama sabachthani?' My God, My God, why hast thou forsaken me?" Matthew (27.46) likewise states that "Jesus
cried with a loud voice" when he was crucified.

THE LORD'S PRAYER

"Pray then like this: Our Father who art in heaven,

hallowed be thy name. Thy kingdom come, thy will be done
on earth as it is in heaven. Give us this day our daily
bread; and forgive us our debts, as we also have forgiven
our debtors; and lead us not into temptation, but deliver
us from evil. For if you forgive men their trespasses, your
heavenly Father also will forgive you; but if you do not
forgive men their trespasses, neither will your Father forgive your trespasses" (Matt. 6.9-15).

The Lord's Prayer is given by Luke in a different version (11.2-4); it is not found in the Sermon on the Plain.
Luke relates (11.1) that the disciples said to Jesus, "Lord,
teach us to pray, as John taught his disciples."

The Gospels never referred to the Lord's Prayer. They
do mention that Jesus prayed on different occasions, but
they do not record the Lord's Prayer. Nowhere in his
Epistles does Paul ever mention the Lord's Prayer. Neither
do the Apostolic Fathers ever refer to the Lord's Prayer,
and we may conjecture that they did not know of it. Clement in the First Epistle to the Corinthians (c. 75-110)
told them that they should pray with eager entreaty, and
he gave them the form of the prayer (§§59-60; ed. K. Lake
in the Loeb Classical Library):

> We beseech thee, Master, to be our 'help and succour.'
> Save those of us who are in affliction, have mercy on
> the lowly, raise the fallen, show thyself to those in
> need, heal the sick, turn again the wanderers of thy
> people, feed the hungry, ransom our prisoners, raise
> up the weak, comfort the faint-hearted; let all 'nations
> know thee, that thou art God alone,' and that Jesus
> Christ is thy child, and that 'we are thy people and
> the sheep of thy pasture.' . . . Thou that art faithful
> in all generations, righteous in judgment, wonderful
> in strength and majesty, wise in thy creation . . . O
> 'merciful and compassionate,' forgive us our iniquities
> and unrighteousness, and transgressions, and short-
> comings. Reckon not every sin of thy servants and
> handmaids, but cleanse us with the cleansing of thy

truth, and 'guide our steps to walk in holiness of heart, to do the things which are good and pleasing before thee.' . . ."

This prayer echoes the doxology of the *Shemoneh Esreh*. If the Apostolic Fathers had known of the Lord's Prayer, Clement in his Epistle to the Corinthians would certainly have referred to it.

After Matthew recorded the Sermon on the Mount, he wrote the following (7.28-29), "And when Jesus finished these sayings, the crowds were astonished at his teaching, for he taught them as one who had authority, and not as their scribes." Luke does not record this passage at the conclusion of the Sermon on the Plain. Both Mark (1.22) and Luke (4.32) wrote that when Jesus was teaching in Capernaum on the Sabbath, "They were astonished at his teaching, for he taught them as one who had authority, and not as the scribes"—except that Luke lacks "and not as the scribes."

The Sermon on the Mount is a conglomeration of the sayings of Jesus. We must stress again that the sayings of Jesus as given in the Sermon on the Mount were recorded at least two generations after his death. His followers had different traditions of his sayings, and so we find confusion and contradictions in the sayings of Jesus as recorded in the Sermon on the Mount and in other passages in the Synoptic Gospels. We have noted that several terms supposedly used by Jesus were not in vogue during the lifetime of Jesus, but came into usage after the destruction of the Temple. The words "Gehenna" and "synagogue"—as a house of prayer—were first used in the Judaean literature after the destruction of the Temple. Similarly the saying in the Sermon on the Mount, "You cannot serve God and mammon,"[29] could not have been uttered by Jesus, since the word "mammon" was not in vogue in his lifetime. The word "mammon" is Hebrew *mamon,* meaning "money, wealth." During the Second Commonwealth the word used

for "money" was *kesef;* and the word *nekhasim* had the
connotation of "property, wealth." The word mammon,
"money, wealth," came into vogue after the destruction of
the Temple.

To make a critical study of the sayings in the Sermon
on the Mount, they must be placed in their proper historical perspective. We must take cognizance of when the
sayings were collated and edited as a unit, as "The Sermon
on the Mount." The Sermon on the Mount as given by
Matthew and Luke is the product of the first part of the
second century. Thus comparisons must be made with the
teachings of the sages of the first two centuries.

Friedlander's book, *The Jewish Sources of the Sermon
on the Mount,* is really a catechism. The author wanted to
instruct the Jewish theologians how to defend Judaism and
how to answer their opponents. Caution must be used in
utilizing this book. It is a polemical treatise. The author
did not exercise historical discipline in his citations from
the Rabbinical Literature. The purport of the book was to
serve as an answer to the well-meaning and sincere Christian theologians who have maintained that the teachings
of Jesus as given in the Sermon on the Mount are superior
to the teachings of the sages.

In our day, particularly after the Ecumenical Council
of Vatican II, many sincere and well-meaning Christian
theologians have propounded the idea of dialogues between
Jews and Christians, i.e., between Judaism and Christianity. Many Jewish theologians and laymen have applauded
this idea. This is contrary to the history of true Judaism.
The Jews never engaged in dialogues with Christians on
religion. It is true that during the Middle Ages there were
dialogues and disputations between Jews and Christians;
but these were forced upon the Jews. The Jews were compelled to defend their religion. Even the famous dialogue
between the Jew Trypho and Justin Martyr never took
place. Justin, in order to refute some of the arguments of
the Jews and to prove the truth of Christianity, himself
composed this dialogue. He placed in the mouth of Trypho

arguments and charges against Christianity so that he might refute them.

The Jewish do not wish to convert the Christians to Judaism, nor to be converted to Christianity. The Jews respect Christianity, as it brought monotheism to the pagan world. Friedlander is correct when he states that the word *goyim* in the Talmud refers to pagans, not to Christians. The Jews are against interfering in the theology of Christianity, and at the same time are strongly opposed to the interference of Christian theologians in Judaism. The Jews follow the eternal words of the prophet Micah (4.5):

> For let all the peoples walk each one in the name of its God, but we will walk in the name of Adonai our God for ever and ever.

During the Middle Ages the Jews engaged in polemical writings against Christianity. To mention two: Rashi was aware that the Christian authorities interpreted many passages in the Bible as relating to Jesus; so in his commentaries on the Bible, Rashi made it a point to deal with these passages. And in the sixteenth century, Isaac of Troki wrote a book *Hizzuk Emunah,* later translated into English as *Faith Strengthened,* a polemic against Christianity.

The time of polemics against Christianity is over. During the Middle Ages when the Christians forced the Jews to embrace Christianity, the Rabbis were impelled to engage in polemics against the New Testament. In our time, the Jews have no interest in engaging in polemics against the New Testament. The Jews are grateful to the Church for preserving the great treasures of Jewish literature, such as the Apochrypha-Apocalyptic literature, the Septuagint, the writings of Josephus, and the writings of Philo. Were it not for the Church, the Hebrew Bible would have remained for the Jews alone, as the Talmud has. Through its adoption by the Church, the Hebrew Bible became a universal Book which has had a tremendous influence on Western civilization.

The need now is to present the historical background of Judaism during the rise of Christianity and to give a true picture of the nature and significance of the "Parting of the Way." Authoritative historical works that present the true spirit of Judaism is a *sine qua non* for our day.

While we are against theological dialogues, we believe that there is considerable ground where Jews and Christians can meet and should meet. They are members of one human society. Having a common interest in the welfare of their country, and of humanity, they are members of one fellowship, although separated by their religions.

January 6, 1969   Solomon Zeitlin
                                   Dropsie College
                                   Philadelphia, Pa.

NOTES

* Personal data about Gerald Friedlander are scant. He was born December 2, 1871 and died August 22, 1923 in London. He served as rabbi in Western Synagogue in London from June 1897 until his death. He wrote the following books— *Jewish Sources of the Sermon on the Mount;* An English rendering of *Pirke de Rabbi Eliezer; Laws and Customs of Israel; Hellenism and Christianity; Rabbinic Philosophy and Ethics; Jewish Fairy Tales; Shakespeare and the Jew.* He was a contributor to the *Jewish Chronicle* of London.

In an editorial which appeared in the *Jewish Chronicle* of August 24, 1923, he was eulogized as a conscientious, consistent, and courageous Jew. He was a faithful worker and lover of learning, and spared neither time nor energy in defending the truth as he saw it.

[1] Cf. S. B. Hoenig, *The Great Sanhedrin* (Phila., 1953), chap. 28.

[1a] S. Zeitlin, "The Takkanot of Rabban Jochanan ben Zakkai," *JQR,* N.S., 54 (1963-64), 288-310.

[2] *JQR,* 55 (1964-65), 267-269.

[3] See H. M. Orlinsky, *"Hā-Rōqdīm* for *Hā-Rēqīm* in II Samuel 6₂₀," *JBL,* 65 (1946), 25 ff., especially n. 10 on pp. 30 ff.

[4] Cf., e.g., Ps. 6.6; 30.4; 49.15; 88.4; Prov. 15.11.

[5] The book of Fourth Ezra was composed in the time of Trajan. The book of Baruch was composed during the time of Hadrian. Cf. S. Zeitlin, "The Apocrypha," *JQR,* 37 (1947), 219-246. Cf. also R. H. Charles, *The Apocrypha and Pseudepigrapha* vol. II, p. 554.

[6] 3.19.

[7] 31.1.

[8] 8.2.

[9] Gittin 9.10. (90[ae]).

[10] *Jewish War,* 2.8.6 (135).

[11] *Ant.,* 15.10.4 (371).

[12] §§ 17.84-85.

[13] Cf. S. Zeitlin, "The Pharisees and the Gospels," in *Essays and Studies in Memory of Linda R. Miller* (1938), 232-286.

[14] *Ant.,* 4.8.35 (280).

[15] Baba Kamma 83b.

[16] 25.21.

[17] 18.2.

[18] Matt. 11.24.

[19] Matt. 10.34; Luke 12.51 reads: "Do you think that I have come to give peace on earth? No, I tell you, but rather division."

[20] Cf. Rashi at Isaiah 48.16.

[21] Shabbath 31.

[22] Tobit 4.15.

[23] Cf. S. Zeitlin, *The Rise and Fall of the Judaean State,* I, p. 340, n. 84.

[24] Cf. Shebuoth 36a.

[25] Cf., e.g., Ex. 14.10; Num. 20.16; Deut. 26.7; Jud. 4.3; Ps. 107; 6, 28.

[26] 9.1.

[27] 5.33; cf. v. 31.

[28] 1.12-13.

[29] Matt. 6.24.

PREFACE

THIS book is intended, in the first place, as a contribution to comparative theology. An attempt is made to set forth the relation of Christianity to Judaism, not only by way of contrast but also by way of comparison. I have limited the scope of inquiry to the Sermon on the Mount, which is undoubtedly the most important document of Christianity.

The Sermon is considered to be the Charter of the Church, containing the ideal summary of the teaching of Jesus. Bishop Gore on the first page of his widely-read exposition of the Sermon says : " it occupies in the New Testament the place which in the Old Testament is occupied by the Ten Commandments."

In order to estimate at its true worth the religious value of the Sermon, it is necessary to compare it with the contemporary religious teaching current among the Jews.

In the first century of the common era Jewish life and thought were not limited to Palestine. Account must also be taken of the literary activity of the Jews of the Diaspora. In other words, we must compare the teaching of the Sermon not only with the Old Testament and its Rabbinic glosses preserved in the Mishna, Tosephta, Gemara, Midrashim and Targumim, but we must refer likewise to the invaluable Jewish Hellenic

literature, which includes the Septuagint, the Apocrypha, Philo and the Apocalyptic writings. Without
this literature the New Testament could never have been
written.

My attempt to read a few chapters of the New Testament in the light of contemporary Jewish thought is a
novel venture, which I hope will meet with the approval
and sympathy of my readers. I have endeavoured to
analyse the Sermon, and I have traced its sources, so
far as they are discoverable.

In the second place, this book is intended to suggest
how the New Testament might be expounded, so as to
enable a Jew or a Christian to read it with interest and
perhaps with profit.

We have reached in these days a turning-point in the
history of Christianity. The famous *Hibbert Journal*
Supplement entitled, " Jesus or Christ," issued in 1909,
clearly demonstrated that the *Jesus of history* was no
longer to be identified with the *Jesus of dogma*. The
late Father Tyrrell spoke of Christianity as being at
the " Cross Roads." The alternative is either blind
belief in the Jesus of the Church, or reasoned historical
inquiry as to his existence and personality.

The most striking contribution to the study of his-
torical Christianity is Dr. Albert Schweitzer's book
Von Reimarus zu Wrede (1906), which has been trans-
lated into English under the title of *the Quest of the
Historical Jesus*. This book has, once for all, dealt the
death-blow to the ordinary accepted life of Jesus. Dr.
Schweitzer says : " There is nothing more negative
than the result of the critical study of the Life of Jesus.
The Jesus of Nazareth who came forward publicly as the
Messiah, who preached the ethic of the Kingdom of God,

who founded the Kingdom of Heaven upon earth, and
died to give his work its final consecration, never had
any existence. He is a figure designed by rationalism,
endowed with life by liberalism, and clothed by modern
theology in an historical garb " (p. 396).

Still more negative and sceptical is the position of
Professor Arthur Drews, whose widely-read book, *Die
Christusmythe*, has just appeared in an English translation—*The Christ Myth*. Drews agrees to a very large
extent with the results arrived at by Mr. J. M. Robertson
in his books *Pagan Christs*, and *Christianity and Mythology*. Drews and Robertson argue that there is no historical proof, that the Jesus of the Gospels ever lived.
The studies in Comparative Religion by Frazer, Gunkel,
and Pfleiderer, have been drawn upon by Robertson
and Drews, especially with reference to Vegetation and
Solar Myths, which formed the basis of the Religions
prevalent in Asia Minor in the first century of the
common era (see Frazer, *Golden Bough*, ii. pp. 115–116 ;
and *Adonis, Attis and Osiris*).

Already as far back as 1889, Usener of Bonn had
maintained that a pagan substratum could be discovered
in the Birth and Childhood-stories of Jesus as contained
in the Gospel of Matthew. Again, the investigations
by Wendland, and the theories of Frazer dealing with
the Gospel story of the Crucifixion, are in line with
Usener's studies, tending to prove that the Gospel
account of the death of Jesus is built up on a widely-
spread heathen custom, which obtained throughout Asia
Minor and elsewhere in the first century.

Wendland refers to Philo's account of the mock coronation, followed by the crucifixion of one named Karabas
(*Against Flaccus*, 6, M. ii. p. 522). A parallel to this is

found in the Gospels, which describe the mock coronation
and crucifixion of Jesus. The Gospels also refer to
Barabbas in connexion with the trial of Jesus. Wendland considers the Gospel narrative concerning Barabbas
to be quite unhistorical (*Hermes*, 1898, p. 178).

Was it likely that Pilate would have attempted to
save Jesus, by substituting Barabbas ? Was it possible
for a Roman Judge to acknowledge to the world, that
he had made a judicial error ? This would be the
meaning of putting Barabbas to death, in place of Jesus.
Such a procedure, in the case of a man of Pilate's harsh
and proud nature, is psychologically unthinkable.
Where, then, did the Gospels find the story of the mock
coronation and crucifixion, and also the name of Barabbas ? I venture to think that Philo is the source used
by the Evangelists.

Philo has been a valuable mine whence the writers
of the New Testament have drawn some of their best
treasures. The " Logos," the " Parable of the Prodigal
Son," the " Gift of Tongues " (associated with Pente-
cost), as well as " Barabbas " have all been derived
from Philo. We saw that Philo spoke of the crucifixion
of Karabas. It is a very short step from Karabas to
Barabbas, if one bears in mind that in Hebrew or Aramaic K (כ) is very similar to B (ב). Moreover, some
of the old texts of Matthew speak of " Jesus Barabbas,"
as contrasted with Jesus, the Son of the Father in Heaven.
The Aramaic for " Son of the Father " is *Barabba.*
Does this not suggest that originally Jesus and Barabbas
were one and the same person ?

Again, can we accept the New Testament account of
the trial of Jesus ? Was Jesus sentenced to death by
the Sanhedrin in which the Rabbis and Scribes deliber-

ated ? This problem has been discussed by Dr. Büchler (*Das Synedrion in Jerusalem*, 1902), who maintains (p. 200) that, in all passages in the Gospels, the word ἀρχιηρεῖς does not mean " chief priests," but it should be translated " temple authorities." Dr. Büchler argues, that, in Jerusalem, there were two bodies, each called Sanhedrin, but exercising different functions (p. 38). One Sanhedrin had exclusive jurisdiction, as far as the Temple was concerned. It had to decide on the purity of the priests and other matters connected with the Temple (pp. 33 ff.). This Sanhedrin was the governing body of the Sanctuary. The High Priest was naturally a member of this body. Dr. Büchler holds that if Jesus was seized, it was by order of this Temple Sanhedrin, which dealt with his case.

If this be so, Jesus did not appear at all before the other Sanhedrin, which is known to us from the Mishna (Synhedrin, xi. 4). In this body, the Scribes and Rabbis deliberated under the presidency of the Nasi. The High Priest was not the president, as one is led to infer from the New Testament. Dr. Büchler's theory has been criticized by Schürer (*Geschichte*, iii. pp. 239 ff. in 4th ed.), and by Dr. George Adam Smith (*Jerusalem*, i. pp. 419 ff.). These scholars reject Dr. Büchler's conclusions, although Dr. Smith admits that " Dr. Büchler bases his theory on no meagre foundation of evidence " (p. 421). Dr. Smith opposes Dr. Büchler by pointing out that : " neither in the Gospels nor in Josephus is there any proof of this duality in the supreme national authority " (ibid.).

I find, however, that the New Testament offers some evidence that may support Dr. Büchler's contention. The Greek word συνέδριον denotes in the New Testament:

(1) the ordinary tribunal (Matt. x. 17) which was to be found in every Jewish town ; (2) the Sanhedrin or Law Court, the Great Council of seventy-one members in Jerusalem (Matt. v. 22, where this court is contrasted with the ordinary tribunal, also called κρίσις or local Beth Din, cf. Matt. v. 21), and (3) the Temple Sanhedrin in which the so-called " High Priests " figure so prominently (Mark xiv. 55, Acts, v. 21.)

It is necessary to compare a few texts, in order to appreciate the meaning of the word and to see before which tribunal Jesus is supposed to have appeared. Mark xiv. 55, after relating that Jesus was led away to the high priest, adds the words :—" Now the chief priests and the *whole Sanhedrin* sought witness against Jesus to put him to death." In Mark (xv. 1) again, it is said:—" And straightway in the morning the chief priests with the *elders and scribes* and the *whole Sanhedrin,* held a consultation " ; but the parallel passage, Matt. xxvii. 1, has simply " All the chief priests and the elders of the people took counsel." In the narrative in Luke the word Sanhedrin is introduced very awkwardly. Thus Luke xxii. 66 has :—" And as soon as it was day the assembly of the elders of the people was gathered together, both chief priests and scribes ; and they led him away into their Sanhedrin, saying, If Thou art the Christ, tell us."

The abruptness with which the clause—" saying, If thou art the Christ, tell us "—comes in, together with the use of Sanhedrin for the place of assembly as well as for the Council itself, suggest the question, whether in an earlier stage of the narrative, the word Sanhedrin was present in any of the passages ? (See *Enc. Bibl.*, col. 4842). In any case, we see that in Mark it is the *Chief*

Priests and the *whole Sanhedrin* who try Jesus. Mark also speaks of " the Chief Priests with the *Elders and Scribes* and the whole Sanhedrin," indicating that the Elders and Scribes are distinct from the Chief Priests and the whole Sanhedrin. In other words, the Chief Priests and the whole Sanhedrin constituted the Temple Sanhedrin, whilst the Elders and the Scribes formed the other Sanhedrin which had. the Nasi as its President. This result agrees with Dr. Büchler's conclusions. Matthew writes from the Jewish standpoint ; he is careful to omit all reference to the Sanhedrin. He only mentions " the Chief Priests and the Elders of the people " (xxvii. 1), who take counsel against Jesus. Luke combines Matthew with Mark and speaks of (1) the Assembly of the Elders of the people, (2) the Scribes in their Sanhedrin, and (3) the Chief Priests in their Sanhedrin.

This discussion tends to show how difficult it is to regard the Gospels as sources of history. In a recent issue of the *Hibbert Journal* (January, 1911) a Christian Clergyman writes :—" As a result of the work of the Higher Criticism the Four Gospels are a complete wreck as historical records. . . . It can never be proved that an historical person uttered the great-teachings of the Fourth Gospel. . . . As authorities for a life of Jesus they (i.e., the Synoptic Gospels) are hopelessly shattered by the assaults of the Higher Criticism. How little they tell us of an historic Jesus " (pp. 346–7).

The *Hibbert Journal* is echoing the voice of unrest in Christian circles throughout the world. Burnouf and Hochart with many more scholars have attempted to prove the non-historicity of Jesus. The storm raised in Germany by Drews' theory of the Christ Myth is bound to give rise to much discussion in other lands.

b

Drews has been taken to task by many eminent theologians. Dr. G. Klein's brochure, *Ist Jesus eine his-
torische Persönlichkeit* (1910), *assumes* that Jesus was a
real person.   The author declines to discuss the issues
raised by Drews.   Dr. Chwolson (*Über die Frage ob
Jesus gelebt hat*, 1910), follows a similar line of attack,
and, like Dr. Klein, argues that Jesus was a Pharisee
who was naturally opposed by the corrupt Sadducean
priesthood.   Apart from this point, the rest of Chwolson's
essay is very unconvincing.   For instance, he accepts
as genuine the famous passage referring to Jesus in
Josephus (*Antiquities* xviii. v. 2,), which Niese as well as
Schürer consider to be spurious.   More important is
Johannes Weiss' reply to Drews.   His book *Jesus von
Nazareth, Mythus oder Geschichte* is probably the best
attack on the Mythological School represented by Drews,
Kalthoff and Jensen.   There is however, more abuse
than criticism in the book.   Thus, on p. 163 we read :—
" But the Words of Jesus—what are they but Jewish
platitudes, which Drews, the learned authority on
Jewish sayings and also on the Talmud, is able to refer
to their original sources.   Drews denies that the sayings
of Jesus can lay any claim to originality.   If he had
only been good enough to have communicated the results of his most thoroughgoing studies !   To say that
the Sermon on the Mount is a mere mosaic, which re-
sembles the Lord's Prayer, by not containing a single
idea, which has not its parallel in the Old Testament or
in the moral proverbial maxims of the Jewish people, is,
indeed, a bold word.   To what extent is it true ?   The
fact is that the first Christians, as well as Jesus, drew
their inspiration from the Sacred Writings of the people,
and that the Gospel of Jesus is but a reconstruction

of the righteousness taught by prophet and psalmist. Who disputes this fact? Perhaps Drews, if he continues to study the Talmud, may yet learn that it was the act of a religious genius to be able to penetrate the rubbish of tradition (Wust der Tradition) and to reach the source." Thus far Weiss.

I have ventured to utter in this book the " bold word " which has roused the ire of Weiss. But I hold no brief for Drews, whose book contains many statements and theories, which I am not prepared to accept. Weiss is exceedingly unfair to Drews, who makes no pretence to Talmudic knowledge. In the passage (pp. 283–4) which Weiss criticizes, Drews refers to Nork's *Rabbinische Quellen und Parallelen zu neutestamentlichen Schriften*, and more particularly to Robertson's *Christianity and Mythology* (pp. 403–423), where the entire Sermon on the Mount is analysed, and traced to some of its Jewish sources. What does Weiss know of the "rubbish of tradition," which is, of course, preserved in the Talmud? How could Jesus be the religious genius who was able to penetrate this "rubbish of tradition," which only arose with the rest of the Talmudic literature long after the date when Jesus is said to have been put to death by the Romans? Of course, Weiss is only repeating the well-worn phrase, invented by Wellhausen, and endorsed by Mr. Montefiore, when he speaks about the Talmudic literature in this wise :—" the great things are scattered around third and fourth-rate material " (*Synoptic Gospels*, p. ciii.). It is quite unhistorical to compare the Gospels with the Talmudic literature. The comparison should lie as between the writings of the Church Fathers of the second, third and fourth centuries and the Talmud. Drews and Robertson discuss the famous article on the

Gospels by Professor Schmiedel in the *Encyclopaedia Biblica*, in which he had accepted nine passages of the Gospels as credible pillars on which a new historic life of Jesus could be based. Drews and Robertson have demolished these pillars.

We shall do well to note the weighty words of Professor Hermann Cohen of Marburg : " In dealing with the personality of Jesus the greatest caution and reserve are necessary. A young man—a so-called philosopher— told me that he had allowed himself to be baptized, because he revered the personality of Jesus. I could only reply, that I was unable to admire his onesidedness in his knowledge of Jewish historical characters. It was useless for me to give him my opinion about using that legendary person (i.e. Jesus) as an exemplar for our moral conduct. But with no show of reason can we, in any case, allow our children to imbibe any sympathetic leanings towards this most involved personality of all mythology and legendary history " (See *Neujüdische Stimmen über Jesum Christum*, by J. de le Roi, p. 16).

Whilst I am not prepared to go quite as far as Drews and Robertson in denying the possibility of the existence of Jesus ; I cannot ignore the fact, confirmed by recent historical criticism, that it is impossible to extract from the Gospels sufficient incontestable evidence necessary for a biography of the Gospel hero. In brief, my view is, that, probably 1900 years ago, a teacher and a claimant to the Messiahship, named Jesus, the son of Joseph and Mary, lived in Galilee. His apocalyptic dreams and his eschatological discourses induced his followers to recognize his Messianic claims, and this led to a conflict with the ruling authorities, i.e. the Roman Procurator.

The death of Jesus did not destroy the movement he had set on foot. His followers awaited his Parousia and meanwhile, they remained within the camp of Pharisaic Judaism. This state continued until the destruction of Jerusalem in 70 C.E. In the early years of the second century the Gospels were written and Christianity arose as a new religion.

Paul, and not Jesus, was the creator of the New Testament theology. The Gospels were not written by eye-witnesses of the events they narrate. The Evangelists wrote in Greek, which was not the language used by Jesus. The Gospels were not written in the land where the events described occurred. Philo, an earlier contemporary of Jesus, does not mention his name. The famous passage in Josephus, which we have already noticed, is considered by the greatest authorities, e.g. Niese, to be spurious. A contemporary of Josephus, Justus of Tiberias, who wrote at the same period, passes over Jesus in silence. The first non-Christian record of Jesus occurs in the *Annals* of Tacitus (xv. 44), in connexion with Nero's persecution, after the Fire of Rome in 64 C.E. Tacitus wrote the *Annals* after the year 100 C.E., and the passage referring to the Christians and Jesus has been held to be a Christian interpolation. According to Tacitus, Jesus was put to death by the procurator Pontius Pilate in the reign of Tiberius. Is this one of the few historical facts vouched for by the New Testament and confirmed by Tacitus—assuming for the moment that this text is quite authentic?

Matthew places the birth of Jesus in the reign of Herod the Great, that is to say, in the year 4 B.C.E. or some time earlier. This is contradicted by Luke, who dates it at the time of the census of Quirinius, which took place

ten years after the death of Herod, i.e. 6 C.E. Luke
says that Jesus was thirty years old in the fifteenth
year of the reign of Tiberius, that is to say, in the year
29 C.E., the date to which he assigns the baptism of
Jesus by John the Baptist. It has been suggested that
Luke took this date from a passage in Josephus which
speaks of the death of John the Baptist in connexion
with an event of the year 36 C.E.

Luke clearly contradicts himself by fixing the birth of
Jesus at the time of the census (6 C.E.), and making
him thirty years old in the year 29 C.E. (the fifteenth year
of Tiberius). In any case, if we assume that Jesus was
thirty years old in the year 29 C.E., he could not have
been born in the days of Herod (i.e. 4 B.C.E.), as Matthew
records.

In spite of all the ingenious arguments of Sir William
Ramsay in his book *Was Christ born at Bethlehem?* in
which he accepts 6 B.C.E. as the date of the birth of
Jesus, the fact remains that there are serious errors in
Luke's narrative, which cannot be explained away by
inventing history so as to make it harmonize with the
Gospels. (See Neumann, *Jesus*, E.T., pp. 25 ff.)

According to John (viii. 57), the Jews said to Jesus,
" Thou art not yet fifty years old," clearly implying that
he was not far off fifty, at any rate over forty, since to a
man between thirty and forty, the phrase would have
been, " Thou art not yet forty years old." The early
Church inferred that he was about forty-nine years old
at his death, so that, if he was born in 4 B.C.E., he must
have died in 45 C.E. In 45 C.E. we are no longer in
the reign of Tiberius, but under Claudius, whose reign
began in 41 C.E. If, however, the phrase in John be
interpreted to mean that Jesus was at least forty years

old at his death, as he was born in 6 C.E. (according to Luke), he died in 46 C.E. (under Claudius). In both cases, we have reason to question the report of Tacitus. Hastings' *Dictionary of the Bible*—a conservative authority—fixes the following limits :—Nativity, 7–6 B.C.E. ; Baptism, 26–27 C.E. ; Crucifixion, 29 C.E. The ministry is made to last between two and three years, and the life of Jesus is extended over thirty-six years. There may be some evidence for these results, but they are contradicted by one or more of the Gospels. Moreover, Luke's reference to the census of Quirinius, which fell in 6 C.E. (see Josephus, *Antiquities*, xvii. xiii. 5 and Acts v. 37), suggests the following dates: Nativity, 6 C.E. ; Crucifixion, 42, C.E. (based on the life of Jesus covering thirty-six years). This result is again against Tacitus, inasmuch as 42 C.E. is later than the reign of Tiberius, who died in 37 C.E. This insoluble chronological difficulty fully justifies my contention, that we cannot obtain from the Gospels, the only available sources at our disposal, the necessary data for a critical and historical life of Jesus.

Dr. Bergmann has pointed out how the New Testament story of Jesus, e.g. his Davidic descent, his birth in Bethlehem, his flight into Egypt, his entry into Jerusalem, and his trial and death, are due to Old Testament influence. The disciples of Jesus believed in the divine inspiration of the Hebrew Bible, and every supposed Messianic prophecy had to find its fulfilment in the life or death of Jesus (*Jüdische Apologetik*, pp. 57 ff. ; see also Reinach, *Orpheus*, E.T., pp. 231 ff.). The Evangelists used the Septuagint with its errors. Reinach (p. 232) points out that in Psalm xxii., the righteous man complains that his enemies have cast lots for his vesture ;

this detail has found a place in the account of the Passion, where it is introduced to " fulfil " the prophecy.
But the righteous man also says :—" They pierced my
hands and feet," i.e. they crucified me.[1] Unless we
insist on using two kinds of weights and measures, we
must admit that this verse in the Psalms *may* be the
origin of the tradition which declares that Jesus was
crucified. What then remains to us of all the Gospel
story ? " In recent years the scholars have turned to the
Talmud for evidence that Jesus is a genuine historical
character. Laible's *Jesus in Talmud* ; Herford's *Christianity in Talmud and Midrash* ; and Strack's *Jesus,
die Häretiker und die Christen* have not succeeded in
discovering any trustworthy traditions confirming the
Gospel story. Thus, according to the Talmud (Synhedrin, 107b), Rabbi Joshua ben Perachjah fled with
Jesus to Egypt to escape the vengeance of Alexander
Jannaeus, who sought his life. The date of this event
is 87 B.C.E. According to another tradition, Jesus
is made to be a contemporary of Rabbi Akiba (120 C.E.).
Thus, if we are to take any account of Talmudic references, the indefinite period of 200 years is the nearest
date in which the career of Jesus can be located. He
may have lived in 87 B.C.E. or in 120 C.E. All the
references to Jesus in the Rabbinic literature are entirely
legendary (see Bergmann, op. cit. p. 36).

The Jews have refused steadfastly to see in the hero

---

[1] The Septuagint which was generally followed by the Evangelists, has a different text in this verse to the Massoretic text,
which reads : "Like a lion" instead of, "they pierced."
It is quite likely that our Septuagint text was not invariably
known to the Evangelists. Perhaps they used Aquila's version
or some other translation in addition to LXX.

of the Gospels either a God, or an inspired prophet, or a
qualified lawgiver, or a teacher in Israel with a new
message for his people. Now that the Christian theologians have begun to reject the Jesus of dogma, and
to attempt to find the Jesus of history, it has been
left to an English Jew to invite his co-religionists to
enter into the heritage that is fast slipping away from
the Christian grasp.

Mr. Montefiore's attempt to inscribe Jesus in the
roll of the prophets of Israel cannot be permitted to
pass without a protest. In these days of scepticism,
it would be strange to hear even a Unitarian using Mr.
Montefiore's words :—" God's nearness was felt by
Jesus directly with a vivid intensity unsurpassed by
any man " (*Jowett Lectures*, p. 88). Coming from a
Jew, this remark suggests, to my mind, an unbalanced
judgment. When Mr. Montefiore says that " Jesus
differs from, or as some would say, goes beyond the
prophets : ' More than a prophet is here ' " (*Jowett
Lectures*, p. 115)—does he really believe that any Jew,
liberal or conservative, or even a Theist, will accept
his view without demur ? In the *Jowett Lectures* for
1910 Mr. Montefiore deals with the religious teaching
of Jesus, and in addition, he has compiled a voluminous
commentary upon the first three Gospels—entitled,
The Synoptic Gospels. It has been specially written for
Jewish readers. It claims to be a Jewish exposition
of the Gospels. The commentary attempts to answer
the questions : " What should be the Jewish interest
in the New Testament, in the Synoptic Gospels, or in
the life and character of Jesus ? " (S.G., p. ci.).

I have attempted to consider in the following pages
some of these points. It seems to me, that Mr. Monte-

fiore's attempt to persuade Jews to *believe* in the " ideal "
and " heroic " character of Jesus of the Gospels is an
indication, either that Mr. Montefiore is totally unaware
of the present crisis in the Christian Church, due to the
failure of the theologians to discover the historic Jesus ;
or that he must imagine his co-religionists to be in
blissful ignorance of this crisis. Before the Jewish
reader turns to Mr. Montefiore's books, he would do
well to read the article by the Rev. R. Roberts, which
appeared in the *Hibbert Journal*, 1909, under the title
" Jesus or Christ ? An Appeal for Consistency." This
was in circulation about a year before the publication
of the *Jowett Lectures* and *Synoptic Gospels*. Then the
Hibbert Journal Supplement for 1909, arising out of the
Rev. R. Roberts' article should be read, in order to
enable the reader to know something about the latest
views concerning Jesus. The reader will then be able
to test the value of Mr. Montefiore's enthusiastic appreciation of Jesus, as well as his unfeigned contempt
for the Rabbis, such as Hillel. Mr. Montefiore's words
are :—" To his eternal dishonour Hillel said " . . .
(S.G., p. 235). The reference should have been to the
School of Hillel. Mr. Montefiore has blundered through
relying on Christian scholars, ignorant of Jewish
sources.

Is it a mere accident that Loisy (*Les Évangiles
Synoptiques*, i. p. 577) has made the same mistake about
Hillel ? Is it not due also to Loisy's suggestion (E.S.i.
p. 634) that, in Mr. Montefiore's commentary, Hillel's
negative form of the Golden Rule is alone contrasted
with the positive form of the Gospel (S.G., p. 550) ?
There were, as we shall see, several positive forms of
the Rule in the pre-Christian literature of the Jews.

The relative attitude adopted by Mr. Montefiore
to the Rabbis and Jesus is summed up in the following
words : " Just ordinary people need, in addition to the
admirable sayings and exhortations of the Rabbis, the
ideal and *heroic* spirit which inspires the teaching of the
Synoptic Gospels " (S.G., p. cv.). " Admirable " suits
the Rabbis, but " ideal " and " heroic " belong to
Jesus. Mr. Montefiore believes not only in the historical accuracy of the Gospel story of the Crucifixion,
but he even says, " Though his (Jesus') death was
primarily caused by the priests and the Romans, yet
doubtless some of the Rabbis in Jerusalem were also
privy to his arrest and assented to his condemnation."
(S.G., p. xci.)

We have already seen how impossible it is to discover
in the Gospels a consistent historical narrative. Moreover, the Gospels do not even mention the Rabbis in
connexion with the trial or condemnation. It has
been left to the historical acumen of a " liberal Jew "
to discover the complicity of the Rabbis. Some of
these Rabbis had names—who were they ? Although
Mr. Montefiore has made good use of M. Loisy's commentary, he has failed to refer to the important essay
by Wendland, which I mentioned in discussing the
Gospel story of the Crucifixion. The essay—Jesus as a
Saturnalian King—appeared in *Hermes*, 1898, pp. 175 ff.
Strange to say, M. Loisy refers to Wendland. Mr.
Montefiore would have done well to place all the available evidence, and the latest theories on this all-important matter, before his Jewish readers. Surely a Jew
would rather learn that his ancestors and the sect of
the Pharisees to which he belongs, were not implicated
in the trial and condemnation of Jesus. This Mr.

Montefiore has entirely failed to do. He does not mention H. Reich's essay *Der König mit der Dornen-Krone* (1905), and no reference is made to Mr. W. R. Paton's article in the *Zeitschrift für die Neutest. Wissenschaft* (1901, pp. 339–341). Perhaps he refers to these writers when he says : " There are curious parallels to the Gospel story, into the details of which I cannot, however, enter" (S.G., p. 367). It would have been more satisfactory to have given some details of these parallels instead of implicating the Rabbis. Has Mr. Montefiore seen the essay by Rabbi Ludwig Philippson, " Haben wirklich die Juden Jesum gekreuzigt ? " If he has, why does he assert without proof or reference, that the Rabbis assented to the condemnation of Jesus ? What are we to say to the following passage, which speaks of a future in which " Christianity and Judaism will be able to shake hands over the Sermon on the Mount and the fundamental elements in the moral and religious doctrine of Jesus " ? (*Synoptic Gospels*, p. cvii.) Mr. Montefiore is convinced that " Judaism has something to gain and absorb from the New Testament. There are teachings in the New Testament, and above all in the Gospels, which supplement and carry forward some essential teachings in the Old Testament. It seems true to say that for moral and religious value neither the Old Testament can dispense with the New Testament nor the New Testament with the Old Testament " (ibid., pp. cii. and ciii.). Can this standpoint endure the test of impartial criticism ? Saint Augustine says : " We do wrong to the Old Testament if we deny that it comes from the same just and good God as the New. On the other hand, we do wrong to the New Testament if we put the Old on a level with it " (de

Gest. Pelag., v. 15, quoted by Bishop Gore, op. cit., p. 2).
The Christian, as well as the Jew, would disagree with
Mr. Montefiore, for placing the Old and New Testaments
on one level. Bishop Gore writes : " We may say
with truth that the Sermon on the Mount supersedes
the Ten Commandments ; but it supersedes them by
including them in a greater, deeper, and more positive
whole " (ibid.). The Christian considers the New Testament as having superseded the Old Testament ;
whereas the Jew believes that all the good things which
he can find in the Gospels, or in the other books of the
New Testament, are to be found either in the Old Testament, or else in Jewish, or Rabbinic literature.

The Jew denies that the New Testament has sup-
plemented or carried forward the great teachings of
the Old Testament, or of the Jewish literature which
has grown out of the Old Testament.

Mr. Montefiore is fond of speaking of the " brilliant
flash of the highest religious genius " evidenced in
Mark xii. 29–31, where we find the combination of
Deuteronomy vi. 4, 5 with Leviticus xix. 18 (see *Hibbert
Journal*, 1905, p. 658). In his commentary (S.G., p. 288),
Mr. Montefiore remarks that the combination of the
two sayings " was first effected in this way by Jesus."
This is, however, not the case. The combination was
effected long before the birth of Jesus by the Jew, the
Pharisee, who wrote the Testaments of the Twelve
Patriarchs :—" I loved the Lord, likewise also every
man with all my heart " (Test. Issachar, v. 2). Surely
Mr. Montefiore will admit that this pre-Christian writer
displayed the " brilliant flash of the highest religious
genius " by this happy combination of the love of God
and the love of man.

Apart from the excellent book of Mr. Paul Goodman, *The Synagogue and the Church*, there is no work in English dealing with Jewish Apologetics. There is an undoubted need of a series of scholarly books, written from the genuine Jewish standpoint, dealing with Judaism and Christianity. The excellent German writings of J. Eschelbacher, L. Bäck and J. Goldschmidt on " What is Judaism " in reply to Harnack's famous course of lectures " What is Christianity " contain good material for future books, which English Jewish scholars may produce. The valuable contributions to Jüdische Apologetik by Güdemann, and Bergmann, as well as the splendid essays by Hermann Cohen of Marburg, dealing with " Judaism and Ethics," are *desiderata* in Anglo-Jewish literature. Some of the books just mentioned have been published by the " Gesellschaft zur Förderung der Wissenschaft des Judentums." When will the Anglo-Jewish Community have a similar institution, ready to publish books dealing with Judaism, its history, its doctrines and its defence ? The Jew should learn something of the relation that his religion bears to Christianity. If, as it is sometimes said, Jews misinterpret Christianity ; it is equally true that not a few Christians fail to understand Judaism. We can all profit by seeking after truth.

I am encouraged to believe that my efforts may be of some service to my co-religionists in helping them to meet the advances made by Missionaries of the Gospel, who suffer the " Reproach of the Gospels " to obtain among the Christians, and prefer to convert the Jew from the belief in the One God to the belief in the Trinity. I have the satisfaction of knowing that at least one

converted Jew has returned to the ancient faith of
Israel, as a result of reading some of the chapters of this
book, which appeared in the *Jewish World*. More
than half of the book was written, before I saw the Dean
of Lichfield's interesting study of the Sermon on the
Mount in the light of contemporary Jewish thought.
I have already mentioned Mr. J. M. Robertson's parallels
to the Sermon on the Mount, drawn chiefly from the
Old Testament. I have not been able to use any of
the parallels he adduces, because my book was in the
press before I saw his. The independent list of parallels
which he has given, is a further justification for regarding the Sermon on the Mount as a compilation. I am
glad to find that Mr. Robertson criticizes also Dr. Erich
Bischoff's book, which attempts to defend the absolute
originality of the Sermon. Some sixty years ago the
late Dr. Zipser wrote a good essay on the Sermon on
the Mount, with parallels from the Talmud and Midrashim. It appeared in the *Jewish Chronicle*, and was
reprinted in pamphlet form. I have made little use of it,
inasmuch as the majority of the parallels are subsequent
to the age of the Gospels. My references to M. Loisy's
monumental work *Les Évangiles Synoptiques* are few
and far between, because the most salient points in his
fascinating exposition have been reproduced by Mr.
Montefiore. For a similar reason I have very rarely
referred to Wellhausen and the other authorities used
by M. Loisy.

In conclusion, I wish to thank Rabbi H. M. Lazarus,
B.A., for the care he has taken in verifying the Rabbinic
quotations in my book. I am also indebted to the
Revs. L. Mendelsohn, M.A., and M. Rosenbaum, and
Mr. J. H. Schneiderman, B.A., for the reading of the
proofs.   G. F.

April 3, 1911.

LIST OF ABBREVIATIONS

Achelis	Achelis, Bergpredigt.
Adv.	Adversus (against).
Alex.	Alexandria.
Antiq.	Antiquities.
b.	ben or bar (son).
Büchler, D.G.A.h.A.	Büchler, *Der Galiläische ' Am ha'-Areş des Zweiten Jahrhunderts.*
B.C.E.	Before the Common Era.
c.	*contra* or *circa.*
Clem.	Clement.
col.	column.
Const. Apost.	Apostolical Constitutions.
D.C.G.	*Dictionary of Christ and the Gospels,* ed. Hastings.
D.B.	*Dictionary of the Bible,* ed. Hastings.
Enc. Bib.	*Encyclopaedia Biblica.*
Expos.	Expositor's.
E.S.	*Les Évangiles Synoptiques.*
E.T.	English Translation.
Holtzmann	*Hand-Commentar zum Neuen Testament.*
J.Q.R.	*Jewish Quarterly Review.*
J.Z.f.W.u.L.	*Jüdische Zeitschrift für Wissenschaft und Leben* (ed. Geiger).
Jülicher	Jülicher, Gleichnisreden Jesu.
Kohler, Theologie	*Grundriss einer Systematischen Theologie des Judentums.*
Levy	*Neuhebräisches und Chaldäisches Wörterbuch.*
Levy, *Targum-Wörterbuch*	*Chaldäisches Wörterbuch über die Targumim* (1881).
Marc.	Marcion.
M.	Mangey, ed. of Philo; or Mishna.
Monatsschrift	*Monatsschrift für Geschichte und Wissenschaft des Judentums.*
N.T.	New Testament.
O.T.	Old Testament.
P.B.	Prayer Book.
Phar. und Sadd.	Pharisäer und Sadducäer.
R.	Rabba or Rabbi.
R.E.	*Real Encyclopädie für Bibel und Talmud* (Hamburger).
S.G.	Synoptic Gospels.
Strom.	Stromateis.
T.B.	Talmud Babli (Babylonian Talmud).
T.J.	Talmud Jerushalmi (Palestinian Talmud).
Test.	Testament.
Weiss (Johannes)	*Die Schriften des Neuen Testaments,* edited by Johannes Weiss.

CHAPTER I

WAS JESUS A PROPHET ?

IN this chapter and in those to follow, I shall consider some of the problems connected with Jesus and the Gospels. It is far from my intention to attack any party or creed. The Jewish standpoint is well known, and while attempting to defend orthodox Judaism, we Jews refuse to offend those who cannot see eye to eye with us. Our problem is—should Jesus be called a prophet ? We are frequently told that he was so regarded. The Gospel of Matthew states that when the people of Jerusalem saw Jesus they asked, " Who is this ? " The reply was, " This is the prophet Jesus, from Nazareth in Galilee " (xxi. 10, 11). This is also the opinion of Mr. Montefiore, as set forth in his edition of the *Synoptic Gospels* and also in his *Jowett Lectures* for 1910.

Mr. Montefiore is probably the first Jew who has seen in Jesus the " last of the prophets." He even believes that Jesus was greater than any of the Hebrew prophets (see *Jowett Lectures*, p. 115). Naturally, the New Testament writers speak of Jesus as a Prophet, a King, and a High Priest, just because they believed him to have been the Christ (Messiah) or the Anointed One. In days of old, high priests, kings, and prophets were anointed.

B

The first question then is : When and how was Jesus anointed ? The answer is that he was anointed Messiah at his baptism at the hands of John the Baptist. The story is to be found in chapter i. of Mark. Mr. Montefiore says, " no critical reader to-day can believe in the literal truth of Mark i. 10 and 11 " (see *Synoptic Gospels*, p. 45). At this baptism, Jesus, after entering and leaving the water, sees the Heavens open, then a dove rests upon him, conveys the holy spirit to him, and he hears a voice from Heaven saying, " Thou art my beloved Son, in thee I am well pleased." According to another account in the Gospels, the Heavenly message or Bath Kol was, " Thou art my Son, this day have I begotten Thee." This is a quotation from the Psalms (ii. 7). Jerome tells us that in the *Gospel according to the Hebrews* (which we no longer possess), the proclamation ran as follows : " My Son, in all the prophets I expected thee, that thou wast destined to come, and I should rest on thee ; for thou art My rest, thou art My only begotten Son, who reigneth for ever " (cf. *Comment.* Isaiah, iv. 11, 12).

Later tradition associated various miraculous features with the event. There was also a fire, probably representing the Old Testament account of the Theophany at the burning-bush. All these elements of miraculous display at once disclose the real nature of the story. Here we have a piece of apocalyptic literature. It would not be difficult to show that part of the baptism story, with the celestial vision and the Bath Kol, are also to be found in the *Testaments of the Twelve Patriarchs*, a Jewish apocalyptic book written more than a hundred years before the birth of Jesus. By " apocalyptic literature " we mean such writings as are intended to reveal the divine secrets concerning the last things, the Messianic age, and the coming of the Kingdom of God. The Book of Daniel is placed in this class. On the whole, the Pharisees rejected this literature. They felt that it did not really express the Jewish spirit. This will explain why Daniel is not counted among the Nebi'im or Prophets, but is classed among the Kethubim or Holy Writings.

Now not only is the baptism story apocalyptic, but as we shall see, practically all the genuine teaching of Jesus is apocalyptic. His message, " the Kingdom of Heaven is at hand " (Matt. iv. 17), plainly indicates the apocalyptic character of his teaching. Again, his frequent use of the term Son of Man, his opposition to wealth, his conflict with the Kingdom of Satan, his preference for celibacy, his hostility to the Pharisees who rejected the apocalyptic teaching, all these (and many more) features force us to see in Jesus not a prophet, but an apocalyptic dreamer and teacher, who, in time, applied his own teachings to himself and believed himself to be the Messiah. The early Christians felt that Jesus must have been a prophet if he was the Messiah. Eusebius says Jesus was the supreme prophet of prophets. The Gnostic Ebionites denied his divinity, but acknowledged that he was an inspired prophet of the highest order (Dr. Hastings' *Dictionary of Christ and the Gospels*, i. p. 506 ; and Hoennicke, *Das Judenchristentum*, p. 228).

According to the Koran, Jesus was merely one among many prophets. At the outset of his career Jesus seems to have claimed the title for himself. The Gospels tell us that in the first address (for he was a teacher) which he delivered in the Synagogue of Nazareth, he applied to himself the words of Isaiah lxi. 1, "The spirit of the Lord is upon me," etc. (see Luke iv. 18, 21). Again at the end of his career, when his death seemed imminent, the Evangelists make him associate himself with the prophets, by letting him assert that just as they had perished in Jerusalem so he also would die there (see Matt. xxiii. 29 ff., and Luke xiii. 33). We need better evidence than the testimony of the Gospels if we are to believe, that it was a sign of a prophet to die in Jerusalem, or that it was a fact that the true prophets had been put to death in the Holy City. The mere fact that Jesus applied to himself the words of Isaiah lxi. 1, would not constitute him a prophet. Something more is needed. The first thing that a prophet had to do was to bring to his fellow-men a message from God and about God's ways with men.

Moses brought the Commandments and revealed God as the God of all spirits. Isaiah taught that the Lord is the God of holiness. Ezekiel laid stress on the value of the individual soul in the eyes of the Heavenly Father, who desires that the sinner should repent and live. Amos dwelt on righteousness as the way to God. Hosea taught that love is the essence of religion. Jeremiah dwelt on the divine pity. And so with all the other prophets—each had his message, eternally true and universally valid. If Jesus is to be considered a prophet, we ask, Did he reveal an aspect of the Deity previously unknown or forgotten in his day ? The Gentiles of the first century would rightly answer this question in the affirmative. Jesus and the Apostles had much to teach them which they did not know. The Jews of the days of Jesus had nothing to learn from his message. If they had relied on him as the Messiah, they would have been deluded, even as they were one hundred years later by Bar Coziba (often spoken of as Bar Cochba). To the Jew, Jesus was no prophet. He came among his fellow-men, but did not say " I will teach you about God," but rather " I will teach you about myself and then you will know God." (See John v. 19 and vi. 35.)

The Gospel makes Jesus invite the weary to find rest under his new yoke—so much easier to bear than the old Torah given by Moses, the chief of the Prophets. " Come unto me, all ye that labour and are heavy laden, and I will give you rest " (Matt. xi. 28). The Psalmist had long ago urged the weary to cast their burden on God, who is ever with the broken-hearted and the humble in spirit. Jesus displaces God. He constitutes himself the only way that leads to the God of all. In the famous verse, " All things have been delivered unto me of my Father (i.e. God) ; and no one knoweth the Son (i.e. Jesus), save the Father, neither doth any know the Father, save the Son, and he to whomsoever the Son willeth to reveal him " (ibid. xi. 27), Jesus limits man's power to know God. Again the Old Testament prophets were " men of God," " servants of the Most High." Jesus does not, according to the Gospels or the Church, belong to this category. He is represented as infinitely higher than this. He is held forth as the only Son of God who (to use his apocalyptic phraseo-logy) " is coming on the clouds " to judge the world. He is to usher in the Kingdom of God on earth, and as a direct result of his own teaching, he was acclaimed the Messiah of Israel.

At this time (circa 33 c.e.) Israel was undoubtedly yearning most passionately for the coming of the Mes-siah, who would break the oppressor's fetters and once for all put an end to the galling tyranny of the proud Romans. Jesus disappointed his followers, who deserted him. His appearance in Jerusalem had caused no little stir, and the Romans treated him as they treated all the Jewish false Messiahs. Pontius Pilate did not ask Jesus if he was a prophet. The charge was that he claimed to be " the King of the Jews," and in accordance with Roman law, he was sentenced to be crucified. The Gospel stories of the crucifixion need careful consideration, in view of the light thrown on the history of the crucifixion of mock-kings among the Romans. Philo, who was born some time before Jesus, has something to tell us on this point. Dr. Frazer in his *Golden Bough* (ii. 71 ff. and iii. 138 ff.) helps us to appreciate the historical meaning and value of the Crucifixion narratives as recorded in the New Testament. We do not care to emphasize now the terrible persecution of Jews by followers of Jesus, just because it was believed that the Jews had been responsible for his condemnation and execution. Both the condemnation and the execution were sanctioned and carried out by the Roman authorities.

The career of Jesus as prophet and Messiah was an entire failure. Men are not even to-day ready for the Messianic age, and after 1,900 years the Kingdom of God has not yet been established. Jesus preached about the coming of the Kingdom, but in vain. For this reason we cannot grant that he was a prophet. Jesus is often spoken of as a prophet because he displayed in a marked degree a strong personal note. The Gospels say he did not teach like the Scribes, but with authority (Matt. vii. 29). The Scribes merely interpreted the Law and the Prophets ; Jesus did something

quite different. He even went, says Mr. Montefiore,
" beyond the prophets." The latter spoke to the people
in the name of God—" Thus saith the Lord." Jesus,
who in his own consciousness was so much greater, had
no need to imitate the Scribes or even the Prophets.
" Ye have heard it said of old " was the cry of the contemporary Scribes. Jesus said : " But I say unto you."
This personal note is certainly new, but what did it
mean ? We are forced to choose between two alterna-
tives : either Jesus imagined himself to be the only Son
of God and therefore knew the Divine will which he was
called upon to reveal, or else he deliberately used the
words " I say unto you " this, that, or the other, without
any authority or justification.

This matter will not be pursued further now, as it
will arise again when we discuss the new law of Jesus.
The fact that he claimed to give a new law—" I say
unto you "—disqualifies his claim to be a prophet.
The Jews have always relied on the passage in Deuteronomy (xiii. 1 ff.), that a prophet who attempts to alter
the Mosaic Law is not to be credited. The Rabbis express this by saying, " No prophet is permitted to intro-
duce a new law in Israel " (Joma, 80 a). The fact that
Jesus abrogated several Mosaic commandments would
also disqualify him as a prophet. None of the Old
Testament Prophets attacked the Law. They frequently
attacked the hollow worship, the irreligious manner in
which the people kept their Sabbaths or Festivals (Isa.
i. 14), but they did not abrogate the Mosaic precepts.
Nay, they told the people to remember the Law of Moses.
This Jesus did not do, and again for this reason we
cannot call him a prophet in Israel. In another way
Jesus displayed the personal note of authority, by for-

giving sins. This seems to the Jewish spirit to be reserved for God alone. Man cannot forgive sins. Whenever we sin we do wrong not only on earth, but we offend also God, whose Kingdom rests on love and righteousness.   The divine grace can be given only by God, not by any prophet or teacher.   The Gospels state that when Jesus claimed power to forgive sins, his opponents said: "Why doth this man thus speak? He blasphemeth; who can forgive sins but one, even God?" (Mark ii. 7).   The prophets of old had always taught that God alone could pardon sin.   This, again, hinders us from seeing in Jesus a prophet sent by God. Had he merely re-echoed the words of Micah iii. 8 :— "I am full of power . . . to declare unto Jacob his transgression, and to Israel his sin "—his words would have given no cause for offence.   The prophets received direct communications from God (see Amos iii. 7).   Did Jesus, apart from the questionable revelation at his baptism, receive such direct communications?   The Synoptic Gospels offer no evidence on this point; and therefore it seems reasonable to say that he did not. This differentiates him from the prophets of Israel.

Now we must consider the question of prediction. The prophets foretold what was going to happen, not to themselves but to Israel or to other nations.   Jesus, indeed, seems to have foretold certain events concerning himself.   In Mark xiv. 62, we have the prophecy of his Parousia or re-appearance on earth as the judge of men.   This prediction has remained unfulfilled till to-day.   He declares that true atonement for sin can only be found in himself, and, again, he predicts that his death was to be sacrificial—he came "to give his life a ransom for many" (Mark x. 45).   This idea, known as " Vicarious Atonement," is entirely un-Jewish, and has been rejected invariably as contrary to the prophetic teaching of Ezekiel that the individual is responsible to God for his own iniquity.

Jesus, we are told, predicted the destruction of Jerusalem and the Temple ; so did Rabban Jochanan ben Zakkai (Joma, 39 b). But we do not, on that account, reckon Jochanan among the prophets, and therefore we have no reason for considering Jesus as one of the prophets. Much of his teaching could justly be called prophetic, but then, in all such cases, it will be found that he is merely repeating the identical words or re-enforcing the messages of the prophets of old. It would be an interesting study to reconstruct any of the Gospels after all Old Testament ideas or phrases had been deleted. We have pointed out that, in addition to the presence of Old Testament elements, we have a large portion of apocalyptic teaching. Some of the most famous parables fall under this head. They have no importance for Jews, who have rejected the entire post-Biblical apocalyptic literature as being opposed to the best Jewish thought and sentiment.

Finally, there is an element in the teaching of Jesus which is antagonistic to Jewish practice. This is hardly likely to meet with approval among orthodox Jews. Far more serious is the fact that the Gospels present Jesus as the only Son of God and as the Messiah. Jews do not believe that he was either. We have given adequate reasons for denying the prophetic claims attributed to Jesus which he himself, at least on one occasion, repudiated (Mark viii. 27 ff.). If, as we hope to show, Jesus had a part to play in the history of men, that part must not be sought in Israel but among the

Gentiles. Let us, however, remember that Jesus believed that he was sent not to the Gentiles, but only to
Israel. Here, again, we believe that Jesus was mistaken. Profoundly significant are the questions at
issue as recorded in the Gospels. We have dealt with
the prophetic claims put forth by Jesus or, on his
behalf, by the Evangelists. We cannot accept these
claims. They are involved with the questions of the
Sonship and the Messiah, and therefore cannot appeal
to the Jew, who believes that every human being is a
child of God, and that the future will herald the coming
of the Messiah, whose mission will be to establish peace
and love in the world.

LITERATURE

See Maimonides, *Moreh Nebuchim*, ii, chapters 32–48, and
Hilchoth Jesode Hatorah, chapters 7–10, on 'Prophecy.' On
'Holy Spirit,' see Dr. H. B. Swete, *The Holy Spirit in the New
Testament*. On 'Authority' in the teaching of Jesus, see
Dr. J. Bergmann, *Jüdische Apologetik* p. 33, n. 3, and Hast-
ings' D. C. G. i. pp. 146 ff. On 'Apocalyptic Literature,'
see Hastings' D. B. i. pp. 109 f, and D. C. G. i. pp. 79 ff.

NOTES

[1] The dove and the holy spirit (p. 2) may be parallcled by
the Talmudic account of the Bath Kol, which is said to have
resembled the cooing of a dove (*see* Berachoth, 3*a*).

[2] The persecution of the prophets (p. 4) mentioned in Luke
xi. 49, owes its origin to the pre-Christian Book of Jubilees i,
12: "And I shall send witnesses against them . . . but they
will . . . slay the witnesses also and persecute those who seek
the law."

CHAPTER II

IN our last chapter, we saw that it was impossible to include Jesus among the prophets of Israel. This negative position will not deter us from acknowledging frankly and unreservedly that Jesus was a preacher and a teacher. There is good reason to believe that he and his followers preached and taught in the Synagogues. This fact, which is vouched for by the New Testament, bears eloquent testimony to the fine spirit of toleration that obtained among the Pharisees in Palestine, in the first century. Jesus felt that he had a message to deliver, and obtained permission to speak to his fellow Jews in their houses of prayer.

What is the Jewish attitude to-day towards the teaching of Jesus ? In the past the Jews looked askance at the Gospels and the other books of the New Testament. They instinctively avoided all contact with this literature. The reason for this is to be found in the attitude of the Church towards the Jews. It was believed that the first duty of the Church was to convert the Jews. In the Middle Ages the persecuted Jews were forced to attend church and to listen to the stories of the Gospels. Again, the Rabbis were compelled to engage in disputations with renegade Jews or with learned Christian divines. At one of the most famous of these public disputations the great scholar Nachmanides defended the Jewish position with remarkable skill. The result of these polemical discussions was invariably disastrous to the Jews. The intellectual victory was always on the side of the Jews, and the enraged opponent found an easy way of defeating his " obstinate and blind " Hebrew antagonist by instigating an attack on all the Jews in the town ; or by persuading the authorities to banish the " disbelieving and accursed " Jews. This frequent experience naturally estranged the Jews from the Church and her sacred scriptures recorded in the New Testament.

If the Gospels were read and studied by Jews, this was only for polemical purposes. We still possess some fine specimens of this class of literature. The *Chizzuk Emunah* by Troki has been translated into English ; it is called *Faith Strengthened* and is divided into two sections. In the first part, the Old Testament passages, which are generally adduced by Christians as proofs that Jesus was the Messiah, are clearly shown to contain no reference to the Founder of Christianity. In the second part, we have a detailed criticism of the Gospels, with a view of demonstrating that Jesus could not be the Messiah. The circumstances in England, both political and intellectual, are different to-day, and again we ask : What is the modern Jewish attitude towards the teaching of Jesus ?

Christian scholars and apologists are naturally concerned to demonstrate the superiority of Christian teaching. They claim that the last word in religion and ethics has been taught by Jesus. They invite Jews and others to learn the " higher morality " revealed in the New Testament. It is almost impossible in a modern Christian country, such as England, for the Jew to refuse to listen to these pressing invitations. We are to-day confronted by honest and well-meaning men, who ask us to be candid, and to acknowledge that the moral teaching of Jesus is higher and better than that of any other teacher. Can we afford to imitate the old Jewish attitude (which was quite right in the dark days of persecution) and shall we still refuse to read the Gospels or to discuss their contents ? If we do, we shall not act in harmony with the old teaching of the Rabbis : " Know how to answer the opponent," whose claims to possess a better religion should be met by a fearless justification of Judaism as the purest of all forms of religion. To remain Jews and to refuse to defend the Jewish religion, or wilfully to ignore the claims made by Christian teachers, when asserting the absolute superiority of their religion, is a cowardly and irreligious attitude.

Two famous German Christian theologians have published within the last few years two books which have been epoch-making. We refer to Dr. Harnack's *What is Christianity ?* and to Dr. Bousset's learned work on the Jewish religion, entitled *Die Religion des Judentums im neutestamentlichen Zeitalter*. Both books are alike in claiming that Christianity teaches religion and morality from a higher standpoint than that taught by Judaism. The German Jewish scholars were not silent. Rabbis Perles, Güdemann, Eschelbacher, and Bäck, among others, took up the challenge, and again, as of old, vindicated the Jewish religion. This, we claim, is the bounden duty of English Jewish scholars. We must know how to answer our opponents and how to defend the religion of Israel. We shall not only show that we appreciate our own religion, but we shall, at the same time, discover how much Jews and Christians have in common.

There is a remarkable difference between the teaching of Jesus and that of the Jewish prophets. If we wish to know what Isaiah taught, we need only read the book that bears the prophet's name. If we desire to ascertain the teaching of Jesus, we are confronted with four chief accounts of his life. The four Gospels do not harmonize with one another. There is, for instance, very little of the teaching to be found in Mark, the oldest of the Gospels. On the other hand, Matthew and Luke contain much more. Much of it was conveyed in parables. This was quite the usual method with the Rabbis. The parables are to a great extent apocalyptic, and refer to the state of the coming Kingdom of God. There is much in them that does not appeal to modern Christian scholars, who acknowledge that Jesus was mistaken in believing that the end of the world was imminent, and that God's Kingdom was about to be inaugurated. We shall have to remember that much of the teaching of Jesus was conditioned by his firm belief that the existing human society was about to come to an end. He believed that the generation which heard his message would witness the new order of things. He, therefore, urged that it was hardly worth while to insist on one's rights, and that the wisest policy was to follow the line of least resistance.

What was the good of opposing evil, when in the immediate future evil would vanish? We shall, therefore, be prepared to find that much of the teaching of Jesus in our modern social life must be considered as hardly practical or even possible. All the sayings in the Gospels, however, are not concerned with the Kingdom of

God. In attempting to investigate some of this teaching, we shall constantly inquire whether it contains
anything new and valuable for the Jew. We shall
accordingly confine ourselves to the famous Sermon on
the Mount which is to be found in Matthew, and in a
shorter form in Luke. There is considerable reason to
believe that the more original form is to be found in
Luke. It has been expanded by Matthew, who writing
for Jews, has added such current teaching as would
probably appeal to his Jewish readers. We quite agree
with Mr. Montefiore, who holds that " it is of profound
importance and interest for Jews to consider whether,
and how far, and in what the moral and religious teaching of the Sermon on the Mount excels the teaching of
the Old Testament and the Rabbis " (*Synoptic Gospels*,
p. 321). In addition to the writings of the Rabbis, we
shall try to find some parallels in the writings of Philo,
Josephus, and in the various Jewish apocalyptic and
pseudo-epigraphic books. This is a necessary procedure,
because the criticism is often raised, that the sayings of
Jesus cannot be justly compared with those of the Rabbis ; because the Mishna, Gemara, and Midrashim were
committed to writing subsequent to the date when the
Gospels were written.

This criticism does not hold good with reference to the
other writings just mentioned. Philo is earlier than
Jesus, and this fact meets another objection that Mr.
Montefiore raises. The teaching of Jesus, he maintains,
is compact and is to be found in the Gospels. On the
other hand, we are told that the sayings of the Rabbis
are scattered through the many folios of the Talmud ;
and that, moreover, we do not get the opinions of one
teacher, but of many Rabbis. As a matter of fact, the

Gospels contain at least half a dozen different sources or accounts of the supposed thought of Jesus. Again, in Philo and in the *Testaments of the Twelve Patriarchs*, we find in a compact form the thought and teaching of two Jews earlier than Jesus, and we venture to believe equally valuable and original. The level of their moral teaching is by no means inferior to that of the Gospels. The Sermon on the Mount might also be called the Sermon in the Plain, for in Luke the locale is a plain, and not, as in Matthew, a mountain. The entire Sermon was probably unknown to Mark. Moreover, Paul is equally silent and does not give a single passage of the entire Sermon.

This at once leads to the question : Did Jesus really teach what is recorded in the Sermon ? Most of the great critics agree that he certainly did not deliver the whole of it on one occasion. They agree generally that the Evangelist has joined together several sayings, delivered on different occasions, and has probably added other matter, which may or may not be original. Very few scholars claim that the Sermon is entirely the genuine utterance of Jesus. Nevertheless, the fact remains that we have in it a remarkable composition, which will certainly repay our careful study.

According to Tertullian (one of the old Church Fathers) the Sermon on the Mount was believed to be in agreement with the spirit and teaching of the Hebrew Scriptures. He quotes (*Adv. Marcion*, iv. 14) verses from the Old Testament to illustrate and explain the Sermon. He clearly indicates that it contains nothing new. It seems to him that it is really a condensed summary of the Old Testament teaching. We think that this is a fair criticism, and it appears to be, to an extent, correct.

This view may explain the fact that the earliest Christian manual of instruction, the Didache, omits the entire Sermon. If the author of the Didache (*circa* 110 C.E.) knew the Sermon, he probably omitted it because it did not teach any doctrine unknown to the people at large, or any new teaching that was specifically Christian.

The Sermon on the Mount occupies the central position in the accepted ethical teaching of the Founder of Christianity. Every sentence in it is therefore of vital importance to all who take an interest in the New Testament. The real question for the Jew is summed up in one sentence: "Does the Sermon teach new truths which the Jew cannot find in his own literature?" If the answer to this question be in the affirmative, then it is the undoubted duty of the Jew to study and assimilate such revelations of new truth, which were hitherto unknown to him. The Jew calls truth "the Seal of God." It must be courted and loved entirely for its own sake. It is like goodness and beauty. These three aspects of life are eternal and universal. They are independent of race and creed, and by their own intrinsic worth appeal to every soul. We should look for truth wherever we can find it.

The first verse of the Sermon in Matthew v. 3, states:— "Happy are the poor in spirit, for theirs is the Kingdom of Heaven." This is an expansion of Luke's version, "Happy are ye poor" (vi. 20). Matthew wishes Jesus to begin his earliest teaching with a Beatitude. This procedure is paralleled by the opening word of the first Psalm, "Happy is the man who walketh," etc.

In the Old Testament there are some thirty sentences beginning with the word "happy." This word "Ashrei" (happy) occurs forty-five times in the Hebrew

c

Bible, including twenty-six instances in the Psalms.
Beatitudes occur in the Psalms of Solomon, in Ecclesiasticus, and in the Secrets of Enoch. By way of contrast
with this first verse of the Sermon " Happy are the poor,"
let us compare (Ps. xli. 1), " Happy is he that considereth
the poor." It does not seem necessary to do more than
to place these two verses together, in order to determine
which is practically more valuable. To remove poverty
or to relieve distress must surely be more meritorious
than to remain resigned to poverty. Why were the
poor told that they were destined to enjoy happiness ?
It would be idle to believe that Jesus honestly believed
that the poor were really happy. The actual experience
of life would contradict this. The reason is that the
Sermon was delivered only to the narrow circle of disciples who were very poor people. The first message is
to encourage them. They are promised happiness in
the coming Kingdom. Here on earth they are poor—
there, in the new Kingdom, they will be rich. The expression " Kingdom of Heaven " is an exact translation
of the Aramaic *Malchuta Dishemaja*. It is peculiar to
Matthew. In Josephus, it is called the Theocracy, and
was believed to designate the present authority of God
over the lives of men (*Contra Apionem*, ii. 165). The
origin of the term is to be found in the Book of Daniel
(ii. 44 ; vii. 14). In these passages a Kingdom is promised. The realization of the divine Kingdom will
afford a striking contrast to the wicked rule of the cruel
heathens on earth. The seventh chapter of Daniel
speaks of the " saints " of the Highest who will inherit
the Kingdom.

In the Gospels, the " saints " become the disciples of
Jesus. Poor they may be now, but if they follow him

and reject the wicked world and its manifold attractions, then they will inherit the Kingdom of Heaven.
In opposition to them, the Jews as a people will be
excluded from the coming Kingdom (Matt. xxii. 13).
The "poor" correspond to the *Ani'im, Anavim,* and
Ebionim—the poor, meek, and humble of the Psalms.
It is evident that the opening verses of the Sermon
were based on the first three verses of the sixty-first
chapter of Isaiah. Luke (iv. 17 ff.) says that this chapter of Isaiah was applied by Jesus to himself at the
opening of his ministry. The passage begins : " The
spirit of the Lord God is upon me ; because the Lord
hath anointed me to preach good tidings (i.e. the Gospel)
to the poor (Anavim)." Parallels to the words of Jesus,
" Happy are the poor," may be seen in Isaiah xi. 4,
and lvii. 15. If the text of Matthew, " Happy are the
poor in spirit " be preferred, then Psalm xxxiv. 18 offers
a fine parallel—" The Lord . . . saveth such as be of a
contrite spirit " (cf. ibid. li. 17 and also see Isa. lxvi. 2).

The next verse of the Sermon (Matt. v. 4) states,
" Happy are they that mourn, for they shall be comforted." This is also based on Isaiah (lxi. 1–3) : " He
hath sent me to bind up the broken-hearted, to proclaim
liberty to the captives, and the opening of the prison to
them that are bound, . . . to comfort all that mourn."
The idea of divine comfort is a commonplace in the Old
Testament (see Isa. xl. 1 ; lvii. 18 ; lx. 20). We suggest,
as additional parallels : " They that sow in tears shall
reap in joy " (Ps. cxxvi. 5), or another passage from the
Psalms : " Happy is the man whom thou chastenest, O
Lord . . . that thou mayest give him rest from the
days of adversity " (xciv. 12, 13). Isaiah (li. 11) promises that " sorrow and sighing shall flee away."

God himself will comfort his people (Isa. lxvi. 13). Another parallel may be given from Tobit : " Happy are as many as were grieved over all thy plagues ; for they shall rejoice " (xiii. 14).

There can be no doubt that Jesus intentionally based the first two verses of the Sermon on Isa. (lxi. 1–3). In his belief that he was the Messiah, he naturally adopted the Old Testament programme—to cheer the poor and to comfort the mourners. The function of comforting the people is peculiar to Isaiah's description of the Messiah. In Hebrew literature, the " Comforter " is one of the designations of the Messiah (Synhedrin, 98*b* and T. J. Berachoth ii, 4. 5*a* ; cf. Levy iii, p. 153). The mourners (in Isaiah) do not lament personal loss but national disaster. The individual must lament the degradation of his people, and he will rejoice and be happy when his people receive the divine comfort.

The next verse of the Sermon reads :—(5) " Happy are the meek, for they shall inherit the earth." This is a direct quotation from Psalm xxxvii. 11 : " The meek shall inherit the earth." See also Psalms xxv. 13. In the Book of Enoch (vi. 9) we have a parallel—" The elect shall possess light, joy and peace, and they shall inherit the earth." The elect are the saints or the meek. The Didache (iii, 7) also used Ps. xxxvii. 11. It has " Be meek, since the meek shall inherit the earth." To " inherit the earth " was understood in the sense of entering the Messianic Kingdom (Isa. lx. 21). The opponents of the Kingdom of God are the arrogant (Zedim). In the Shemoneh Esreh (Eighteen Benedictions) the Zedim are mentioned as destined to be humbled by God. When this is accomplished, the divine Kingdom will be established.

Luke has no parallel to the last two Beatitudes. It is remarkable that Luke omits all the blessings pronounced on such virtues as meekness, peacemaking, purity, mercy or charity. It is possible that the original teaching of Jesus did not deal with these virtues. The Sermon continues :—(6) " Happy are they who hunger and thirst after righteousness, for they shall be filled." Luke (vi. 21) has " Happy are ye that hunger now ; for ye shall be filled." This version is again considered to be the original. It is probably merely another aspect of the first Beatitude. Philo (Mangey ii. 651) has the phrase, " to hunger and to thirst." In the forty-second Psalm (v. 2), we have the beautiful expression, " My soul thirsteth for God, for the living God." The idea of righteousness is peculiar to the Old Testament. God himself (Jer. xxiii. 6) promises to become the righteousness whereby the people will be saved. A few parallels to Matthew's version will suffice :—" Thou shalt follow after that which is altogether righteous, that thou mayest live and inherit the land which the Lord thy God giveth thee " (Deut. xvi. 20). " And the effect of righteousness is quietness and confidence for ever " (Isa. xxxii. 17). " Hearken unto me, ye that follow after righteousness, ye that seek the Lord " (ibid. li. 1). " The meek shall eat and be satisfied, they shall praise the Lord that seek after him " (Ps. xxii. 26). " He that followeth after righteousness and mercy findeth life, righteousness, and honour " (Prov. xxi. 21). God " loveth him that followeth after righteousness " (ibid. xv. 9).

The next Beatitude (v. 7) says : " Happy are the merciful ; for they shall obtain mercy." This is not found in Luke. It is possible that " righteousness " in the previous verse (v. 6) suggested " mercy " in this. The Hebrew " Tzedakah " means righteousness as well as charity (or mercy). The Septuagint frequently translates the Hebrew by either term. Good parallels are Psalm xli. 1, " Happy is he that considereth the poor, the Lord will deliver him in the day of evil " (see next verse); and, " He that hath pity on the poor, happy is he " (Prov. xiv. 21). The Talmud says : " He who has mercy on his fellow-creatures obtains mercy from Heaven " (Sabbath, 151b; cf. Tosephta Baba Kama, ix, 30).

The next Beatitude (v. 8), " Happy are the pure in heart, for they shall see God," does not occur in Luke. The " pure in heart " occurs in Psalm xxiv. 4, in connexion with ascending God's mount. Philo uses the term " seeing God " as the connotation of Israel. Perhaps Matthew used this in connexion with Psalm lxxiii. 1 : " Surely God is good to Israel, even to such as are pure in heart." We have here a good parallel to this Beatitude, connecting the " pure in heart " with " Israel " (i.e. seeing God). Other parallels are Psalms vii. 10 ; xi. 7 ; xvii. 15 ; and xcvii. 11. The next Beatitude (v. 9), " Happy are the peacemakers for they shall be called sons of God," is also missing in Luke. Isaiah again offers a parallel : " How beautiful upon the mountains are the feet of him that bringeth good tidings, that publisheth peace " (lii. 7, and cf. Zech. viii. 16, 17, 19; Ps. xxxiv. 14, and Prov. xii. 20).

Hillel, who lived before Jesus, taught " love peace, pursue peace, and love mankind " (Aboth i. 12). For " Sons of God," as a title acquired by nobility of character, see Sirach iv. 10. Philo says, " All who have real knowledge of the one Father of all are rightly called Sons of God " (*Confusion of Languages*, 28, M. i. 426).

Knowledge of God, according to Philo and the Rabbis, means the "Imitation of God." God creates peace (Isa. lvii. 19) and therefore let man imitate the Heavenly Father, whose name is Peace (Leviticus Rabba, ix, 9). The last Beatitude (v. 10) is, " Happy are they that have been persecuted for righteousness' sake, for theirs is the Kingdom of Heaven." The fine passage in Isaiah (l. 6 and 7) is an excellent parallel. " I gave my back to the smiters, and my cheeks to them that plucked off the hair, I hid not my face from shame and spitting. For the Lord God will help me ; therefore have I not been confounded ; therefore have I set my face like a flint, and I know that I shall not be ashamed " (cf. li. 7 and 12).

Israel's heroic suffering during the last nineteen hundred years is an actual parallel to the words of Jesus. The persecution by the Church is the living commentary on the higher morality said to have been enunciated by her Founder. Deeds speak louder than words. The Beatitudes have undoubtedly a lofty tone, but let us not forget that all that they teach can be found in Isaiah and the Psalms. Israel finds nothing new here. The Jew rejoices to think that such fine teaching is common to Judaism and Christianity. Would that the practice of these noble words were realized by all the children of men, then would happiness be established in the Kingdom of God on earth.

LITERATURE

The best authorities on the Jewish parallels to the Sermon on the Mount are Lightfoot (*Horae Hebraicae*) ; Schöttgen (*Horae Hebraicae*) ; Soloweyczyk (*La Bible, Le Talmud et l'Évangile*) ; Zipser, *The Sermon on the Mount* (1852) ; Wünsche, *Neue Beiträge*, etc; Hamburger, R.E. Suppl. iii. pp. 48 ff. ; Delitzsch and Siegfried have also given Rabbinic parallels. On 'Beatitudes' see H. Weinel, *Jesus im Neunzehnten Jahrhundert*, pp. 151 ff. ; and *The Expositor's Greek Testament*, i, pp. 95 ff.

CHAPTER III

WE shall now turn to the next section of the Sermon according to Matthew's version (v. 11–20). Owing to limitations of space we cannot give more than one or two parallels to each verse. It is hardly necessary to observe that there are many more parallels in Jewish literature that might aptly be quoted. Again, we cannot discuss at length the various important problems that will arise in the course of our investigations. We shall, however, give references to the leading authorities, in order that the reader may obtain full information.

In the next two verses of the Sermon, Matthew expands the last Beatitude (v. 10) : " Happy are they that have been persecuted for righteousness' sake," into " Happy are ye when men shall reproach you, and persecute you, and say all manner of evil against you falsely, for my sake. Rejoice, and be exceeding glad ; for great is your reward in Heaven ; for so persecuted they the prophets which were before you " (v. 11 and 12). In Luke (vi. 22, 23) we find an interesting variation of this expansion, " Happy are ye, when men shall hate you, and when they shall separate you from their company, and reproach you, and cast out your name as evil, for the Son of Man's sake. Rejoice in that day, and leap for joy ; for behold, your reward is great in

Heaven ; for in the same manner did their fathers unto the prophets."

This expansion by both Evangelists is evidently an interpolation. It destroys the simplicity and beauty of the last Beatitude, by introducing the personal note " for my sake "—" Happy are ye when men shall persecute you for my sake." This is infinitely inferior to the belief that men shall eventually be happy if they suffer now for the sake of righteousness. For " Jesus' sake," rather than for the sake of justice or righteousness, is undoubtedly a new note. We confess that we are unable to give any parallel to this idea from Jewish literature. Judaism certainly insists on the duty and privilege of living for, and if needs be, of dying for the sake of God (Kiddush Ha-shem). It has never taught that we should rejoice in being persecuted for the sake of any prophet or leader. The Glory of God has been the only incentive. Israel has never failed in making every sacrifice in order to sanctify God's name.

Mr. Montefiore (*Jowett Lectures*, p. 132) sees in the motive " for my sake " a tremendous power and effect in the religious history of the world. He goes on to urge that " even if, in the sentences where they occur, the words ' for my sake ' are not always genuine, yet the thought and the motive assuredly go back to the historic Jesus." We cannot agree with this appreciation. We are monotheists, and we protest that the higher motive " for the sake of God " is in danger of being forgotten when men are taught to act for " Jesus' sake." Mr. Montefiore, in a note (p. 169), draws attention to the view that the authenticity of *every* passage in the Gospels, where the expression " for my sake " is found, is not above suspicion. Be this as it may, the fact remains that the motive for " Jesus' sake " has displaced the higher motive " for the sake of God." The version of Luke is very important. He does not say " for my sake," but " for the Son of Man's sake." Some authorities (e.g. Schmidt, *The Prophet of Nazareth,* p. 123) hold that Luke's text here is later than Matthew's, which has also been subjected to emendation. In other words, the phrase " for my sake " is not a genuine utterance of Jesus. It seems to me, however, that Luke's text is more original than Matthew's ; and that Jesus may have spoken of himself as the " Son of Man." This was an eschatological term used to designate the Messiah. Dr. Schmidt's contention that Jesus never used this term concerning himself in a Messianic sense has not been universally adopted. We cannot stay now to discuss this subject. Canon Driver's learned article on " Son of Man " in Hastings' *Bible Dictionary,* and Dr. Schmidt's article on the same subject in the *Encyclopædia Biblica,* will enable the reader to appreciate the difficulty involved in explaining the term.

We have said that the term was part of the eschatological terminology. It is necessary to support this contention by references (e.g. Enoch xlvi. 2, 3, 4 ; 4. Ezra xiii. 3 ff.). It is probable that the origin of these verses (Matt. v. 11 and 12, or Luke vi. 22 and 23) of the Sermon on the Mount is to be sought in Isaiah li. 7, " Hearken unto me, ye that know righteousness . . . ; fear ye not the reproach of men, neither be ye dismayed at their revilings." It is noteworthy that the Gospels do not discard the promise of a " reward in Heaven." Jews are told so often by Christian writers that in Judaism you have a regular " tit for tat " morality. God must promise a heavenly reward in return for man's

service. This motive is lacking in the parallel passage
(to Matt. v. 11, 12) which we have just quoted from
Isaiah. The fact, however, is beyond dispute that the
Rabbis taught the people that God would judge each man
according to his merit. There was good authority for
this belief. The Old Testament holds out the promise
of rewards and punishments. The prophets especially
insist that every man is destined to be recompensed
according to the " fruit of his works." The ethical
problems which had vexed the souls of the writers of
Job and the Psalms are solved by the teaching that the
wages are not all paid now, but that some of them are
in the keeping of the Father in Heaven. When the
Mishna (Peah i. 1) speaks of the " Keren Kayyemeth,"
i.e. the capital that remains in Heaven, or when Jesus
says " Great are your wages in Heaven," the idea is the
same. God is also the judge and taskmaster.

There is just one other point that we must discuss in
connexion with these two verses of the Sermon. The
disciples are told that they will have to endure persecution, " for so persecuted they the prophets which were
before you." Luke xi. 51, speaks of the " blood of
Abel and the blood of Zachariah, who perished between
the altar and the sanctuary." This Zachariah is not
the prophet of the same name. Graetz deals with this
question in his *History of the Jews*. He agrees that
Luke has used Josephus' *Wars* (iv. v, 4) where the
murder of Zachariah, son of Berachiah, in 68 C.E. is
narrated (see *Geschichte der Juden*, 4th ed., vol. iii. p.
754). Josephus published his history in 97 C.E., and
consequently the third Gospel was written after this date.
Apart from the exceptional cases of Elijah and Jeremiah,
we are unaware of any persecutions of the true pro-

phets. Elijah was certainly in danger owing to the hatred of Jezebel and of the heathen prophets of Baal. There is absolutely no proof that the people generally were hostile to the prophet. As regards Jeremiah, it is true that a party at court was strongly opposed to him. The thirty-eighth chapter of his book will show that although he was persecuted, yet he was not put to death. Jesus even declares that he will have to suffer death, because this was the fate of the prophets (Luke xiii. 33). There is no proof whatsoever for this statement. The supposed martyrdom of Isaiah lacks historical support. The legend is found in the Talmud. The prophets were not killed, nor as a rule were they subjected to persecution. It may be necessary later on to return to this question of persecution.

The Sermon continues (v. 13): "Ye are the salt of the earth; but if the salt have lost its savour, wherewith shall it be salted? It is thenceforth good for nothing, but to be cast out and trodden under foot of men." This is an instance of the teaching in allegory, so common among the Jews in the days of Jesus. He compares his disciples with salt. What was the lesson he wished to convey to his followers? Jesus undoubtedly knew that salt was the essential element in a sacrifice (Lev. ii. 13, and Ex. xxx. 35–38). Its value in daily life as a necessary part of food would naturally suggest that the disciples were to consider themselves as an essential element in the coming Kingdom. Salt was used to keep food wholesome. So likewise, the disciples were to sweeten the life of the new community which was about to be inaugurated. There is nothing very original in telling one's disciples that they are called upon to prove themselves useful members of society. It seems perfectly reasonable to assume that there is no connexion between this part of the Sermon and the previous section. This conclusion is forced upon us, when we consider the fact that this passage of the Sermon occurs also in Mark ix. 49 and 50, as well as in Luke xiv. 34 and 35. It seems to be obvious that Mark, the oldest Evangelist, should record the earliest form of this allegory. It forms in Mark part of the earliest eschatological teaching. The context begins in verse 48, which is a direct quotation from the Septuagint version of Isaiah lxvi. 24, and is used to describe Gehenna, as opposed to the coming Kingdom. " It is good for thee to enter into the Kingdom of God with one eye, rather than having two eyes to be cast into hell ; where their worm dieth not, and the fire is not quenched. For every one shall be salted with fire. Salt is good ; but if the salt have lost its saltness, wherewith will ye season it ? Have salt in yourselves, and be at peace one with another " (47–50).

It is easy to see that Matthew and Luke have borrowed from Mark the passage dealing with salt. Matthew has rather inartistically inserted it in the Sermon, whereas Luke has joined it on to the parable of the tower. Jülicher (ii. p. 74) argues that this allegory was not an original part of the Sermon. He believes that Mark ix. 49, is merely an elaboration of Leviticus (ii. 13) " neither shalt thou suffer the salt of the covenant of thy God to be lacking from thy meal offering : with all thine oblations thou shalt offer salt." The Evangelist also used Job vi. 6 : " Can that which hath no savour be eaten without salt ? " and probably also Zechariah xiii. 9 : " And I will bring the third part (of the people) through the fire, and will refine them as silver is refined," etc.   The verse in Mark ix. 49 : " For every one shall be salted with fire," seems rather diffi-cult to understand.   Coming after the words, " and the fire is not quenched," we would expect " purified " or " refined " instead of " salted."   It is quite possible that this verse of Mark influenced the practice of the early Christian Church in more than one direction.   Salt was used as an essential element in the ancient Church rites.   The Catechumen before baptism had to be exor-cized.   Then he took a small quantity of salt and was anointed all over with exorcized oil, which, by invocation to God, purified him from the burning traces of sin, and also put to flight the countless invisible powers of the devil.   For further details, see Hatch, *The Influence of Greek Ideas and Usages upon the Christian Church* (p. 308), and cf. Hoennicke (*op. cit.*, p. 239).

Then there was a belief that fire was also miracu-lously associated with the water of baptism.   It was supposed that a fire came from heaven upon all who entered into the water.   The influence of the Gnostics is probably at work here.   The next verses of the Ser-mon according to Matthew (v. 14–16) state : " Ye are the light of the world.   A city set on a hill cannot be hid.   Neither do men light a lamp, and put it under a bushel, but on the stand ; and it shineth unto all that are in the house.   Even so let your light shine before men, that they may see your good works, and glorify your Father who is in Heaven."   The Old Testament affords a good parallel to the first sentence.   " I the Lord . . . will give thee for a covenant of the people, for a light of the Gentiles " (Isa. xlii. 6 ; cf. xlix. 6 and lx. 3).   The next verse in Isaiah xlii. explains how Israel, the Servant of God, can be a light to the Gentiles.

He is " to open the blind eyes, to bring out the prisoners from the dungeon, and them that sit in darkness out of the prison house." This is somewhat loftier in tone than the corresponding passage in the Sermon—" even so let your light shine before men, that they may see your good works." We note that Jesus also insists on " good works." This refutes the notion that Judaism alone demands good works, whilst Christianity demands good motives. It also denies the superficial contrast that sees in Judaism an external religion and in Christianity a spiritual religion of the heart. The final words of the passage " Glorify your Father who is in Heaven," may be based on Isaiah lxvi. 19, " And they shall declare my glory among the nations."

The parable of the lamp is also found in Mark iv. 21, and twice in Luke (viii. 16, and xi. 33). Jülicher (ii. p. 88) considers the sayings " Ye are the light of the world," and " Even so let your light shine before men, that they may see your good works," as genuine utterances, but without any real connexion with the context. It is only in Matthew (v. 14b) that we find the parable of the " city on the hill." Again, we find a parallel in Isaiah (ii. 2) : " And it shall come to pass in the latter days, that the mountain of the Lord's house shall be established on the top of the mountains, and shall be exalted above the hills ; and all nations shall flow unto it."

The Sermon continues (Matt. v. 17–19): " Think not that I came to destroy the law or the prophets ; I came not to destroy, but to fulfil. For verily I say unto you, Till Heaven and earth pass away, one jot or one tittle shall in no wise pass away from the law, till all things be accomplished. Whosoever therefore shall break one of these least commandments, and shall teach men so, shall be called least in the Kingdom of Heaven ; but whosoever shall do and teach them, he shall be called great in the Kingdom of Heaven." The following Old Testament passage will serve as a parallel : " Ye shall not add unto the word which I command you, neither shall ye diminish from it, that ye may keep the commandments " (Deut. iv. 2). The teaching attributed here by Matthew to Jesus is quite in accord with Jewish sentiment. Philo also dwells on the immutability of the Law which is to continue as " immortal, so long as the sun and moon and the whole heaven and universe exist " (*Life of Moses*, ii. 3., M. ii, p. 136 ; cf. Josephus, c. Ap. ii. 228). There is, moreover, a parallel to Matthew's text in Luke xvi. 17 : " It is easier for Heaven and earth to pass away, than for one tittle of the law to fall." This is probably the source used by Matthew. The fact that Luke and Matthew both refer to the eternity of the Law seems sufficient reason to lead one to believe that Jesus may have expressed this view.

How are we to reconcile this with Jesus' remarkable hostility to the Law (Matt. xii. 1 ff.) ? One answer is that the Gospel of Matthew contains two strands or tendencies, one pro-legal and the other anti-legal. Another view is that at first Jesus intended to keep the Law ; but towards the end of his career, he modified this attitude. Some authorities see in the Gospels a reflection of the early history of the Christian community. This would be at a period long after the death of Jesus. There was then a conflict between Paul and the Apostles at Jerusalem. Paul wished to discard the Law, the Apostles strove to carry on the orthodox attitude attributed to Jesus. Where, then, in Matthew, as

In the case in point, we find a pro-legal attitude, we are probably reading the work of a supporter of the Apostles. There are good reasons for believing that Paul is referred to in Matthew in a very hostile manner. We shall have to deal with this subject again, and for the present we can only mention the fact that for about a century after the death of Jesus, there were many Christians who observed the Jewish law very strictly. This subject has been dealt with in a very able manner by Dr. Hoennicke in his book, *Das Judenchristentum im ersten und zweiten Jahrhundert*, which we have already quoted.

The expressions " jot " and " tittle " refer respectively to the tenth letter (yod) of the Hebrew alphabet and to the strokes or marks added to certain letters (e.g. beth or kaf). Schöttgen (p. 28) gives the following saying of Rabbi Alexander, the Reader : " If all men in the world were gathered together to destroy ' yod,' which is the smallest letter in the Law, they would not succeed." (Canticles Rabba, v, 11. For the meaning of " tittle" see also Levy, *Neuhebräisches und Chaldäisches Wörterbuch*, iv. p. 272, s.v. "Kôtz".) The phrase " till heaven and earth pass away " is probably derived from Psalm cii. 25, 26 : " Of old hast thou laid the foundation of the earth ; and the Heavens are the work of thy hands. They shall perish, but thou shalt endure." The eternity of the written law was an accepted belief among all classes of Jews in the age of Jesus. It continued also to be the belief of the early Palestinian Church and of the Ebionites. Until the destruction of Jerusalem in 70 C.E., the Christians belonged to the Jewish people. They frequented the Temple and the Synagogues. When, however, the Romans invested Jerusalem, and the hopeless fate of the Jews was seen

D

to be inevitable, the Christian community withdrew from the Holy City. They settled in Pella (see Eusebius, *Hist. Eccl.* iii. 5) and refused to identify themselves with their fellow-countrymen. Then the cleavage was made, and the Christians ceased to count themselves as members of the Synagogue.

Judaism did not cast off Christianity, but the latter arose as an independent faith when the Jews were left to their horrible fate in 70 C.E. At this period the success of Paul's missionary work proved of incalculable value in support of the anti-legal party in the Church. Moreover, the destruction of the Temple and the penalties attached to the observance of the Jewish religion were factors that induced the Christians to reject the Law. This determined the future history of the Christian Church. In place of the Holy Law a new system of dogma arose. The Jewish affection for the Law grew into the Christian worship of Jesus, first as Messiah, then as Son of God, and finally as part of the Trinity. If the followers of Jesus had only faithfully adhered to the Law and the Prophets, there would never have been a Christian Church.

LITERATURE

On the 'Origin of Christianity,' see Geiger, *Das Judenthum und seine Geschichte*, i. pp. 116 ff. ; Joël, *Blicke in die Religionsgeschichte;* Hamburger, *Real Encyclopädie*, ii. pp. 140 ff. ; Graetz, *Geschichte der Juden*, iii. chapter xi. ; *Jewish Encyclopedia*, vol. iv., pp. 49 ff. ; Bergmann, *op. cit.* p. 27 and Geiger, *Z. f. W. u. L.* xi. pp. 8 ff. On 'Son of Man,' see Schweitzer, *The Quest of the Historical Jesus*, pp. 279 ff. On the 'Martyrdom of Isaiah,' see *The Ascension of Isaiah* in Kautzsch, *Die Apokryphen und Pseudepigraphen*, edited by G. Beer who gives the Talmudic literature, cf. Dr. Charles' edition.

NOTE TO PAGE 31

Matthew v. 17, is quoted in the Talmud Sabbath, 116*b* ; see Güdemann, *Religionsgeschichtliche Studien*, pp. 65 ff., and cf. Strack (*op. cit.*) p. 20.

CHAPTER IV

THE UNFAIR TREATMENT OF THE PHARISEES

JESUS is said to have declared (Matt. v. 17), that he came " to fulfil the Law." This was the ideal of the Pharisaic Scribes, and accordingly needed qualification if Jesus was to be better and wiser than the Pharisees. The editor of the Gospel of Matthew has therefore added a remarkable verse, which is intended to modify the pro-legal sentiments in the preceding verses. " For I say unto you, that except your righteousness shall exceed the righteousness of the Scribes and Pharisees, ye shall in no wise enter into the Kingdom of Heaven " (Matt. v. 20). Here the Gospel denies the possibility of the Pharisees or Scribes being able to enter into the Kingdom of Heaven. Their righteousness is sin, only the new and higher righteousness of Jesus will enable his disciples to enter into the coming Kingdom.

One would like to know how and why the righteousness of the Scribes and Pharisees was believed to be so hollow and unreal as to exclude the whole class from the divine Kingdom ? This wholesale exclusion from future happiness is a marked feature of the Gospel teaching. It will recur several times in the course of our study. This verse is undoubtedly an interpolation. It is not found in any of the other Gospels. It is also in direct contradiction to the preceding verses. Is it likely that Jesus would have said the words in this verse (20), and also have said, " The Scribes and the Pharisees sit on Moses' seat : all things therefore whatsoever they bid you, these do and observe " (Matt. xxiii. 2, 3) ? The verse is missing in Beza's codex (fourth century). Wellhausen believes it is later than Jesus. It is, however, of considerable importance, because it speaks of the insufficient righteousness of the Scribes and Pharisees, and implies the higher righteousness of Jesus.

We are now facing the chief problem of the Sermon— the relation of the religion of Jesus to Judaism. The Church claims that the moral teaching of Christianity is infinitely superior to that of Judaism. Why ? Because the New Testament says so. But the New Testament has drawn a prejudiced, untrue and unfair picture of the Pharisees. Mr. Montefiore, in his *Jowett Lectures*, p. 37, adds : " The picture of the Pharisee in Luke's parable " is " a ludicrous caricature of the average Pharisee, a monstrous caricature of the Pharisaic ideal." He says, without the slightest proof, that this caricature " may yet be true enough of one particular perversion of the Pharisaic religion." Mr. Montefiore has not only erred in making this admission, but also in limiting his criticism to the single case of Luke's parable.

The words " ludicrous and monstrous caricature " should apply to the entire picture of the Pharisees in the Gospels. They are party documents, written long after the events they record. The Pharisees refused to believe in the Messianic and apocalyptic claims of Jesus. Should we not really expect in the Gospels a biassed account, if not a wretched caricature, of the " disbelieving " Pharisees ? Again, the Evangelists believed that Jesus had a new and genuine message—a " higher righteousness " that replaced the Jewish religion and its interpretations by the Scribes and Pharisees. The great difficulty is to know where we are to look for an honest account of the Pharisee of the first century. It will not be found in the New Testament, nor in the important modern Dictionaries of the *Bible,* and of *Christ and the Gospels,* edited by Dr. Hastings. The fact that in the latter work, H. S. Chamberlain, the noted anti-Semite, is frequently quoted with approval, will indicate the tendency of the article on the Pharisee.

It is remarkable that Mr. Montefiore in his extensive commentary on the Synoptic Gospels should have refrained from criticizing the exceedingly unfair account of the Pharisees contained in these standard Dictionaries. He never refers to this monstrous caricature of the most important party among the Jews of the first century. Readers of Dr. Hastings' works will continue to believe all the silly statements about the Pharisees, unless they are made to understand that the Pharisees were as full of ideals, and as true to these ideals, as were Jews or Christians of any age. The Pharisees of the first century produced Philo as well as Jesus ; Hillel and his disciples were Pharisees, who led a life as pure and as simple as the disciples of Jesus. We ask, in no sarcastic spirit, where is the higher morality of the Gospels, and where can one trace its effect ? The history of the Church is the only source at our disposal to which we can look for an answer to our question.

Failure is written across its pages. Bloodshed, wars, persecution, inquisition, crusades and hatred stare us in the face in every land, at one time or another in the course of the last nineteen hundred years. The reproach of the Gospels is the record of the long life of the Church. A modern book dealing with the failure of Christianity is Peile's Bampton Lectures for 1907, entitled *The Reproach of the Gospel.* There is no sign in Christendom of the righteousness which is higher than that of the Scribes and Pharisees. If one dares to speak the truth, history proves that the Jews have done infinitely better than the Christians, in spite of the " lower " righteousness of the Scribes and Pharisees. Better by far to belong to the persecuted Pharisees (for Jews are still Pharisees), than to the persecuting Church with its higher righteousness. Mr. Montefiore speaks of the " pure and intense ethical and religious insight of Jesus " and of his " prophetic conception of religion " (*S.G.*, p. 489). Why does he never apply the same words to any of the Pharisees or Scribes ? Are we to infer from his silence that the Pharisees and Scribes lacked the pure inwardness of the ethical and religious teaching which he has discovered in the Gospels ? If these words apply to Jesus, then they apply equally well to many of his contemporaries.

To put all the Pharisees in one class doomed to damnation may be the method of the New Testament, or of modern Biblical and Gospel Dictionaries, but it is neither charitable nor just. It is repugnant to me to draw attention to this one-sided view of history. The Christian writers generally know so little of the Jewish literature that they are naturally influenced by the New Testament picture of the Pharisee. Just let us see how the authorities we have mentioned describe the Pharisee and his views on religion.

" Pharisaic ethics taught (Jews) to hate Gentiles as enemies " (*Dictionary of Christ and the Gospels*, ii. p. 354) This is a falsehood. We are surprised to learn that " a bad man's body was impure, and to touch it would bring uncleanness to another man's soul." The Pharisees would have denied the statement that they " had no idea that the Messiah would be a Saviour of all men." Dr. Bousset holds that " later Judaism is through and through Pharisaism and nothing but Pharisaism " (*Jesu Predigt*, 1892, p. 32). In a later work on the *Jewish Religion in New Testament Times* (p. 65), Dr. Bousset adds : " Jesus broke through the transcendental ascetic spirit of Judaism." Another theologian of the same school, Baldensperger in his *Selbstbewusstsein Jesu* (p. 45), informs us that " the Pharisees had an abstract, transcendental view of God, which gave rise to the legalism that marks their teaching."

They all agree in describing the God of the Pharisees as " transcendental," because He was called " The Father in Heaven," or because, instead of using the divine name, the term " Heaven " was substituted. Strange to say, Jesus also uses these identical expressions. Words used by a Pharisee mean something quite different from that conveyed by the same words used by Jesus. This is the only conclusion we can arrive at, when we are told that the God of the Pharisees was transcendental, whereas " Jesus broke through this transcendental spirit." Wellhausen (*Phar. und Sadd.*, p. 19) asserts that " the Pharisees killed nature by legal prescriptions." If the Christian hears thunder or sees lightning he is unconcerned, but the Jew utters a benediction in which the majesty and power of God are asserted. Is this what Wellhausen would call " killing nature " ? Such criticisms are to be found in almost every Christian book dealing with Judaism. As far as

I know, Mr. Montefiore has not dealt with any of the above-mentioned statements. They are entirely untrue, and can be easily refuted. This is not our purpose now, but we hope to return to this problem.

There is one point of interest in Matthew v. 20, which should be considered before we turn to the next section of the Sermon. The word " Scribe " does not occur in the Gospel of John. Luke occasionally uses νομικοί or lawyers, instead. This word occurs only once in Matthew (xxii. 35). The Gospels never seem to be quite sure of the parties among the Jews. This is due to the fact that the Gospels were committed to writing more than half a century after the death of Jesus.

The Sermon now gives the higher righteousness of Jesus : " Ye have heard that it was said to them of old time, Thou shalt not kill ; and whosoever shall kill shall be in danger of the judgment : but I say unto you, that every one who is angry with his brother [without cause] shall be in danger of the judgment ; and whosoever shall say to his brother, Raca, shall be in danger of the council ; and whosoever shall say, Moreh (Thou fool), shall be in danger of the hell of fire " (Matt. v. 21, 22). This is the first great interpretative antithesis of the new law as against the old. The critics point out that in the doctrine of Jesus the crimes of the Mosaic code are traced to their sources in the heart. Thus murder is traced to the passion of anger. Dr. Schmidt says : " The searching criticism of fundamental principles of the Mosaic law and of the common practices of piety, as well as the unfolding of the higher righteousness of the Kingdom of Heaven may plausibly be regarded as having formed part of Jesus' private instruction " (*The Prophet of Nazareth*, p. 272).

A statement of this kind can be found in almost every commentary dealing with the passage from the Sermon now under consideration. Just note the contrast: "Ye have heard that it was said to them of old time, Thou shalt not kill, but I say unto you every one who is angry with his brother shall be in danger." Does this not seem to be something new and valuable? Mr. Montefiore (*S.G.*, p. 499) says that "Jesus, as the prophetic teacher of inwardness, wanted to show that the true fulfilment of the Law included and implied an inward and enlarged interpretation of the leading moral enactments." Quite so, the true fulfilment of the Law included and implied an inward and enlarged interpretation. This was the work of the Scribes, who, although they are not called by Mr. Montefiore "the prophetic teachers of inwardness," agreed with Jesus in his interpretation of the sixth commandment. Mr. Montefiore truly remarks (p. 501) that "the Rabbinic Jew has nothing here to learn from the Sermon." Jesus, like the Rabbis, made a fence to the Law.

The Extra Volume (fifth) of Hastings' *Dictionary of the Bible* (p. 26) has the following interesting passage:—
"Jesus' ideal of human brotherhood is first illustrated by an exposition of the principle which lay behind the sixth commandment. In this commandment the act of murder was explicitly forbidden, and the Jews conscientiously abstained from murder; they kept the letter of the precept. But there existed also the spirit of the commandment, the principle on which it was founded, that brethren should not hate one another; for it was out of hatred that murder came. Since the commandment did not explicitly forbid hatred, men had allowed themselves to cherish anger, hatred, and

contempt against others without regarding themselves as disobedient to the Law."

We must observe that Jesus' new commandment is strictly limited to one's *brother*. Therefore, to speak of " Jesus' ideal of human brotherhood " is quite out of place. All that one can say is, that Jesus lays down a regulation which prohibits the cherishing of anger against one's blood relation, one's actual brother. To argue otherwise, would necessitate an alteration of the text. The words are " every one who is angry with his brother "—not with his neighbour (πλησίον), or with any man (ἄνθρωπός τις). The word used for brother (ἀδελφός) cannot possibly be interpreted as meaning one's fellow creatures. Such a use is not warranted by any passage in the New Testament. Moreover, Jesus was not giving a new law at all, or even a new interpretation of the law. The same law that said " Thou shalt not murder " (Exod. xx. 13), also said, " Thou shalt not hate thy brother in thy heart," and " Thou shalt not take vengeance nor bear any grudge against the children of thy people " (Lev. xix. 17 and 18). Not only did Jesus forget to say that this law against hatred, vengeance, or bearing any grudge, was also " said to them of old," but he claims to be the originator of this precept.

The law of murder is older than the Decalogue. It is based on the fundamental principle (which is again and again emphasized in the Old Testament and by the Rabbis) that all men are created in the image of God (see Gen. ix. 6). It is gratifying to learn from the passage just quoted from Hastings' *Bible Dictionary* that the Jews kept the letter of the precept (" Thou shalt not murder "). We should like to inquire how does the writer justify the following sentence : " Since the commandment did not explicitly forbid hatred, men had allowed themselves to cherish anger, hatred and contempt against others without regarding themselves as disobedient to the Law " ? The Law explicitly prohibited hatred and revenge (Lev. xix. 17 and 18). The Israelites were specially reminded that they were not to abhor the Egyptian, although they had been enslaved in his land (Deut. xxiii. 7). This leads to a more universal outlook than Jesus seems to have contemplated.

We have now seen that in the Sermon the new interpretation is really the old law. Thus far we are on old ground, at least in theory. How about practice ? Did Jesus always show the charity and love that drives out anger and hatred ? His attitude to his mother and brothers was marked by anger and contempt (see Mark iii. 31 ff.). He looked upon his fellow citizens (Mark iii. 5) in anger, and again and again gave way to passionate vituperation. The second half of verse 22 in the Sermon is difficult. Parallel to the climax in penalties, we expect a similar climax in the offences. We should have expected (1) hatred in the heart, (2) expressed contempt, and (3) expressed abuse. Instead of this, the two terms of abuse " Raca " and " Moreh," probably mean the same. Jesus used the latter word on several occasions (Matt. vii. 26 ; xxv. 2, 3 and 8). A further difficulty is raised by the penalties. If one hates his brother (in his heart), how can the local court know of the offence ? God alone can read the heart. Again, if Moreh (fool) be not identical with Raca (emptyheaded), is it reasonable to maintain that for saying the one word, the Sanhedrin will inflict the sufficient penalty, whilst for the other the eternal fires of hell are required to impose the requisite punishment ? The Beth Din, as far as we know, did not inflict a punishment if one called another " Raca " or " Moreh."

Nevertheless, there was a moral punishment. The Rabbis declared that " if one put his fellow to the blush in public, then the offender would forfeit his portion in the world to come " (Aboth iii. 15). Again they say, " it were better for a man to cast himself into a fiery furnace than shame his fellow-man in public." To call one's fellow nicknames was considered one of the grave sins that deprived the offender of the future bliss (B. Mezia, 58b). Jesus warns his disciples that they must not call their brothers " Raca " or " Moreh." Both words are Aramaic. The Greek word " Moreh " ($\mu\omega\rho\acute{e}$—the same sound as the Aramaic) means fool. The Hebrew word " Moreh " means rebel (Num. xx. 10). Moses called his brethren rebels, and as a punishment he was forbidden to enter Palestine (Tanchuma, Chukkath § 9 on Num. xx. 10). A Rabbi of the third century, Reuben by name, was asked the meaning of the word Moreh. He answered that it meant the same as the Greek word which was used to connote a fool (Pesikta, ed. Buber, p. 118b). The Revised Version, which we have used, is somewhat misleading. The passage (v. 22) should be translated, " But I say unto you, that every one who is angry with his brother [without cause] shall be in danger of the judgment (i.e. the local court) ; and whosoever shall say to his brother, Raca, shall be in danger of the Sanhedrin," etc.

The Revised Version has placed the words " without cause," which are in the first clause of Jesus' statement, in the margin. We are told that many ancient authorities insert this reading. As a matter of fact, " without cause " (Greek, εἰκῆ) is as old as the second century (see Merx, *Die vier kanonischen Evangelien*, pp. 231 ff.). It is an explanatory gloss, intended to justify the conduct of Jesus, who was so often angry. If the qualification be omitted, then the practice of Jesus contradicted his theory. In the *Testaments of the Twelve Patriarchs*, we have a parallel which is more universal in scope than the words of Jesus : " As love would quicken even the dead, so hatred would slay the living " (Gad iv. 6). Another parallel is in the same Testament : " Fearing lest he should offend the Lord, he willeth not to do wrong to any man, even in thought " (ibid. v. 5). The Rabbis teach that he who gives way to anger is considered to be a worshipper of idols (Sabbath, 105b). Again, " he who hates his fellow-man is held to be a murderer." (Derech Eretz xi ; cf. Sifrê, §§ 186, 187 on Deut. xix. 11.)

As a last parallel, we suggest Psalm xv. 3, describing the man fit to sojourn in God's tabernacle : " He that slandereth not with his tongue, nor doeth evil to his friend, nor taketh up a reproach against his neighbour." The Gospels do not teach a better or higher morality than this. Thus far we have not seen any good reason to prefer the teaching of Jesus to that of the Old Testament, or of the Scribes and Pharisees.

LITERATURE

On ' Pharisees,' see Hamburger, R.E., ii. pp. 1,038 ff. ; Geiger, *Sadducäer und Pharisäer* (1863) ; J. Cohen, *Les Pharisiens* (1877) ; Schürer, II. ii. pp. 1–43 (the best literature is given here) ; also *Jewish Encyclopedia*, vol. ix., pp. 661 ff. ; and from a different standpoint, Dr. Elbogen's *Die Religionsanschauung der Pharisäer ;* and see Rev. C. T. Dimont's article, *The Synoptic Evangelists and the Pharisee*, in *The Expositor* (March, 1911).

CHAPTER V

THE Sermon in Matthew continues :—" If therefore thou art offering thy gift at the altar, and there rememberest that thy brother hath aught against thee, leave there thy gift before the altar, and go thy way, first be reconciled to thy brother, and then come and offer thy gift " (v. 23, 24). Here we are taught that it is better by far to postpone sacrifice than to postpone reconciliation. This is quite in accord with Pharisaic teaching. If a man had wronged his fellow, he was bound to become reconciled with him before he could obtain the divine grace. The Mishna points out that even the Day of Atonement cannot bring pardon for sins committed by man against his fellow-man. Repentance would not even suffice ; reconciliation is the indispensable condition (Joma, 85b). The underlying principle is the prophetic message that God does not really wish for our sacrifices when we have evil in our hearts ; but He asks for love to Him, expressed by our love to one another. " I desire love, and not sacrifice " (Hos. vi. 6). A parallel to Matthew's passage is to be found in the Pentateuch :—" If any one commit a trespass, and sin unwittingly, in the holy things of the Lord, then he shall bring his guilt offering unto the Lord . . . and he shall make restitution for that which he hath done amiss in

46

the holy thing" (Lev. v. 15, 16). Another parallel is given in the following passage from Philo : " It is necessary for those who are about to go into the temple to partake in the sacrifice, to be pure in body and soul, and also to be adorned with virtues expressed by praiseworthy actions. But let him whose heart harbours covetousness and a desire of unjust things, cover his head in shame and be silent. Truly the temple of the living God may not be approached by unholy sacrifices." (*On Those who Offer Sacrifices*, 3, M. ii. p. 253.)

The Talmud points out that a man's guilt is not purged by bringing a trespass-offering. Before he brings his offering he must repair the wrong done and then his sin can be forgiven (Baba Kama, 109*a*). New Testament commentators have questioned the authenticity of the passage (v. 23, 24). Jesus, or the author, dwells on the folly of a man seeking God's grace when, at the same time, he remembers that his brother has a grievance against him. It seems, however, that this passage belongs to the preceding section, as in both we find duties to one's brother set forth. Our former observations in explaining the limitations implied by speaking of a brother only, apply to the passage we are now considering. There is no such limitation in Philo or in the Rabbinic teaching. We shall do well to bear in mind that Jesus never thinks of humanity at large, but only of his disciples and followers. His rules and precepts apply to them only. He believed that the great majority of men would be excluded from the coming kingdom, where his new law would be observed. We are fully aware that this view will be severely criticized.

Perhaps the following consideration will justify our standpoint. The Sermon says that if one's brother has aught against him, he must go to the offended brother and seek reconciliation. Just assume that this is not limited as we contend ; suppose a Christian knows that a Jew or a Mohammedan has some objection to his belief or conduct ; then he must become reconciled by modifying his belief or by rectifying his conduct. This would mean the effacement of Christian life and thought. This is, of course, impossible, although it would lessen religious controversy. The thought underlying these verses has been well expressed in the fine words, " reconciliare, ut Deo reconcilieris," which can be rendered " forgive and God will forgive thee." It must not, however, be limited in its interpretation. Men must forgive one another (not only one's brother) in order to hope for God's grace. Here again the " Imitation of God " is the motive according to Jewish teaching.[1] " Just as God is merciful and forgiving, so be thou merciful and forgiving." (See Mechilta, Shira § 3, 44*b*.)

The next two verses of the Sermon are probably eschatological. They warn man to lose no time before the coming judgment in becoming reconciled with any adversary. Jülicher (ii. pp. 240 ff.) says that the passage does not form part of the original Sermon. The verses are :—" Agree with thine adversary quickly, while thou art with him in the way ; lest haply the adversary deliver thee to the judge, and the judge deliver thee to the officer, and thou be cast into prison. Verily I say unto thee, thou shalt by no means come out thence till thou have paid the last farthing " (Matt. v. 25, 26).

---

[1] On the *Imitation of God* as the Jewish ideal, see Dr. Schechter's *Aspects of Rabbinic Theology* pp. 199 ff, where holiness is identified with *Imitatio Dei*. See also Lazarus, *Die Ethik des Judenthums* pp. 87 f, 94, 114.

Most of the critics agree that a new and not wholly harmonious thought is introduced here. The passage is said to be highly metaphorical, and metaphors, we are told, must not be pressed. This is a very convenient system of exegesis. If you do not like the spirit of a passage when read literally, explain it away by saying it is highly metaphorical. We have never seen this standard of criticism applied to the teaching of the Pharisees. We request the reader to note this fact. The Greek for *adversary* (ἀντίδικος) in v. 25, occurs in the Midrash (Gen. Rab. lxxx ii, 8 ; cf. also Pesikta, Nachmu p. 126*a*). Again, the Greek word for *farthing* (κοδράντης) is also to be found in the Palestinian Talmud (Kiddushin i. 1 58*d*).

This passage (Matt. v. 25, 26) also occurs in Luke (xii. 58) in quite another context. In Matthew it seems to follow quite properly the previous section which recommended reconciliation. This, as we have already shown, is but a restatement of the old Law, which not only says " love thy neighbour as thyself," but also prohibits anger or resentment. The passage in Matthew (vv. 25, 26) advises a man to become reconciled, because his adversary will otherwise cast him into prison. This is an instance of the " morality of expediency " sometimes advocated in the New Testament. Unless the passage be considered to be allegory, then Jesus was uttering a commonplace of every-day experience. It could hardly be called " the higher righteousness." It is a lesson in practical prudence, probably well-known in every age and society. If we apply the allegorical form, we must assume that God is prosecutor, judge, and executor of judgment. This can be matched by a fine Rabbinic parallel in the Ethics of the Fathers :—

E

" They that are born are destined to die ; and the dead to be brought to life again ; and the living to be judged, to know and to be made conscious that He is God, He is the Maker, Creator, Discerner, the Judge, the Witness as well as the Adversary " (Aboth iv. 29). If the literal and practical interpretation be adopted, then we offer as a parallel the following :—" If thou hast done harm to any one, be it ever so trivial, consider it as very serious . . . but if thy neighbour has done thee an injury, take care not to exaggerate it " (Aboth de R. Nathan 41, ed. Schechter p. 133).

In the next section of the Sermon we have another illustration of the new interpretation of the old Law. It is more revolutionary than anything we have so far considered. If Jesus intended to enforce a new lesson in dealing with the seventh commandment, he should have expressed his meaning in clear and simple words that could never have been misinterpreted. We shall for the sake of clearness divide the passage (vv. 27–32) dealing with woman into three sections. The first part says :—" Ye have heard that it was said, thou shalt not commit adultery ; but I say unto you, that every one that looketh on a woman to lust after her hath committed adultery with her already in his heart " (27, 28). Does Jesus teach anything new in these words ? We cannot help answering this question in the negative. The Decalogue not only said : " Thou shalt not commit adultery," it also said : " Thou shalt not *covet* thy neighbour's wife." To covet or to lust after (Deut. v. 21) another man's wife is strictly prohibited. David's conduct towards the wife of the heathen Hittite, Uriah, met with the sternest reprobation and was swiftly punished by God. Apart from the parallels that might be cited from the Old Testament, the following Pharisaic teachings may be compared with the words of Jesus : " Renunciation of worldly pleasures leads to purity, purity leads to holiness " (Aboda Zara, 20b). " Immoral thoughts are worse than immoral deeds " (Joma, 29a). " Do not think that he is an adulterer who, by his sinful act, has sinned ; he also is an adulterer who lusts with his eyes " (cf. Job xxiv. 15 ; Pesikta Rabbati 124b). " He who excites evil thoughts cannot approach God " (Nidda, 13b). " When a man has the intention to sin, it is as though he had already sinned against God " (Num. Rab. viii, 5). The ethics enforced by Job (xxxi. 1 ff.), or by the example of Joseph (Gen. xxxix. 7 ff.), or by the precept, " not to go about after your own heart and your own eyes, after which ye go astray " (Num. xv. 39) are all good parallels to the words of Jesus. The *Testaments of the Twelve Patriarchs* also offer a fine parallel :—" He that hath a pure mind in love looketh not on a woman with thought of fornication " (Benjamin viii. 2. See Dr. Charles' edition, p. lxxix.). This superb teaching is more than one hundred years earlier than that of Jesus, and enforces the lesson of chastity as finely as any passage in the New Testament.

The next section of the Sermon reads :—" And if thy right eye cause thee to stumble, pluck it out, and cast it from thee : for it is profitable for thee that one of thy members should perish, and not thy whole body be cast into hell. And if thy right hand causeth thee to stumble, cut it off, and cast it from thee : for it is profitable for thee that one of thy members should perish, and not thy whole body go into hell " (29, 30). Is this to be taken literally or figuratively ? If we were to interpret

the words literally we should bear in mind the fact that
Jesus never married.   He prefers celibacy to the married life.   He even recommends absolute continence.
He speaks in a strange un-Jewish strain when he says :
" There are eunuchs, who have made themselves eunuchs
for the sake of the Kingdom of Heaven.   He that is
able to receive it, let him receive it " (Matt. xix. 10–12).
If, however, the words are to be interpreted figuratively,
then we must understand them to mean that for the
sake of purity no sacrifice is too great.   The result of
such teaching has been seen in monasticism, which has
been to the present day a marked feature of Christendom.   Another result has been the celibacy of the
Roman Catholic priest.   We need not dwell on these
two aspects of religious life ; they are un-Jewish.

The third part of this section of the Sermon is as
follows : " It was said also, whosoever shall put away
his wife, let him give her a writing of divorcement : but
I say unto you, that every one that putteth away his
wife, saving for the cause of fornication, maketh her
an adulteress : and whosoever shall marry her when she
is put away committeth adultery " (Matt. v. 31, 32).

This is the most important of the three sections.   The
words " saving for the cause of fornication " are generally acknowledged to be an interpolation.   If this be
denied, then Jesus had no right to say " I say unto you "
as opposed to what the people had previously been
taught.   Taking the words as they stand, they contain
nothing new or startling.   The School of Shammai
taught exactly the same as Jesus is said here to have
done.   We must, however, pay a little attention to
this important, if delicate, question.   Mr. Montefiore
says : " The originality of Jesus seems strikingly shown

in his treatment of women. . . . We may infer that Jesus appears to have rebelled against that more Oriental view of women which is indicated or expressed in certain passages of the Law " (*Jowett Lectures*, p. 44). Mr. Montefiore sums up the Mosaic law of divorce in the words " a man can put away his wife, but a woman cannot put away her husband." He agrees that Jesus probably " declared himself against all divorce whatever and on whatever ground." In the conflict between the Rabbis and Jesus on this matter, Mr. Montefiore finds that Jesus was " from a higher point of view prophetically right " (ibid., p. 46). This is practically identical with the conclusions arrived at by Christian commentators.

Mr. Montefiore adopts the views advocated by Dr. Schmidt in his book, the *Prophet of Nazareth*. Now Dr. Schmidt acknowledges (although Mr. Montefiore does not quote this) that Jesus did not " consider the possibility of woman's economic independence, or the desirability of her political emancipation." Paul refused to accept the equality of the sexes, which, Mr. Montefiore insists (*Synoptic Gospels*, p. 689), was taught by Jesus. To this day the Church has followed Paul and *not* Jesus. Again, we are told (*S. G.* p. 508):—"Jesus saw that a weak spot in the social order of his time, as it has been a weak spot in all later Judaism till the present hour, was its lax law of divorce." What was the remedy suggested by Jesus ? No divorce at all. If Mr. Montefiore thinks this shows the "originality of Jesus," or believes that in this " he made himself one of the great champions of woman's cause," he is welcome to the belief. We prefer to agree with Dr. Schmidt that Jesus, by forbidding divorce under any circumstances, not only annulled her existing rights, but, by perpetuating immoral relations, made her slavery complete (*Prophet of Nazareth*, p. 370).

The Mosaic law, which Mr. Montefiore condemned as " lax," secured to women real protection. Was not the bill of divorce instituted solely in her favour ? The husband was forced to renounce all his rights over her. He could not prevent her marriage to another man. (Jesus prohibited this, and interfered with her freedom after her divorce.)   Mr. Montefiore quotes Dr. Schmidt's note that the Mosaic Law was " decidedly inferior to the Law of Hammurabi, which recognizes the right of a woman to divorce a husband she cannot love " (*S.G.*, p. 510).   Mr. Montefiore and Dr. Schmidt would be surprised to learn that the penal code of Babylon clearly described the abject humiliation of a woman by enacting that, " If a husband say unto his wife, thou art not my wife, he shall pay one-third of a mina and be free.   But if a woman repudiate her husband, she shall be drowned in the river " (§§ 140, 143).   Is this superior to the enactments contained in the Mosaic code ?   But stay. Mr. Montefiore (p. 689) notes that Hillel allowed divorce for " ' every cause '—if a man saw a woman he liked better, or if a woman spoiled a man's soup."   As a matter of historical accuracy, Hillel did not say these words.   The question of divorce was debated by the *Schools* of Hillel and Shammai.   Are we to suppose that only Jesus is allowed to use figurative language ? Rabbi Akiba said the words attributed to Hillel some ninety or a hundred years after the death of Jesus. They have therefore no place in comparing Jewish contemporary teaching with that of Jesus.   Are words used in debate always to be cited as law ?   Did not

Rabbi Akiba frequently indulge in hyperbolical or figurative speech ? This same Rabbi Akiba also said, " If a man wishes to see his children happy and prosperous, let him not only obey God, but also his wife in love " (Kallah 1).

Dr. Schmidt acknowledges that " the policy of Christian society has differed little from that of Jewish society, attacked by Jesus." His attitude towards women has not been copied by his followers. It is untrue to say that Christianity has raised the status of women, whereas Judaism has done the reverse. If Christianity adopted the teaching of Jesus that divorce cannot be sanctioned under any conditions, then it would be possible to compare the status of woman in the Church and in the Synagogue. Jesus legislated, we are often told, for the ideal society in the Kingdom of God. He was a celibate, and despised marriage. In this he followed the example of John the Baptist and the Essenes (Josephus, *Antiquities*, xviii. i, 5, and *Wars*, ii. viii., 2). In view of his law that marriage should be indissoluble, his disciples asked him whether it was wise to marry at all. His reply clearly shows that, in his opinion, celibacy was to be preferred (see Matt. xix. 10–12). The Church had to deal all along with ordinary human beings, and found it quite impossible to follow the lines laid down by Jesus. This fact will account for the contradictory accounts as to the law of divorce found in the Gospels. Mark (x. 2–12) gives the oldest account of the discussion on divorce. Jesus denies the right of divorce in any case whatsoever. Matthew introduces a qualification, and makes Jesus follow the opinion held by the School of Shammai. Divorce is only allowable in case of unchastity on the part of the

wife. Jesus does not give the woman the power of
divorcing her husband. The old Oriental view of man's
superiority to woman is still maintained. Perhaps it
is even aggravated. Jesus would not allow the woman,
who had been divorced, to remarry. She cannot enjoy
her freedom. This was not the custom among the
Jews, and, in this respect, the Jewish law is more con-
siderate to the woman than the present-day practice of
the Church. Luke (xvi. 18) has a combination of the
law contained in Mark and Matthew. There is reason
to question the authenticity of Mark's version. He
seems to have confused Jewish-Egyptian law with
Jewish-Palestinian law. Again, Jesus is said to have
been original in laying down the principle of the equality
of the sexes. His proof is based on Genesis ii. 24,
according to Matthew xix. 5, 6 :—" And the twain
shall become one flesh. So that they are no more twain,
but one flesh." Now, it is quite impossible for Jesus to
have said these words. He did not use the Septuagint,
and only there do we find this version. It is not warranted by the Hebrew text. It is clearly the opinion
of the Evangelist. Jesus is nowadays called the " cham-
pion of woman." Clement of Alexandria and other
Church Fathers would not share this view. Clement
refers to a saying of Jesus, preserved in the *Gospel of
the Egyptians :* " I came to destroy the works of the
female " (Strom. iii. ix. 63). He also reports two other
sayings of Jesus which are highly interesting : " Eat
every herb, but that which hath bitterness (i.e. mater-
nity) eat not," and " He who is married, let him not
put away his wife ; and he who is not married, let him
not marry ; he who with purpose of chastity has determined not to marry, let him remain unmarried " (ibid.

xv. 97). If Jesus could say to his mother : " Woman, what have I to do with thee ? " or if he could venture to refuse to see his mother when she wished to see him (see Mark iii. 31 ff.), we question the accuracy of Mr. Montefiore's statement that " the originality of Jesus seems strikingly shown in his treatment of women " (*Jowett Lectures*, p. 44).

We have shown that the Jewish Law permitted divorce. When the Rabbis allowed divorce for reasons other than adultery, they took into account human nature as it exists in every-day life. One Rabbi, Jose of Galilee, said that a woman who refused to give food to the poor forfeited her rights and could be divorced (Gen. Rab. xvii, 3). Another Rabbi, Ben Azzai, said : " He who hates his wife is held to be a murderer " (Derech Eretz xi.). It is easy to talk of the lax law of divorce among the Jews. It is frivolous to say that a bad dinner, or another woman with a pretty face, was sufficient ground for divorce. The Rabbis also deprecated divorce. The Talmud says, " He who divorces his first wife causes the altar to shed tears " (Gittin, 90 *b*). This means that divorce is to be deprecated as much as sacrilege. Jewish law to-day insists on the wife's right to give or withhold her consent to divorce. If she refuses to be divorced, there is no remedy and divorce cannot take place. This shows that it is really the woman who allows or disallows divorce. In this respect Jewish law gives greater power to woman than is to be found in any other law. If writers on the laws of Jewish divorce would study and understand the seventh chapter of Ketuboth and the fourteenth chapter of Maimonides' Laws of Marriage there would be no more talk of lax laws of divorce in Judaism.

According to the Mosaic Law a man could not under any and every circumstance divorce his wife. If a man falsely accused his wife (see Deut. xxii. 19), he could not divorce her. In Egypt in the time of Philo (about 20 C.E.) this case seems to have allowed the wife the right of divorcing her husband. Philo's words are very important :—" For the law permits them (the women) at their own choice to remain with their husbands or to abandon them, and will not allow the husbands any option either way, on account of the false accusations which they brought " (Special Laws, 14, M. ii. p. 313). If Mark knew this, perhaps we have the explanation of the otherwise difficult case referred to by him (x. 12) :— " and if she herself shall put away her husband." The Pentateuch gives another instance prohibiting a man to divorce his wife, viz., if he had been compelled to marry a girl whom he had wronged (see Deut. xxii. 29). Jesus was not the first to condemn divorce. Malachi (ii. 16) had already said :—" For I hate divorce, saith the Lord." God had sanctified the marriage bond in Israel by representing his relation to Israel under the figure of a marriage. He is said to be the witness at man's marriage (Malachi ii. 14). Divorce is then not absolutely prohibited, but it is not to be recklessly granted. Jesus tried to abolish divorce, but he failed. Human nature, being what it is, requires divorce as a necessary and expedient consequence of the sin of adultery. We cannot enter now into the question whether in our days divorce should be allowed for other reasons. Should a marriage of a woman to a lunatic or to a criminal condemned to a life sentence remain indissoluble ? The law of the land may, in the near future, deal with this question. The law of the Church

has already answered by saying :—"No divorce."
Judaism has again nothing to learn from this negative
teaching of Jesus.

LITERATURE

See Amram's Bibliography appended to his article on ' Divorce ' in the *Jewish Encyclopedia*, vol. iv. p. 628 ; likewise
the two articles on ' Scheidung ' in Hamburger, and see S.
Holdheim, *Maamar Haishuth* (pp. 26 ff.) for the Law of Divorce
in the Gospels. Dr. Gaster's article on Jewish Divorce in the
Jewish Review i, vi. (March, 1911) is noteworthy.

NOTE TO PAGE 46

The Greek word for gift (δῶρον) which is used here (v. 23) and
by the Septuagint for the Hebrew " Mincha " and " Corban," has
been borrowed by the Jews (see Targum Psalm xx. 4, Zebachim
7*b*, and Pesachim 118*b*).

NOTE TO PAGE 50

Additional parallels (to Matt. v. 27, 28) from Rabbinical
literature may be found in : Jer. Shekalim iii. 5, 47*c*. ; T. B.
Aboda Zara, 20*a* ; Nedarim, 20*a* ; Aboth i. 5 ; Berachoth, 24*a*,
61*a* ; Kallah i; Pesikta Rabbati 125*a*, and Aboth de R. Nathan
ii. (ed. Schechter, pp. 8, 9).

CHAPTER VI

FALSIFYING THE TORAH TO PRAISE THE GOSPEL

THE fourth illustration of the contrast between the new
Law and the old Law is taken from the third and ninth
commandments :—" Again, ye have heard that it was
said to them of old time, Thou shalt not forswear thyself, but shalt perform unto the Lord thine oaths ; but
I say unto you, Swear not at all ; neither by the heaven,
for it is the throne of God ; nor by the earth, for it is
the footstool of his feet ; nor by Jerusalem, for it is the
city of the great King.   Neither shalt thou swear by
thy head, for thou canst not make one hair white or
black.   But let your speech be, Yea, yea ; Nay, nay :
and whatsoever is more than these is of the evil one "
(Matt. v. 33-37).   Jesus here opposes the Jewish Law,
which permits the taking of oaths, by forbidding this in
the words, " Swear not at all."   Jesus, however, did
not always refrain from swearing.   He frequently emphasizes his statements by the phrase, " Amen, I say
to you."   The English Bible renders this by " Verily, I
say to you."   " Amen " in this connexion is simply an
oath.   This was the opinion of the old Church Father,
Origen.   Modern critics (e.g. Holtzmann, Achelis) say
that Jesus took an oath at his trial (Matt. xxvi. 63, 64).
Paul also swore (2 Cor. i. 23, and Rom. ix. 1 ff.).   What
then did Jesus really intend to achieve by his new law ?

Mr. Montefiore (*Synoptic Gospels*, p. 511) quotes Mr. Allen's Commentary on Matthew, *ad loc.* : that Jesus had in view not the solemn use of oaths in religion, but " the casuistical distinctions made by the Jews between different formulæ in swearing. In other words, his teaching is opposed to Jewish tradition." It is a pity that Mr. Montefiore allows this statement to pass unchallenged.

We should like to know something about the " casuistical distinctions made by the Jews between different formulæ in swearing " ? What was the Jewish tradition which Jesus opposed ? From the context in Matthew, we must assume that Jesus attacked the supposed " casuistical distinctions made by the Jews," that only oaths in which the Divine name was mentioned were binding ; all other oaths, including such examples as Jesus gives, were not held to be binding at all. This is the only inference to be drawn from the Gospel narrative. The question now arises : Is there any justification for this view ? It is quite beside the question to say that some Jews thought that only certain forms of oaths were binding. Some Christians also may believe that only certain forms of oaths are really binding. Mental reservation is not necessarily a Jewish characteristic. A Jesuit might also find it useful. Taking human nature as it is, there is no historical testimony to justify the belief that the Jews in the first century were a people steeped in perjury, lying, and casuistry. The Law was no dead letter. The Jews, we are told, ignored the spirit, but faithfully kept the letter of the Law. What did the Law teach ? " Thou shalt not take the name of the Lord thy God in vain ; for the Lord will not hold him guiltless that taketh His name

in vain." " In vain " meant falsely. This was the
third commandment (Exod. xx. 7). Then there was
the ninth commandment : " Thou shalt not bear false
witness against thy neighbour " (Exod. xx. 16). The
Law nowhere lays down a rule that a man must worship God by taking an oath ; Deut. vi. 13 merely enacts
that oaths must be sanctified by the Divine name. (See
Nachmanides *in loc.*).

In Dr. Hastings' *Dictionary of the Bible*, v., p. 28,
" Jesus," we are told, " had the intention of sweeping
away the whole system of oaths as resting upon a false
theory, namely, that a man might use two qualities of
statement—one with an oath, which pledged him to
truth and fulfilment, and one without the oath, which
required neither truth nor fulfilment. As against this
double-dealing and authorization of falsehood, Jesus
demands that a man shall speak only the truth, and
implies that an oath is not only unnecessary, but harmful." It is surprising how this modern scientific work
can venture to say that the Jews in the days of Jesus
authorized falsehood. There is not a shadow of proof
that could be adduced to substantiate this monstrous
libel. Bishop Gore has practically the same :—" To
the Jew it had been a great thing to forswear himself,
but little or nothing to speak in ordinary talk what was
not true " (*The Sermon on the Mount*, p. 80). The Law
not only prohibited false swearing, but also falsehood :
" Ye shall not steal . . . nor lie one to another " (Lev.
xix. 11) ; " Keep thee far from a falsehood " (Exod. xxiii.
7). The only proof for the charge of " double-dealing
and authorization of falsehood " is to be found in Matthew. Is he a competent witness ? Long before his
time the Essenes had protested against the use of oaths.

They regarded their word as stronger than an oath, and they avoided swearing as worse than perjury (see Josephus' *Wars*, ii. viii, 6 and 7). Holtzmann (in view of the fact that Jesus and Paul both took oaths) thinks that Matthew was influenced here by Essenic tendencies (see also Schürer, II. ii. 209, 210). If Matthew was merely repeating the teaching of the Essenes, the fact remains that he did not reveal here the spirit of the genuine teaching of Jesus, whose practice did not harmonize with the words " Swear not at all." Jesus was not the first, nor will he be the last, preacher to forbid lying or perjury.

As a parallel to this section of the Sermon, the following passage from the Book of the Secrets of Enoch (xlix. 1, 2) is very interesting :—" For I swear to you, my children, but I will not swear by a single oath ; neither by heaven, nor by earth, nor by anything else made by God. God said : ' There is no swearing in me, nor injustice, but truth.' If there is no truth in men, let them swear by a word—Yea, yea, or Nay, nay. But I swear to you Yea, yea." Dr. Charles believes that the author was a contemporary of Philo. His book is earlier than Matthew (see *Enc. Bib. col.* 226). Philo also advises men to avoid oaths :—" That being who is the most beautiful, and the most beneficial to human life, and suitable to rational nature, swears not, because truth on every point is so innate within him that his bare word is accounted an oath. Next to not swearing at all, the second best thing is to keep one's oath " (*On the Decalogue*, 17, M. ii. p. 194 ; cf. the second note in Cohn's German translation of Philo, ii. p. 107). *Yea, yea*, or *nay, nay*, are considered by the Talmud to be forms of oaths (Shebuot, 36a). This is, indeed, sound proof that Jesus, if he used these words, did not really consider such formulae to be oaths. Sirach also condemned oaths (see Ecclus. xxiii. 9–11): "Accustom not thy mouth to swearing. Neither use thyself to the naming of the Holy One." This was written about 180 years before the birth of Jesus.

There is just one point in the section we are considering that needs attention. The saying in the Sermon: "Thou shalt not forswear thyself, but shalt perform unto the Lord thine oaths," is not a literal quotation from the Hebrew Bible. It is a combination of different passages (Lev. xix. 12 ; Num. xxx. 2 ; and Deut. xxiii. 21). The first of these passages deals with oaths, the others with vows. This peculiarity forces one to ask, whether the entire passage is a genuine utterance of Jesus. Whatever be the answer to this question, the fact remains that nothing new is enunciated. The Psalmist (xv. 2) demands of the man who would dwell in God's house that he should speak the truth in his heart. There is nothing better or loftier than this in all the teaching attributed to Jesus. The theme of the Law, Prophets, Psalms and other writings in the Hebrew Bible is righteousness of the heart. This was well understood by the Rabbis and Scribes who summed up the teaching of Judaism in the fine words : " God requires the heart " and nothing more {Synhedrin, 106b). The Rabbis declare that it is unbecoming to substantiate the truth by an oath (Num. R. xxii, 1). " God hates all who speak with their lips contrary to the truth of the heart " (Pesachim, 113b). " Let thy yea be a truthful yea, and also let thy nay be a truthful nay " (Baba Mezia, 49a). " He who deceives any of his fellow-creatures (not only relatives or co-religionists) is reckoned as the most sinful among deceivers " (Mechilta, Mishpatim § 13, p. 96*a*, cf. Chulin, 94*a*).

The next section of the Sermon (Matt. v. 38–42) deals with the law of retaliation, generally spoken of as " lex talionis." The verses are :—" Ye have heard that it was said, an eye for an eye, and a tooth for a tooth ; but I say unto you, resist not evil, but whosoever smiteth thee on thy right cheek, turn to him the other also. And if any man would go to law with thee, and take away thy coat, let him have thy cloke also. And whosoever shall compel thee to go one mile, go with him twain. Give to him that asketh thee, and from him that would borrow of thee turn not thou away." Mr. Montefiore says, " we here come to the most striking, and not the least famous, of the teachings of the Sermon on the Mount " (*S.G.*, p. 513). " Jesus fulfils the Law by correcting the Law," i.e. by laying down the principle ' resist not evil.' Now let us see how this works. Jesus modifies the legal part of the Law that was concerned with the correction of crime, by denying the right of the law to exact any penalty. We can well understand Mr. Montefiore's difficulties in dealing with the teaching of Jesus. It must at all costs be superior to the Law as interpreted by the Scribes and Pharisees. They had abolished the literal application of the law of retaliation and had substituted a monetary fine, just as obtains in modern courts of law. Jesus must correct this and does so, by proclaiming the new law, ' resist not evil.' Mr. Montefiore feels the danger of this position. He adds, " Jesus was hardly thinking here of public justice." If that be the case, we have an unfortunate confusion in the words of Jesus. The phrase : " If any man would *go to law* with thee " surely refers to public justice.

F

There never was at any period of the history of Israel a *lex talionis* outside the domain of public justice. The Law, as we have already seen, explicitly prohibits the right of private revenge :—" Thou shalt not take vengeance, nor bear any grudge against the children of thy people ; but thou shalt love thy neighbour as thyself : I am the Lord " (Lev. xix. 18). Mr. Montefiore tries another solution. " It is clear that Jesus does not mean his injunction to be taken literally " (*S.G.*, p. 514). This criticism is so very accommodating. " Eye for eye " was also not meant to be taken literally, according to the Rabbis ; but Jesus did not heed their interpretations. He revolutionized the spirit of all law by teaching non-resistance. How this works in modern life has been illustrated by Tolstoy, who says that the doctrine of the Gospel would do away with States and tribunals, property and individual rights (see Schroeder's *Der Tolstoismus* and Rappoport's *Tolstoy*, p. 56 ff.).

The fact is that Jesus here, as elsewhere, enunciates a principle that would destroy the structure of society. If no man can count as his own that which he has, there can be no such thing as private property. Anarchy would reign supreme, and love would change into hatred. How shall we account for this strange law ? It is hardly cogent to urge that " Jesus is giving counsels of perfection for those who want to enter the Kingdom." This is Mr. Montefiore's opinion (*S.G.*, p. 515). We believe we can give a better solution. Jesus, in his apocalyptic outlook on life, recognized two principles in deadly conflict with one another. Good and evil are the combatants. He and his followers have been sent to overthrow evil. The world, with its lusts and sins, is identified with evil (see James i. 27). How shall the conflict be waged ? Only by the utmost abnegation, the completest self-denial on the part of all who despise the world and desire heaven (see Gal. vi. 14). The last word of the preceding section in Matthew probably refers to the Evil One. Oaths are a characteristic of the world (the Evil One) ; therefore the disciples, who desire Heaven or the New Kingdom, must not swear at all. Again, the world claims justice, through the assistance given by oaths (for discovering truth). Justice is originally based on the principle that a wrong-doer must have " as good as he gave." This idea is also connected with Jesus's famous saying : " What ye would that men should do unto you, even so do ye unto them " (Matt. vii. 12).

The claim of the world that justice should prevail is denied by Jesus. Leave the Evil One, i.e. the world, alone ; and only try to enter the Kingdom. Resist not the Evil One, but rather be persecuted here, for happiness awaits you hereafter. The disciples of Jesus must be prepared to encounter all sorts of temptations, and by pursuing the line of least resistance all the trials will be surmounted. Judaism has rejected this view of the world. It has not identified the Devil or the Evil One with the world. It has never taught man to despise God's creation. The spirit of abnegation and self-denial that sacrifices individuality and personal freedom is alien to Jewish teaching. There are times when the Jew can and should overcome evil by good, but justice cannot be forgotten in an attempt to fulfil the divine law of love. Justice and love together rule supreme. God is both Father and Judge. The great fact to be emphasized is that man in his private capacity must forego all claims for revenge.

It cannot be repeated too often that Judaism forbids the exercise of revenge (see Prov. xx. 22 ; xxiv. 29 ; Lam. iii. 30 ; Job xvi. 10 ; and Ecclus. xxviii. 1, 2). In the religion of the heart there is only room for love and righteousness ; retaliation has no place there. Rabbi Ishmael said : "Be pliant of disposition and yielding to impressment, and receive every man with cheerfulness " (Aboth iii. 16). The *Testaments of the Twelve Patriarchs* protest against any kind of revenge :—" Love one another in the heart, and if any one sin against thee, so speak with him in peace and banish the venom of hatred, and do not let revenge abide in thine heart. If he confess and repent, forgive him ; if he refuse, then do not quarrel with him, lest thou sin doubly by enraging him and making him swear " (Gad. vi. 3 f.). This entire chapter is full of sweet counsel and ideal teaching that cannot be surpassed by any section of the Sermon on the Mount. ' Tit for tat ' in private life was always rebuked by the Rabbis. There is a fine passage in the Siphra to Lev. xix. 18, on this subject (see *The Law of Love in the Old and New Testaments*, p. 15). In public life a different law obtained. Justice demanded that wrong should be resisted. Judaism, unlike Christianity (as taught in the Sermon on the Mount), recognizes the duty of fighting against evil. It repudiates the ' higher and newer ' law, " resist not evil."

Matthew (v. 41) uses the rare verb ἀγγαρεύειν (to impress), which does not occur in Aramaic, whereas ἀγγαρεία (impressment) occurs in the Talmud, Jer. Berachoth i., 1. 2d and T. B. Baba Mezia, 78a and b (see Levy op. cit. i p. 105). The word μίλιον (mile) is not connected with the Talmudic word Mil.

The last verse of this section : " Give to him that asketh thee, and from him that would borrow of thee turn not thou away " is practically a quotation from Deuteronomy, chapter xv., 7 ff. (see also Lev. xxv. 35, 36 and Ecclus. iv. 4, 5). The next section of the Sermon (43–48) is well known and deserves close attention. " Ye have heard that it was said : Thou shalt love thy neighbour, and hate thine enemy ; but I say unto you, Love your enemies and pray for them that persecute you ; that ye may be sons of your Father who is in heaven : for he maketh his sun to rise on the evil and the good, and sendeth rain on the just and the unjust. For if ye love them that love you, what reward have ye ? Do not even the publicans the same ? And if ye salute your brethren only, what do ye more than others ? Do not even the Gentiles the same ? Ye therefore shall be perfect as your heavenly Father is perfect " (Matt. v. 43–48). This passage is usually known as the new law of love. Both this section and the preceding passage dealing with the law of retaliation occur in Luke vi. 27–36. Matthew has probably re-arranged the material and has divided this portion of the Sermon into two parts, whereas in Luke we only have one section. He deals with love as excluding retaliation.

There are important differences in the use of words between the two accounts, clearly showing that Matthew writes from a Jewish standpoint, whilst Luke considers the Gentile standpoint. Our first consideration must be the version in Matthew. In the first verse we read : " Ye have heard that it was said, thou shalt love thy neighbour, and hate thine enemy " (v. 43). This is a fine example of deliberate invention. The first half of the quotation is true (Lev. xix. 18), the second half is false. In no part of the Law, or Prophets, or Writings, or in any book of the Rabbis do we find the law, " hate thine enemy." Mr. Montefiore tells us : " We need not suppose that Jesus was guilty of such a misquotation in order to score a point and to sharpen a contrast " (*S.G.*, p. 518). If this be so,where is the new law ? " Thou shalt love thy neighbour " precludes the hatred of any man. The Torah said " Love thy neighbour," and Jesus says " Love your enemies." But your enemy is also your neighbour. This leads one to suspect that Jesus really said that the old Law taught " hate thine enemy." He corrects this by saying " love your enemies." Epiphanius admits that the orthodox Christians deliberately altered the Gospel text (Luke xxii. 43, 44), dreading a too human view of Jesus (Ancoratus 31 ed. Dindorf i. p. 123).

In order to show that Jesus teaches a new law, it is necessary to falsify the old law, and to invent the un-Jewish sentence : " Hate thine enemy." This sample of the Gospel morality proves the abiding value of the simple, old Jewish law : " Thou shalt not bear false witness." Mr. Montefiore is determined at all costs to defend the new teaching of Jesus. He actually grants that the equivalent of " thou shalt hate thine enemy " is found " in the Pentateuch, or in the Hebrew Bible, or in the Talmud "—but " only as regards the attitude of the Jew to the non-Jew " (*S.G.*, p. 519). This is justified in the following words : " True it is that the universalism of Paul was never attained by Rabbinic teaching. True it is that the Old Testament is, on the whole, particularistic and identifies the enemies of the Jews with the enemies of God." The universalism of

Paul has surely nothing to do with the Sermon on the Mount. Moreover, his universalism was strictly defined. It was limited to such believers in Jesus who agreed with Paul's metaphysics. He speaks of the "household of faith." Let us listen to his own words in order to appreciate his "universalism that was never attained by Rabbinic teaching." He says : "Be not unequally yoked with unbelievers, for what fellowship have righteousness and iniquity ? . . . What portion hath a believer with an unbeliever ? . . . Wherefore come ye out from among them and be ye separate, saith the Lord, and touch no unclean thing and I will receive you" (2 Cor. vi. 14–17). Paul also indulges in misquotations ; here we have an interesting example.

Mr. Montefiore says that on the whole the Old Testament is particularistic. We challenge this statement. The Old Testament, from Genesis to Malachi, is full of the universal spirit of God's love, mercy and grace. The spirit of the Old Testament is summed up in the words (Gen. v. 1) : "This is the book of Man's history." The Old Testament is the Charter of Humanity (see *The Law of Love in the Old and New Testaments*, p. 17). Finally, Mr. Montefiore says, "that the Old Testament identifies the enemies of the Jews with the enemies of God." This is a very wild statement, utterly untrue. Deuteronomy (xxiii. 7) tells Israel not to despise the Egyptian. The Egyptians were the enemies of the Hebrews, but were not to be identified with the enemies of God, and therefore not to be despised. Amos reminds Israel : "Are ye not as the children of the Ethiopians unto me, O children of Israel ? saith the Lord. Have I not brought up Israel out of the land of Egypt, and the Philistines from Caphtor, and the Syrians from Kir " ? (ix. 7). The Grace of God is not limited to Israel. God is the only God, and therefore all the children of men are protected by the Divine Providence. The Philistines and the Syrians were the enemies of Israel, but they are not on that account the enemies of God. The enemies of the Jews arose from political or economical causes. The enemies of God, whether Jews or non-Jews, are absolutely independent of these causes. Their sin is in the moral sphere and here alone can they become enemies of God. In ancient life the alien was necessarily an enemy. Only in Israel was the alien considered as a friend who is to be loved (Lev. xix. 34). This is the message of the Old Testament.

Verse 44 of the Sermon teaches :—" But I say unto you, Love your enemies, and pray for them who persecute you." If Jesus said these words, which is doubtful, he certainly did not practise what he taught. We are told by the New Testament that the Pharisees, the Sadducees, and the Scribes attacked Jesus, but we are not told that he loved them or prayed for them. He condemned them to everlasting damnation, and called them " a generation of vipers," and " children of the devil." The Gospels give no instance of any love shown by Jesus to his opponents.

We shall now give a few parallels to the " new " law of love. The *Testaments of the Twelve Patriarchs* afford several instances, e.g. " If any one seeketh to do evil unto you, do you in well-doing pray for him " (Joseph xviii. 2). " Love one another, and with long suffering hide ye one another's faults " (ibid. xvii. 2). The Book of the Secrets of Enoch says : " When you might have vengeance, do not repay, either your neighbour or your enemy" (l. 4). Philo has : "Bestow benefits on your enemy, and then will follow of necessity the end of your enmity" (*On Humanity*, 15, M. ii. p. 395). "Who is strong ? He who turns an enemy into a friend" (Aboth de R. Nathan xxiii.). There are also several parallels in the Old Testament :—"If thine enemy be hungry, give him bread to eat ; and if he be thirsty, give him water to drink" (Prov. xxv. 21). Again, "Did I rejoice at the destruction of him that hated me, or lift up myself when evil found him ? Yea, I suffered not my mouth to sin by asking his life with a curse" (Job xxxi. 29, 30). The basis of Jewish morality is *humanity*. The Talmud, as well as the Bible, insist on the rights inherent in men as children of God. The stranger as well as the homeborn are the recipients of the divine love (cf. Pss. cxlv., cxlvi.). The Midrash says : " If thou wilt use thy tongue to speak evil of thy brother who does not belong to thy race, then thou wilt also bring shame on the son of thy mother" (Deut. R. vi. 9). The Rabbis speak of "Kebod Habberioth" —the honour due to every man. Josephus has truly said : "For I suppose it will become evident that the laws (of the Torah) are for the general love of mankind" (*Contra Apionem* ii. 146).

Jesus then was not teaching his contemporaries anything new in saying, "Love your enemies and pray for them who persecute you." We have had during the last 1,900 years sad opportunities of realizing the lesson, that "it is better to be cursed than to curse" (Synhedrin, 48*b*). We have returned good for evil in the lands where we have been persecuted and dishonoured. In our own days, Jews in Russia have lamented the shameful massacres of their brethren and friends ; and yet in the same breath they prayed to God to " bless, guard, protect and help, exalt, magnify and highly aggrandize the Tsar." Long before the dawn of Christianity Jeremiah told his people to pray for the welfare of the city where they lived as exiles (Jer. xxix. 7). Daily we pray " To such as curse me let my soul be dumb ; yea, let my soul be unto all as the dust " (Berachoth, 17*a*). It is noteworthy that Jesus, in a parable (Luke xix. 27), says : " Howbeit these my enemies, who would not .that I should reign over them, bring hither, and slay them before me." The well-known verses, " Think not that I came to send peace on the earth. I came not to send peace, but a sword. For I came to set a man at variance against his father, and the daughter against her mother . . . and a man's enemies shall be they of his own household " (Matt. x. 34–36) do not fit in with the higher law of love.

" If thy brother sin (adds Luke xvii. 3), rebuke him ; and if he repent, forgive him." If he repent, he is to be forgiven ; if he will not repent—does the law of love still hold good ? The Church has to this day retained the right of excommunication. In Matthew (xviii. 17) the offending brother, who refuses to repent, is to be considered as the " Gentile and the publican."[1] That is to say, he is an outcast and will be excluded from the Kingdom of God. Holtzmann (Hand-Commentar zum N.T., *in loc.*) holds that what we have in this passage of Matthew is not an actual saying of Jesus, but a reflection of the ecclesiastical practice in the Jewish-Christian circles for which this Gospel was written. This convenient method of exegesis absolves Jesus, but

[1] Compare this with the above quoted passage (p. 68) from the *Testaments of the Twelve Patriarchs* (Gad. vi. 3 f.).

makes the Evangelist guilty of contradicting the law of love by instituting the right of excommunication. The verse in the Sermon (44) seems to reflect a period of persecution when the enemies were the opponents who caused strife. The enemies were not Jews, as Mr. Montefiore most generously suggests (*S.G.*, 520), but a section among the Christians, namely, Paul and his party (see *Enc. Bib.*, col. 4,545).

LITERATURE

Dr. Güdemann, *Die Nächstenliebe*; Friedlander, *The Law of Love in the Old and New Testaments* (1909) ; E. Grünebaum, *Die Sittenlehre des Judenthums*, pp. 121 ff.; Dr. Hermann Cohen, *Die Nächstenliebe im Talmud* ; and Dr. C. H. Cornill, *Das Alte Testament und die Humanität.*

NOTE TO PAGE 63

The expressions " Yea, yea " and " nay, nay " occur in a somewhat different form in James v. 12. See Resch, Agrapha ii. p. 96, where parallels from Justin, Clement of Alexandria and other Church Fathers are given.

CHAPTER VII

THE IDEAL LIFE IN THE GOSPELS AND THE TORAH

IN this chapter I propose to deal with the last four verses of the fifth chapter of Matthew. The first verse of this section reads :—" That ye may be sons of your Father who is in heaven : for he maketh his sun to rise on the evil and the good, and sendeth rain on the just and the unjust " (v. 45). Thus far we have seen how Jesus sketches the ideal life which he wishes to see realized in the coming Kingdom. While there is a considerable amount of agreement between this teaching and that current among the Jews of his day, there are also important fundamental differences. We shall dwell on the common teaching before we discuss the points of difference. The basis of the ideal life is love. Jesus therefore asks his disciples to love one another, even the enemies among them. We have already seen that this law of love is part of the old Jewish teaching. In the Sermon on the Mount we have a series of precepts that are to form the rule of life for the disciples in the Messianic Kingdom about to be inaugurated. All outside the Kingdom are sinners and lawless. They are without rights and privileges. The disciples were to look upon all these excluded people as though they were " dogs." " Do not give the holy thing to the dogs " (Matt. vii. 6 ; Rev. xxii. 15 ; and Phil. iii. 2). The new

revelation was only for the disciples, not for the disbelieving Jews. So also " love your enemies " was strictly
limited to believers (i.e. disciples, see Bishop Gore, *op.
cit.* p. 15). Jesus himself did not love his enemies. He
was very harsh to the Gentile woman (Matt. xv. 26),
and full of fierce anger towards the Scribes and Pharisees
(Matt. xxiii. 13 ff.). He denounced the entire community and called them " hypocrites " and " children
of hell."

According to Jewish theology, God's righteous love
makes Him infinitely merciful to the penitent sinner,
and makes Him also stern to the impenitent. Here we
are confronted by a difficulty that cannot be ignored.
We are told that Jesus demands that men should love
their enemies, because they are to be perfect as their
Father in Heaven is perfect. Our contention that this
is strictly limited to the disciples (i.e. the members of
the Kingdom—see John i. 12) will probably be disputed.
Whatever Jesus teaches, we are told, must be universal,
because it is based on God's character. The argument
is : God sends his rain on the just and the unjust, and
makes his sun to rise on the evil and the good ; therefore,
men are to love their unjust and their evil fellows, even
their enemies. Is this reasoning valid ? God's action
in sending the rain and in making the sun to shine is
limited to the material world. This offers no real analogy applicable to the moral world. The sun would still
shine and the rain would continue to fall whether men
inhabited the earth or not. We have seen that although
God is full of infinite love and mercy, nevertheless He
cannot withhold the divine justice that, together with
love, forms the foundation on which His throne rests.
Can God love the impenitent in the same measure that

He loves the righteous ? Are not the impenitent the
enemies who disturb the peace of the world ? God is
slow to anger, full of tender mercy and love, ever ready
to forgive, when forgiveness is sincerely sought after by
the penitent. From this point of view, God loves the
just and the unjust, provided the latter have abandoned
their evil ways. God even helps the penitent to return
to the right path. As long as man lives he can return
to the Heavenly Father ; even the greatest sinners are
still children of God, who never refuses to listen to the
cry of His erring children.

When Jesus tells his disciples to become " sons of
God " (Matt. v. 45, cf. v. 9), he was using a term that
was common among his contemporaries. Quite apart
from the many passages in the Old Testament, which
speak of the " sons of God " and the " fatherhood of
God," the great Jewish writers of the pre-Christian age
speak of *men* as the " sons of God." A few examples
will show that it is not Israel as a nation, not the individual Israelite, that bears this title ; but that it can
belong to all men, without reference to creed or race.
This is not the case in the Gospels where " son of God "
has a very limited application. In the *Testaments of
the Twelve Patriarchs* we read : " Therefore the Most
High hath heard thy prayer to separate thee from iniquity, and that thou shouldest become to Him a son "
(Levi iv. 2). Dr. Charles (*Testaments of the Twelve
Patriarchs*), has a note on this passage (p. 37), and
says :—" The view that the individual Israelite was a
son of God was already current in the second century
B.C." Reference is made by Dr. Charles to Ecclesiasticus
xxiii. 1 ; li. 10 (Syriac), and to Jubilees i. 24 (see Charles'
edition). The Wisdom of Solomon (*circa* 75 B.C.E.)

says that the " righteous man nameth himself a child
of the Lord " (ii. 13). Again we have, " For if the
righteous man is God's son, he will uphold him " (ii. 18).
There is good reason to believe that this last passage
was used by Matthew (xxvii. 43). In the third book of
the Maccabees (the date is uncertain ; Kautzsch places
it somewhere between 200 B.C.E. and 70 C.E.) God is
called the Merciful Father. Josephus adds that men
" need to be taught that God is the Father and Lord of
All " (Preface to *Antiquities*, § 4).

What do we find in the Gospels ? That the sonship
is strictly limited to such disciples to whom Jesus is
willing to reveal the knowledge of the Fatherhood of
God. How is it possible to say that the Gospels speak
of the universal Fatherhood of God, which implies the
divine sonship belonging to all men, when Jesus declares :
" No one knoweth the son, save the Father ; neither
doth any know the Father, save the son, and he to
whomsoever the son willeth to reveal him " (Matt. xi.
27) ? Jesus, of set purpose, desired to exclude the
masses of the people from all knowledge revealing their
divine sonship. He purposely expounds this teaching
in parables, so that only his disciples should understand.
" And he said unto them, unto you is given the mystery
of the Kingdom of God, but unto them that are without,
all things are done in parables ; that seeing they may
see and not perceive . . . lest haply they should repent
and it should be forgiven them " (Mark iv. 11, 12). Is
this the universal law of love to one's enemies ? Is this
how the Gospel teaches all men that God is the Father,
who seeks all his children in infinite love and compassion ? It is important to remember that the term " son
of God " is used in two different ways in the Old Testa-

ment. First of all, it explains the wonderful spiritual relationship uniting all men to God : " for in the image of God made He man " (Gen. i. 27 ; see also Aboth iii. 18). In this sense Philo also speaks of God as " the Father and Creator " (*On Monarchy*, I. § 4, M. ii. p. 216). God is our Father because He is the giver of life and the creator of our soul. It is noteworthy that the Church Fathers speak of God as the Father and Maker of all in the same way as any of the old Greek writers. Justin (*Apol.* ii. 10), Tertullian (*Apol.* 46), and Clement (*Strom.* v. 78, 92), quote the well-known passage from Plato (*Timaeus*, p. 28) which speaks of God as the " Father and Maker of this All." There can be little doubt that the Church was led to adopt this current term for describing the Deity, because it was a Gentile term and the Church had to appeal to the Gentiles. Then, secondly, we are His children because we have chosen Him as our God. We have really created the bond by attaching ourselves to the worship and service of the one God. In return, God has accepted our sonship, and sanctified the bond by appointing us His " Kingdom of priests " and His " holy nation " (Exod. xix. 6). This is the religious or ethical sonship as opposed to the previous interpretation, which may be called the natural sonship.

Some writers would speak of this Divine paternal relation as referring to the nation as a whole. God, we are told, is the Father of Israel, because He made them a nation and established them by His mighty power (Deut. xxxii. 6). We cannot accept this view which is given in the article " Father " (p. 581), in Dr. Hastings' *Dictionary of Christ and the Gospels.* God made other people into nations, and also established them by His infinite power. He redeemed the Philistines and the Syrians (Amos ix. 7), but this was not enough to establish the divine Fatherhood. The Philistines and Syrians preferred to worship idols, and consequently could not claim God's sonship in the religious sense. The writer just quoted points out that in the Old Testament, God's Fatherhood " is wholly national." This is far from the truth. God's Fatherhood is universal according to Genesis ; it is *man* who is created in the divine image. God claims the title of " Father of the orphan " and " like as a father pitieth his children, so the Lord pitieth them that fear him " (Ps. ciii. 13). Here there is no idea of a national limitation. It is a universal thought that has played no small part in the history of the world. In the olden days of Israel's national life, it was sufficient for a heathen to " fear God " in order to be admitted into the rank of the proselytes of the Gate (Gerê Toshab). They were called " Sebomenoi " ($\sigma\epsilon\beta\acute{o}\mu\epsilon\nu\omicron\iota$) or " Phoboumenoi " ($\phi\omicron\beta\omicron\acute{\nu}\mu\epsilon\nu\omicron\iota$), and their obligations were summed up in the seven " Precepts of the Sons of Noah " (Tosephta Aboda Zara, ix. 4, and Synhedrin, 56*a*). These precepts were supposed to be already binding upon mankind at large. They were absolutely necessary, if society was not to revert to barbarism and anarchy. The term " fearing God " has nothing to do with actual fear. It is used in Hebrew as the equivalent of religion or morality.

All who fear God (i.e. all righteous men, whether Jews or Gentiles) are sons of God. Philo means the same when he declares : " All who have real knowledge of the one Creator and Father of all things are rightly called sons of God " (On the Confusion of Languages, 28, M. i. p. 426). Man, by his conduct and his principles,

G

can be a son of God without reference to his race.

According to Ecclesiasticus : " All who are fathers to the fatherless shall be sons of the Most High " (iv. 10). This is surely an ethical relation. God, being loving and merciful, is brought into contact with any man who is loving and merciful (Sotah, 14a). The love shown to the orphan shows that man is imitating God, following Him (Deut. xi. 22), walking with him (Deut. xiii. 4), cleaving to Him (Deut. iv. 4), and therefore he is His son. We have laid great stress on this side of Jewish theology because it is always ignored by Christian writers. Hastings' *D.C.G.*, i. (p. 581), asserts : " The Old Testament gave to Jesus the name of ' Father ' for God, but he filled it with a new content." In a sense this is true, but then the new content has marked no advance upon the Jewish conception of the Divine Fatherhood. In fact, it has greatly obscured the pure Jewish belief in the one supreme God ever near to all who call upon Him in truth (Ps. cxlv. 18). The Gospel introduces the idea of one divine son, apart from all men, becoming a mediator between God and humanity (Matt. xi. 27 ; Luke x. 22 ; and Mark x. 45). Judaism refuses to accept this view of the Fatherhood of God, and denies the right of any man to be considered as the only son of God, apart from all other men. The Jew has no need of a mediator, since God is his Father, ever near and ever watching. The idea of a transcendental God, only to be approached through a mediator, belongs rather to the Gospels, and is quite alien to Jewish belief. A believer in the Gospels and its hero might be tempted " to doubt the divinity of God, but scarcely the divinity of Jesus " (see *Hibbert Journal Supplement*, 1909, p. 156).

The following passages are close parallels to the rest

of the forty-fifth verse of the fifth chapter of Matthew.
" Why does God not destroy the various objects of
heathen worship, such as the sun ? Because the sun is
beneficial to humanity, and must not be destroyed because some men are sinful and foolish " (Mishna Aboda
Zara, iv. 7). Again, " the rain is a blessing for the
righteous and the wicked " (Taanith, 7a). There is a
good parallel in Seneca, *de Beneficiis*, iv. 26.

The Sermon proceeds to state :—" For if ye love them
that love you, what reward have ye ? Do not even
the Publicans the same ? And if ye salute your brethren
only, what do ye more than others ? Do not even the
Gentiles the same ? " (46, 47). In the parallel passage
in Luke (vi. 32) instead of " publicans " and " Gentiles "
(or heathens) we find " sinners." The Didache (i. 3)
has " heathens " instead of " publicans." I have dealt
with this point in my essay, *The Grace of God* (pp. 18
and 19). The disciples are to be better than the publicans (i.e. collectors of Roman taxes) or the Gentiles.
To respond to love is not enough, it is the duty of the
sons of God to love their neighbours, whether the latter
display love or not. This is also clearly the lesson conveyed by the nineteenth chapter of Leviticus, which tells
us : Do not bear a grudge, do not return evil for evil,
do not hate, but love thy neighbour. We are to see
our neighbour in every man who is, as we are, created
in the image divine. The Mosaic Law explains how
we are to love our neighbour, even though he be our
enemy :—" If thou meet thine enemy's ox or his ass
going astray, thou shalt surely bring it back to him
again. If thou see the ass of him that hateth thee
lying under his burden and wouldst forbear to help him,
thou shalt surely help with him " (Exod. xxiii. 4, 5).

" Say not, I will recompense evil ; wait on the Lord and He shall save thee " (Prov. xx. 22). " Say not, I will do so to him as he hath done to me ; I will render to the man according to his work " (ibid. xxiv. 29). Does the law of love as set forth in the Sermon on the Mount teach us more than these Old Testament precepts ? We grant that the last verses of this fifth chapter of Matthew (and the parallel passages in Luke) contain splendid ethical maxims. But it adds nothing to the Law or to its interpretation by the Rabbis.

It is well to bear in mind the fact, which Dr. Sanday readily acknowledges, that parts of the teaching set forth in the Sermon on the Mount " would become impracticable if they were transferred from the individual standing alone to Governments or individuals representing society " (Hastings' *D.B.*, ii. p. 621). Such a distinction between social ethics and individual ethics is entirely alien to Jewish law. Nevertheless, the principles of Jewish ethics express themselves in various ways, according to circumstances ; but there is only one ethical standard, viz., God, for the individual and for the community.

The next verse in the Sermon teaches :—" Ye therefore shall be perfect, as your heavenly Father is perfect " (48). This statement is clearly intended to be a summary of all that Jesus has said in the Sermon up to this point. From the artistic standpoint, it must be granted that no finer culminating passage could possibly have been selected. Whatever was to be impressed on the disciples is contained in these beautiful words. Like so much in the Sermon, they are practically a direct quotation from the Old Testament. " Thou shalt be perfect with the Lord thy God " (Deut. xviii. 13) is undoubtedly the source, although the form of the wording is borrowed from Lev. xix. 2 : " Ye shall be holy, for I, the Lord your God, am holy."

Is it fair to say, that the thought of these Old Testament passages, as their contexts show, is of levitical purity and national separateness, and therefore superficial as compared with the deep meaning which Jesus puts into the words (Hastings' *D.B.*, v. p. 31) ? In the Torah the command, " Be ye holy " is immediately followed by precepts dealing with the duty of honouring one's parents, with the observance of the Sabbath, and with the prohibition of idolatry (Lev. xix. 3, 4, 5). To argue that these precepts deal with " levitical purity and national separateness " is, to my mind, absolutely unfair. The nineteenth chapter of Leviticus is a far more complete moral code than the Sermon on the Mount, in spite of the important Jewish teaching that makes up the greater part of the contents of the Sermon.

Mr. Montefiore has a fine criticism of Loisy's sneer at the holiness required in Leviticus xix. 2 (see *S.G.*, p. 522). This code of holiness includes, in addition to (1) reverence of parents and (2) observance of the Sabbath (one of the most merciful and gracious of the Jewish laws), the following : (3) charity to the poor, (4) truth of word and deed, (5) justice in all business transactions, (6) honour shown to the aged, (7) equal justice before the law to rich and poor, (8) no talebearing, (9) no malice, (10) the love of one's neighbour, and (11) the love of the stranger. Mr. Montefiore adds : " It does not seem to me that this moral code need fear comparison in holiness with any other teaching. Has the Christian world greatly advanced beyond it in practice as well as in theory ? " (ibid. p. 522). I cordially endorse every word of this fine defence of the Jewish moral code. I do not, however, agree with Mr. Montefiore's remarkable opinion that " we need the correction of the Gospel " (p. 527).   There is nothing in the Gospel that is superior to the divine commandments : " Thou shalt be perfect with the Lord thy God " ; and " Ye shall be holy, for I, the Lord your God, am holy." We have here, in the Law, the divine ideal of perfection based on the *Imitation of God*. Because God is holy, man must strive to become holy and perfect. The Torah is the only code that insists on the necessity and possibility of growth towards perfection. If the Gospels repeat these wonderful laws of the moral and spiritual life, the Evangelist should have remembered the formula, " Ye have heard that it was said "—" be ye perfect." The mere fact that the Gospels have borrowed from the Torah such ideal teachings proves the unequalled superiority of the Jewish law.   It is so perfect that the Gospel is content to repeat its precepts (see also Matt. xxii. 37 ff. and parallel passages).

Mr. Montefiore has practically contradicted himself by asserting, on the one hand, that the holiness demanded by the Law need not fear comparison with any other teaching, and, on the other hand, by telling us that the Jews need the " correction of the Gospel." If the ideal embodied in the law of holiness is incomparable, it is surely not in need of the correction of the Gospel that has borrowed this ideal.   It is a remarkable fact that, in the Synoptic Gospels, Jesus never speaks of the holiness of God. Dr. Gilbert (Hastings' *D.C.G.*, i., p. 651) adds : " in the thought of Jesus the holiness of God did not imply, as with the Scribes, that He was far removed from sinful men, being Himself subject to defile-

ment. His holiness is not ritual, but purely ethical."
This is a sample of the modern scholarship of Christian
writers. They know so little about the Scribes and
Judaism that they feel at liberty to write anything and
everything likely to exalt Jesus at the expense of his
contemporaries. Apart from the fact that Jesus never
speaks of the holiness of God, it must not be forgotten
that he has caused a profound modification of the old
Jewish conception of pure monotheism (see John xiv.
10 ; Matt. xxvi. 64 ff. ; and xxiv. 42), and this has
tended to materialize the spiritual ideal of holiness
associated with God (see Matt. i. 18 ; Luke i. 35).   In
view of this change in the Gospel of the conception of
divine holiness, it is amazing that Christian theologians
should venture to assert that " the Old Testament idea
of moral perfection is distinguished from the New Testament one in three respects. It is negative rather than
positive, refers to outward act rather than to inner disposition and spirit, and may be summed up in righteousness rather than in love " (Hastings' D.B., iii. p. 745).

The fact that God's holiness is man's ideal according
to the Torah, should effectively disprove this unwar-
ranted statement. " Be ye perfect," or " be ye holy " ;
love God with all thy heart, soul and might ; love your
neighbour ; love the stranger—these precepts, among
many others, show that the Old Testament idea of moral
perfection is positive rather than negative, refers to
inner disposition and spirit rather than to outward act,
and must be summed up in righteousness and love.   It
can hardly be gainsaid that, according to the Sermon on
the Mount, righteousness is also to be sought after by
the disciples in the Messianic Kingdom. This subject
will be fully dealt with when we come to treat of the

sixth chapter of Matthew. We would only just mention that the Gospel conception of righteousness is not confined to inner disposition ; but includes such formal and external matters as almsgiving, prayer, and fasting. We have already seen that the Sermon pronounced a blessing on those who are persecuted for righteousness' sake. This is not the real ideal of the Gospel. In place of righteousness, the abstract ideal of the divine character, the Gospels substitute Jesus. "Happy are ye when men shall reproach you and persecute you . . . for my sake" (Matt. v. 11). In the Gospel Jesus becomes the ideal, whereas in the Old Testament the ideal is God :—"Whosoever shall lose his life for my sake, and the Gospel's shall save it" (Mark viii. 35). Jews prefer to sanctify their lives for the glory of God (Kiddush Ha-shem), and can only recognize God as the source of their inspiration.

In concluding our study of this last section of the fifth chapter of Matthew, we shall deal briefly with one or two points in the parallel passage in Luke. In place of "Be ye perfect," Luke (vi. 36) has "Be ye merciful even as your Father is merciful." Even this version has its parallels in Jewish thought :—"With the merciful thou, O God, wilt show thyself merciful ; with the perfect man thou wilt show thyself perfect" (Ps. xviii. 25. This passage gave rise to the variant readings— perfect and merciful in Matthew and Luke respectively). God is gracious unto *all* . . . that the righteous must be a lover of *men* (Wisdom xii. 19). Abba Saul explained the text "And I will praise Him (Exod. xv. 2) as teaching the *Imitation of God.* "Just as He is loving and merciful, so shalt thou be loving and merciful" (Sabbath, 133*b*). According to Luke (xx. 36)

Jesus uses the expression, " sons of God " with reference to believers. All who believe in him and his claims are called " sons of God," and will enter the Kingdom of God (see also John v. 24). The mark of the believers or disciples is love :—" By this shall all men know that ye are my disciples, if ye have love one to another " (John xiii. 35). It is not the love of one's enemies that is insisted on by the writer of the Fourth Gospel—his own hatred of the Jews was too strong, and probably for this reason, his ideal of perfection is limited to the disciples. It must also be remembered that the ideal of perfection as set forth in the Gospel could only appeal to such as believed that the end of the present world was at hand. " If thou wilt be perfect," says Jesus, " sell all that thou hast " (Matt. xix. 21). This is impossible in every-day life. It has led to the belief that wealth is accursed, whilst poverty ensures blessedness. It cannot be denied that from very early times there were circles of Christian ascetics who pointed to Jesus as the founder and example of the ascetic life (see Clem. Alex. *Strom*. iii. 6). We cannot enter now into the question whether this ideal of poverty is due to the influence of the Essenes, who practised voluntary poverty, or whether it is connected with the Gnostic belief that matter (including wealth) was the seat and abode of evil. The fact remains that the Church has identified the ideal life with that *vita religiosa* which has found its fullest expression in Monasticism. Judaism has, on the whole, avoided asceticism, and has rather sought to live the ideal life on earth, and enjoy the good gifts of God. Judaism does not admit that it is impossible for the rich to be saved (Matt. xix. 24). " The loving deeds of the Gentiles," taught Rabban Jochanan b. Zakkai, " are accepted by God as their sin-offering " (Baba Bathra, 10*b*). The righteous and pious of all nations, rich or poor, will inherit the Kingdom of God (Tosephta Synhedrin, xiii. 2). This is the teaching of the Scribes and Pharisees as opposed to the Gospel, which reports Jesus as saying :—" I pray not for the world, but for those whom thou hast given me " (John xvii. 9).

LITERATURE

On 'The Ideal Life,' see last chapter in Maimonides, *Moreh Nebuchim*, and also Maimonides, *Hilchoth Deoth*, v–vii ; Bachya's *Chobot Halebabot*, chapter v, and Luzzato's *Mesilath Yesharim*. On 'Proselytes,' see Schürer, *History* (*E. T.* II. ii. 315–319) ; and Bertholet, *Die Stellung der Israeliten und der Juden zu den Fremden* pp. 323. ff. (The discussion concerning the *Ger Toshab* on page 325 is noteworthy and invites criticism). '*For my sake*' in the New Testament, see Heitmüller, *Im Namen Jesu* (1903) pp. 237, 252 ff. On 'Ger Toshab,' see Grünebaum's article in Geiger's *J.Z.f.W.u.L.* ix. pp. 164 ff.

NOTE TO PAGE 81

According to Rabbi Meir, the Ger Toshab, or 'Proselyte of the Gate,' need only declare before three pious men (Chabêrim) that he disavows idolatry and thereupon he ceases to be regarded as one of the heathens (Aboda Zara, 64*b*), see also Numb. Rabba viii. 9.

NOTE TO PAGE 84

Clemen (*Religionsgeschichtliche Erklärung des Neuen Testaments*, p. 34), admits that Matthew v. 48, has been borrowed from Greek philosophy. We prefer to suggest that the original source is to be found in the Old Testament.

CHAPTER VIII

THE WORKS OF RIGHTEOUSNESS IN THE GOSPELS

THE Sermon on the Mount has thus far set forth the indispensable characteristics demanded of all who would enter the Messianic Kingdom. One class will be ex-cluded, not one of them shall enter. They are the Scribes and the Pharisees, who are " hypocrites." Jesus demands a righteousness higher than that of the Scribes and the Pharisees (Matt. v. 20). The faulty Jewish practice must be replaced by the ideal conduct which he has sketched in the Beatitudes and in his new inter-pretation of the Law. We have seen how the old laws dealing with murder, adultery, oaths, retaliation, and love have been expounded. Jesus now proceeds, accord-ing to the sixth chapter of Matthew, to criticize the works of righteousness in vogue among the Pharisees. The subjects dealt with are (1) almsgiving, (2) prayer, and (3) fasting. These three elements of the religious life are all mentioned in the Book of Tobit (*circa* 100 B.C.E.). This book has exercised no small influence in the Church. The Didache and Pseudo-Clementine Epistles adapt its views with reference to almsgiving. The Council of Trent declared this apocryphal book to be canonical. The passage we refer to is xii. 7–9 : " Do good and evil shall not find you. Good is prayer with fasting and alms and righteousness. A little with righteousness is better than much with unrighteousness. It is better to give alms than to lay up gold : alms doth deliver from death, and it shall purge away all sin. They that do alms and righteousness shall be filled with life."

This Pharisaic principle was transplanted into the Church (see Polycarp ad. Phil., ch. x. ; Pseudo-Clem. ad Cor. xvi. ; and see also Hoennicke, op. cit., pp. 266, 340 f., 362, and 384). The first verse of Matthew vi. says : " Take heed that ye do not your righteousness before men, to be seen of them : else ye have no reward with your Father who is in heaven." This is a general introduction. It emphasizes the old Jewish principle that religion is essentially *inward*. God wishes for the heart. " Rend your heart, and not your garments," cries the prophet (Joel ii. 13). Righteousness which occurs in our context, and so frequently in the New Testament, has been borrowed from the Old Testament. It is one of the fundamental terms in Jewish theology. As we shall see, it has lost part of its meaning in the New Testament. The Hebrew root occurs no less than 520 times in the Old Testament (Hastings' *D.B.*, iv. p. 272). Righteousness does not fully express the meaning of the Hebrew word Tzedakah. Speaking quite generally, morality would be a better rendering. The Septuagint sometimes translates the word by $\dot{\epsilon}\lambda\epsilon\eta\mu\sigma\acute{v}\nu\eta$ (charity), and sometimes by $\delta\iota\kappa\alpha\iota\sigma\acute{v}\nu\eta$ (righteousness). Some commentators have suggested that the New Testament Greek word for *righteousness* should include also the meaning of charity ; just like the Hebrew word Tzedakah, which means both righteousness and charity. The opinion of modern scholars does not support this contention. The fact seems to be, that the word righteousness in this context does not mean charity, which is specially referred to in the next verses—" When therefore thou doest alms, sound not a trumpet before thee, as the hypocrites do in the Synagogues and in the streets, that they may have the glory of men. Verily I say unto you, They have received their reward. But when thou doest alms, let not thy left hand know what thy right hand doeth : that thine alms may be in secret and thy Father who seeth in secret shall recompense thee " (Matt. vi. 2–4).

Votaw adds that " the connexion of these verses with the historical Sermon cannot well be doubted ; they follow in logical consecution upon the material contained in Matthew v. 3–48, illustrating the true righteousness still further and on another side " (Hastings' *D.B.*, v. p. 31). Pfleiderer and Loisy believe that chapter six did not originally belong to the Sermon. We shall see that the other two sections, dealing with prayer (5–8) and fasting (16–18), are set forth in a form closely parallel with the section on almsgiving (2–4) which we are now considering. Each section concludes with the identical rhythmic refrain :—" The Father who seeth in secret shall recompense thee." This artificial character of the structure of the sections seems to indicate editorial composition. The author (Jesus or the Evangelist) of this part of the Sermon does not condemn almsgiving. He quite approves of the Pharisaic works of righteousness. He only attacks the manner of doing these works. Instead of the Pharisaic ostentation, secrecy must mark the performance of these works of righteousness. What is especially required of the disciples is that their outward conduct (practical righteousness) should totally differ from that of the hated Scribes and Pharisees.

People see that the latter give charity in the Synagogues and in the streets ; the disciples are not to do this at all. If they give charity it must be so secret that no one knows anything about it.

In the Synoptic Gospels we do not find a single instance showing that the disciples or their Master were accustomed to give alms. How could they ? They had no property, and if they had wealth they had to renounce it (Luke xiv. 33 ; Matt. xix. 29). The Acts of the Apostles give us a few glimpses of the social life of the first Christian community in Jerusalem. We read that " all that believed were together, and had all things common " (Acts ii. 44). There was no need of almsgiving when all shared alike. As soon as this communism was abandoned, it was necessary to revert to the old Jewish practice. In every case where the Sermon on the Mount lays down a new law in opposition to the Pharisaic customs, the Church has ultimately abandoned the teaching of the Sermon, and has consciously adopted Jewish practice. This is acknowledged by Dr. Schmidt (*The Prophet of Nazareth*, p. 316), who admits : " The Church has too often failed to take this ground (of secret charity) and encouraged, rather than rebuked, ostentatious giving to the Lord." Jesus, like the Rabbis, attacks all kinds of self-advertisement. The Rabbis never weary of demanding *purity of motive.* Jesus calls the Pharisees hypocrites, because he assumes that their motive is not to do good for its own sake, but only to achieve notoriety. They, in giving their charity, are paying for a popular reputation. This is their recompense. Ostentatious religion reaps its reward among men, but forfeits its heavenly reward. Jesus quite naïvely assures his disciples that God rewards man's righteousness. He does not tell his followers to act righteously for righteousness' sake, but he encourages them to be good by promising them a divine reward. The Rabbis undoubtedly speak of a heavenly reward, but they also insist on the duty of acting for the sake of virtue. This is expressed by the term " Lishmoh " —for its own sake (see Lazarus, *Die Ethik des Juden-thums*, p. 110). Jesus says that the Pharisees display their ostentation and hypocrisy by sounding a trumpet before themselves in the Synagogues and in the streets when distributing their alms (v. 2). Is this a fact ? We cannot do better than quote Lightfoot (*in loc.*), whose *Horæ Hebraicæ et Talmudicæ* are invaluable even in these later days of critical research. He says :—" I have not found, although I have sought for it much and seriously, even the least mention of a trumpet in connexion with almsgiving." This opinion is also shared by the learned Hebraist, Schöttgen, and many modern scholars who find themselves in a quandary. They cannot explain the phrase literally ; because, as a matter of fact, there is no reference in early Jewish literature to people giving alms in the Synagogues or streets and at the same time parading their bounty to the accompaniment of the trumpet.

Dr. A. Büchler's brilliant suggestion, that the three sections dealing with almsgiving, prayer, and fasting referred to the procedure on public fasts on the occasion of a drought, will undoubtedly receive the attention it deserves. The Talmudic passages quoted by Dr. Büchler show that the scene of these services was the street or market-place (Mishna Taanith ii., § 1 *seq.*) ; further that the trumpet (Shofar) was blown on such occasions (T.B. Taanith, 15*b*), and that the distribution of alms was considered to be an essential element in the service. This is inferred from the saying of Rabbi Elazer :— " Whosoever postpones overnight the distribution of alms in connexion with the fast is as though he shed blood " (T.B. Synhedrin, 35a). This goes to show that alms were promised on fast-days, but were not always given then and there. Rabbi Elazer considered alms-giving to be the primary condition of the acceptance of the worshipper's prayer on fast-days (T.J. Taanith ii., 1, 65b, line 14 seq. ; see *The Journal of Theological Studies*, vol. x. pp. 266 ff., for Dr. Büchler's article). It must be granted that we have here good evidence that almsgiving was associated with the public fasts which were held in the streets, but there is one difficulty that does not seem to be solved. The sin of the " hypo-crites " was their ostentation, evinced by sounding the trumpets before themselves when giving charity. The passages quoted by Dr. Büchler do not really estab-lish any direct connexion between almsgiving and the blowing of the trumpets. We require further evidence to show that the sounding of trumpets was used to pro-claim individual almsgiving in the streets and in the Synagogues. Gifts to the poor were frequently pro-mised in the Synagogues on Sabbaths and Festivals. Owing to the non-fulfilment of these promises, droughts were believed to be sent as a punishment (T.J. Kiddushin, iv. 1, 65b, and see Dr. Büchler, *The Political and the Social Leaders of the Jewish Community of Sepphoris in the Second and Third Centuries*, pp. 36 and 37). Matthew does not connect almsgiving with fasting or with prayer, but only with the sounding of the trumpet. Some commentators say that the phrase, " sound not a trumpet before thee " (Matt. vi. 2), is a proverbial metaphor. Others take the words quite literally and assure us that the Pharisees actually blew a trumpet to summon the beggars.

Zahn (*in loc.*) compares the phrase with Juvenal's *bucina famæ* (xiv. 152). There is, however, no parallel in Rabbinical literature, and therefore we cannot accept the explanation that " sound a trumpet " is figurative. Matthew has undoubtedly confused two different customs, and by associating them as though almsgiving was accompanied by blowing the trumpet, he shows how unreliable his Jewish knowledge really is. Care must be taken to distinguish between the obligatory almsgiving of which the Sermon speaks and the voluntary charity determined by the generosity of the donor. The obligatory almsgiving is known as Tzedakah, or Mattenoth Aniyyim ; whereas the optional charity is called Chesed, or Gemiluth Chesed. This latter term becomes in the New Testament Greek—" Agape " (charity or love). All the fine things written and said about Agape really apply to the Hebrew ideal of Gemiluth Chesed (see also Lazarus, op. cit., p. 167). Tzedakah is the gift made under a sense of religious obligation. It is not a spontaneous gift. Gemiluth Chesed is the love of God and of man, and is infinitely higher than Tzedakah (charity). If the world were so poor that no one could make a gift, or so rich that no one needed a gift, there would still be room for the deeds of love that sweeten life and make the poor less poor and the rich more rich. This benevolence that unites all men could only arise when the thought of the Unity of God became dominant. This thought begat a standard of moral judgment that for the first time was applicable to humanity. The ideal Israelite, says the Talmud, possesses

H

three attributes ; " he is merciful, modest, and benevo-
lent ; any human being who possesses these three attributes is worthy of being reckoned as a true son of
Israel " (Jebamoth, 79a). The Unity of God implies
the unity of humanity. All men are spiritually of one
kith and kin. This is the imperishable foundation of
Jewish philanthropy, and is finely set out in Philo's
essay on Charity, usually quoted as the essay on
Humanity.

Jesus unmercifully condemned the Pharisaic righteousness—its theory and practice. It is not reasonable to
assume that there were not, here and there, some men
who loved ostentation. The Parish Magazine and the
weekly Church newspapers, as well as the weekly Jewish
press, testify that self-advertisement and ostentation
are not characteristics peculiar to the " hypocrites " of
the first century of the common era. In practice the
Jews do not generally make a display of their generosity.
Secret charity has always been a strongly-marked
feature of Jewish social life. The sixteenth and seventeenth chapters of Mr. Israel Abrahams' *Jewish Life in
the Middle Ages* will afford ample proof to bear out this
contention. The Pharisaic teaching as to the rights
and privileges of the poor is admirably summarized in
Maimonides' Code, in the section, " Hilchoth Mattenoth
Aniyyim." It deals with the laws regulating the rights
of the poor in connexion with the corners of the field,
the gleanings of the harvest, the forgotten sheaf, the
produce of the seventh year, and the poor tithe. Pharisaic Judaism is the only religion in the world that has
special laws preserving the inalienable rights and privileges of the poor. These laws are known as " Kebod
Aniyyim " or " Honour due to the Poor " (see Moed

Katon, 27*a* and *b*, and Tosephta Nidda, ix. 16, 17).
There existed, in the time of Jesus, in every town a
Kuppa (box) in which was placed the money for distribution among the poor. The collection for the Kuppa
took place every Friday (Baba Bathra, 8*b*; see also
I Cor. xvi. 2 for the custom of the early Church).
It was a house-to-house collection. There was also
another custom on Friday, which had nothing whatever
to do with the Kuppa. The trumpet was sounded six
times to remind the people of the approach of the
Sabbath (T.B. Sabbath, 35*b*).

Is it not possible that these customs of collecting
provisions for the poor and of blowing the trumpet were
connected together by the Evangelist, who evidently
delights to refer to Jewish customs, even though he is
not quite sure of his facts ? There is another instance
of his inaccuracy in connexion with the case of Corban
(Matt. xv. 5 ; cf. Mark vii. 10–13).

We must now turn to the title " hypocrites," bestowed
by Jesus on his opponents, the Scribes and Pharisees
(Matt. vi. 2, and xv. 7). He also called them " whited
sepulchres " (ibid. xxiii. 27) " the offspring of vipers "
(ibid. xxiii. 33), " an evil and adulterous generation "
(ibid. xii. 39), and " blind guides " (ibid. xv. 14). These
terms of abuse do not reveal the intense love for humanity, especially for sinners, which is said to have been a
marked feature of the ministry of Jesus. Let us assume, for the sake of argument, that the account of
occasional Pharisaic almsgiving is correct ; is it then
proper to stigmatize the entire community as hypocrites ? The word "hypocrite" in the New Testament
has lost its classical meaning of actor, and indicates an
evil deceiver. Jesus calls all the Pharisees hypocrites,

because " they wore a mask of piety over their selfish lives " (Hastings' *D.B.*, v. p. 31). It would really be most interesting to compare the opinions of the various Christian commentators who define the Pharisaic hypocrisy. We can give only two or three examples, but they are typical of all the rest.

" The Pharisee is really the world's hireling, and receives his wages from it, viz., honour, consideration, power, wealth, and not from God, whom nominally he serves " (Matt. vi. 2, 5, 16 ; see Hastings' *D.C.G.*, ii. p. 811). Dr. Bousset finds that " lack of sincerity " is the characteristic feature of Pharisaism (*Die Religion des Judentums*, p. 161). Let us not forget Dr. Bousset's opinion, that the Judaism of to-day is Pharisaism through and through. Again we are told that " Pharisaism is the deadly enemy of humility or the religion of healthy-mindedness " (*D.C.G.*, i. p. 758). Speaking of the denunciation in Matthew xxiii., Dr. J. Donald says, " in it, Jesus pronounces woe against the Scribes and Pharisees for their ' hypocrisy ' or their dishonesty and love of stage-effect in religion, which was to him the most hateful impiety " (*D.C.G.*, ii. p. 833). " The religious self-advertisement which characterized the Pharisees eviscerated their (religious) exercises of all their value " (ibid. ii. p. 12).

Jesus upbraided them for rejecting him. He denied their right to criticize him (John v. 17), although he never omitted an opportunity to attack them and their theories. He told them that unless they accepted him as the Saviour, they would die in their sins (ibid. viii. 24). He sentenced them in terrible words—" Ye serpents, ye offspring of vipers, how shall ye escape the judgment of hell ? " (Matt. xxiii. 33). " Without attributing such conspicuous sins as theft and adultery and murder to the Pharisees, it is clear that in establishing their own righteousness they laid excessive stress on the details of the law, on Sabbath-keeping, on tithes, and Temple ritual, on the washing of pots and plates— still rigorously maintained by the modern Jew—and all this was supposed to constitute holiness. Jesus, with the clear, incisive word of genius, dismissed it all as ' acting.' The Pharisee was essentially an actor— playing to himself the most contemptible little comedies of holiness " (T. R. Glover, *The Conflict of Religions in the Early Roman Empire*, p. 131). What does the modern Jew, who also is a Pharisee, say to all this ? If hypocrite describes the Pharisee, it applies equally well to the Christian.   In the first instance, we are not going to ignore the fact, that in the thinking Christian Church there are innumerable so-called " believers," who disbelieve the fundamental dogmas which they continue to profess with their lips.   How many priests are loyal to their ordination vows ?   There are not many men like Charles Voysey and Gustav Frensen.   The present day attitude of the clergy to the fundamental dogmas of the Church may be gauged from the remarkable collection of essays contained in the volume entitled *Jesus or Christ ?* which formed the *Hibbert Journal Supplement* for 1909.   In the stirring novel of Frensen, called *Hilligenlei*, we read how the girl Anna Boje says to her boy companion :—" Do you know what often troubles me ? God is three in one.   Well, what frightens me is, that I am often so tired at night, that I don't get the order right.   I'm sure I pray least to the Holy Ghost, and He must be angry with me."   Again, there are many other rites, ceremonies, and beliefs that would be called

" hypocrisy " if performed by the Pharisees, whereas
" higher righteousness " is the label if performed by
Christians. Conybeare, in his *Myth, Magic, and Morals*
shows to what a large extent heathen superstitions have
survived in the Church of to-day. The great scholars
in Germany, such as Johannes Weiss, Harnack, Pfleiderer, and Bousset, have given up the creeds of the
Church. They deny the divinity of Jesus, and look upon
the stories of the Immaculate Conception or the Resur-
rection as legends. Nevertheless, they are not able to
shake off entirely the Christianity which they deny.
And now let us return to consider the indictment drawn
up by Mr. Glover.

" Excessive stress " was laid on the " Temple ritual,"
says Mr. Glover. This was dismissed as " acting " by
Jesus. The Pharisees do not stand alone in taking a
deep interest in the Temple ritual (as a matter of fact,
there is good reason to doubt whether the Scribes and
Pharisees of the age of Jesus really concerned themselves
very much with the heterodox procedure of the Sadducean priesthood). The Church also has devoted no
inconsiderable attention to questions of ritual. We
are told that the " Prayer Book Revision " remains as
one of the most pressing needs of the day, and was
discussed at one of the meetings of the recent Church
Congress. The endless disputes to-day about Church
ritual and ceremonial observances, the acrimonious
controversies concerning the liturgy or the pattern of
the vestments, may be signs of Christian righteousness,
whilst the Pharisaic discussion of the Temple ritual is
mere hypocrisy. Finally, Mr. Glover urges that " the
washing of pots and plates " among the Pharisees is a
proof that they were hypocrites. Apart from the prin-

ciple of self-discipline, cleanliness is, after all, next to
godliness, at least according to the teaching of the
Scribes and Pharisees.   Washings or baptisms are also
part of the rites and ceremonies of the Church.   The
interminable debates as to the sacramental and religious
value of baptism will furnish interesting material for
reflection.   Jews will be surprised to learn that the
Church teaches that infants, who die unbaptized are
forthwith consigned to hell.   Equally interesting is the
fact that the Church, in the earlier period of her history,
tolerated the practice of vicarious baptism.   This meant
the custom of baptizing living proxies in place of those
who had died unbaptized (Tertullian, Adv. Marcion, v,
10, and De Resur. 48).   Here let us ask, did the Law
demand nothing else beyond the " washing of pots and
plates " and the other items mentioned by Mr. Glover ?
He seems to have forgotten the great precepts of loving
God and man, of striving after holiness, and of " being
perfect with God."   We are unaware that should an
adult Jew or Jewess disregard the " washing of pots
and plates," he or she would be doomed to hell.

To return to the Sermon.   Jesus says that the hypocrites have their reward in their popularity.   As a
parallel we submit the following passage from Philo :—
" For they who give, hoping to receive a requital, such
as praise or honour, and seeking for a return of the
favour which they are conferring, under the specious
name of a gift, are really making a bargain. . ." (On
the Cherubim, § 34, M. i. p. 161).

The Sermon has " that thy alms may be in secret."
What do the Rabbis, Scribes, and Pharisees , say ?
" Almsgiving should be done in secret " (Baba Bathra,
9b ; see also Derech Eretz Zutta, ix. 4 based on Prov.

xxi. 14), and not before men, for " he who gives before men is a sinner," as it is said, " for God will bring every work before (His) judgment " (Eccles. xii. 14, and Chagiga, 5a, Baba Bathra, 10a, and Sabbath, 104a). The Siphrê (§ 117, p. 98 b) explains Deut. xv. 9, 10—" Let not thine eye be evil against thy poor brother . . . thou shalt surely give him," as though it implied " thou shalt surely give him—to him directly and secretly—and let no one stand between him and thee."

There was a " Silent Chamber " (Lishkath Chashaim) in the Temple, so that both the donor and the recipient remained unobserved (Mishna Shekalim, v. 6). Such a secret treasury existed in every town, in order that the poor of good families could receive their gifts in perfect seclusion (Tosephta Shekalim, ii, 16). Charity (Tzedakah) and acts of loving-kindness (Gemiluth Chasadim) counterbalance all the other precepts of the Law. Charity applies to the living, loving-kindness applies to the living and also to the dead ; charity is given to the poor, whilst loving-kindness is bestowed on poor and rich. Charity is given in money, whilst loving-kindness is rendered by personal service as well as by money (Tosephta Pea, iv. 19 ; and see Sukka, 49b), Rabbi Elazar, the son of Rabbi Jose, said :—" Whence do we know that charity and loving-kindness are a great Paraclete (advocate) and a cause of great peace between Israel and the Father in Heaven ? Because it is said : ' For thus saith the Lord, enter not into the house of mourning . . . for I have taken away my peace from this people, saith the Lord, even loving-kindness and tender mercies " (i.e. charity) (Jer. xvi. 5 ; Tosephta Pea, iv, 21). The word *Paraclete* occurs in the New Testament (1 John ii. 1), and is applied to

Jesus, who is called the " Advocate " (see Hatch, *Essays in Biblical Greek*, 1899, p. 82 f.).   Philo frequently uses the word Paraclete in the sense of "intercessor " or " advocate," which is its classical meaning.   He makes Joseph say to his brethren, after he had discovered himself to them : " I grant you forgiveness for all that you have done against me ; you need no one else as Paraclete or intercessor," (*On Joseph*, 40, M. ii. pp. 74, 75).   Rabbi Elazar said :—" Loving-kindness is better than charity."   This is based on Hosea x. 12— " Sow to yourselves in charity, reap according to loving-kindness " (Sukka, 49*b*).   From these teachings of the Pharisees we see that great stress was laid on deeds of mercy and charity.   " If a man does these good deeds for his own advantage (e.g. self-display) it would have been better for him if he had never been born " (Berachoth, 17*a*).   Again the Rabbis say :—" Do not put the poor man to shame by giving him your gift in public " (Chagiga, 5*a*).   " It were better for a man to hurl himself into a fiery furnace than to put his fellow to shame in public " (Ketuboth, 67*b*).   This Rabbinic teaching is not surpassed by that contained in the Sermon on the Mount.   We have already referred to Philo's fine essay on Charity.   He says it is a human obligation. Man owes it to his fellow-man as a brother.   It is expected of all men and towards all men (§§ 17, 18, M. ii. pp. 396 ff.).   There are many passages on charity and benevolence in the *Testaments of the Twelve Patriarchs* (see Zebulun vi. 4–7 ; and Issachar iii. 8–11), where the duty of " sharing every gift of God with the needy " is inculcated.   We contend that it is only the Old Testament which has given to the world the true ideal of Humanity.   Man possesses inalienable privileges, quite

apart from race or faith. In the long run a mono-
theistic religion, such as Judaism, cannot exclude any
human soul from the Heavenly Father, who has created
all His children for His glory. The whole of Jewish
literature is permeated by the thought that the highest
effort of life must be directed towards the realization of
loving-kindness uniting all men in a universal brotherhood. Charity in its widest meaning hastens the advent of the Messianic age when this universal brotherhood will be realized (Baba Bathra, 10*a*, and Tana de bê
Elijahu Zutta, 1, p. 170).

Mr. Glover sneers at the Sabbath observance. Jews
have nothing to be ashamed of in observing the Sabbath,
which gives rest to servants and animals. Paul considered that God was too holy to bother about oxen
(1 Cor. ix. 9). He could have learned otherwise from
the Pharisees, who were the first people (more than two
thousand years ago) to possess a " society for the protection of dumb creatures " (see Sabbath, 128*b*). Tithes
are also included in Mr. Glover's indictment. Tithes
can help towards the practice of a holy life—only there
is this difference between the Pharisaic and the Christian
usage. The entire tithe of the third year, and of the
sixth year, and all the produce of the seventh year
belonged to the *poor* in the land of Israel, whilst it is
only the *priest* of the Christian Church who is allowed
to enjoy the tithe. The tithe of the poor (Ma'aser 'Ani)
gave rise to the tithing of one's earnings. This tenth
of one's total income was distributed among the needy
(Sifrê §105, p. 95*b*, Deut. xiv. 22 ; see Ketuboth, 50*a*, T. J.
Peah i. 1. 15*b*, and Tosaphoth, T. B. Taanith, 9*a*). By
way of contrast, let us see how the Church dealt with
the duty of helping the needy. St. Alphonsus, whose

views are shared by many modern moralists of the
Church, holds that an outlay corresponding to two per
cent. of temporalities, superfluous to social prestige,
suffices to satisfy the obligation of almsgiving in extreme or pressing indigence ; because, were all concerned
to adopt this method, ordinary indigence could easily
be remedied (see Lehmkuhl, Theologia Moralis, Specialis
II., ii. No. 609). It is perfectly evident that the disciples of St. Alphonsus will inevitably shun the transient
glory of self-display in almsgiving, if they limit their
benefactions—not to one-tenth of their total income, as
the Pharisaic custom demands—but to two per cent. of
their *superfluous* wealth. Even then this insignificant
dole is to be given only in cases of " *extreme and pressing
indigence.*" We again see no reason to abandon the
Jewish spirit of charity and benevolence. The Sermon
on the Mount does well to impress on the generous the
need of secrecy in their almsgiving, but it has nothing
to offer which is not found in the teaching of the Scribes
and Pharisees.

LITERATURE

Bachya ibn Chalwah, *Kad Hakkemach, sub voc.* ' Tzedakah,'
Hamburger, article ' Liebeswerke' in *R.E.* ii. p. 688. On the
ethical value of Jewish Charity, see Lazarus, *Ethik des Judenthums*, pp. 368–9. On ' Paraclete,' see Hastings, *D.B.*, vol. iii.
p. 666. The section on the " Use of the Word by Philo " needs
modification, see the new German translation of Philo, (II.,
p. 329, note 1.). On Baptism, see Brandt's treatise on Jewish
Baptisms, *Die Jüdischen Baptismen*, 1910. On Corban, see
J. H. A. Hart's article in *Jewish Quarterly Review*, xix., July,
1907. On ' Lishmoh,' see Schechter's *Aspects of Rabbinic Theology*, pp. 159 ff. On ' Poor Relief,' see Weinberg in *Monatsschrift*,
1897.

NOTE TO PAGE 93

The poetical structure of the Sermon has been discussed by
D. H. Müller, in *Die Bergpredigt im Lichte der Strophenbau* (1908).

CHAPTER IX

THE DIFFERENCES BETWEEN THE PRECEPTS AND PRACTICE OF JESUS

FROM Almsgiving the Sermon on the Mount passes to Prayer :—" And when ye pray, ye shall not be as the hypocrites : for they love to stand and pray in the Synagogues and at the corners of the streets, that they may be seen of men. Verily I say unto you, They have their reward. But thou, when thou prayest, enter into thine inner chamber, and having shut thy door, pray to the Father who is in secret, and thy Father who seeth in secret shall recompense thee " (Matt. vi. 5, 6). In its structure this passage is parallel with the preceding section dealing with almsgiving. Again the Scribes and Pharisees are stigmatized as " hypocrites." Jesus then lays down his new law as to prayer, which must differ from that practised by the hypocrites. He demands secrecy in prayer. " Enter into thine inner chamber, and having shut thy door, pray to the Father who is in secret." Mr. Montefiore (*S.G.*, p. 530) holds that " he seems to strike a new note in somewhat depreciating public prayer in comparison with private prayer. The Rabbis tended to do the reverse. . . . Jesus is doubtless right. He would probably have maintained that the higher, purer, more difficult, and more essential prayer is that prayed in private. The essence of *prayer*, contrasted, by way of abstraction, with *praise*, is a

private and personal communion between the individual
and God. . . . As to hypocrisy, that is derided by the
Rabbis as well as by Jesus." These remarks seem to be
very misleading, both with reference to the teaching of
the Sermon, as well as with reference to the place of
private prayer in Jewish teaching and practice. There
is no question of Jesus " *somewhat* depreciating public
prayer in comparison with private prayer." The hypocrites (i.e. Scribes and Pharisees) laid equal stress on
private prayer and public prayer.

Surely Mr. Montefiore knows that in the Jewish homes
there are many occasions when private prayers are
recommended by the Rabbis. Some of the finest
prayers incorporated to-day in our daily prayer-book
were, in the time of Jesus, said by the pious Jew in his
" inner chamber, with his door shut." Such prayers as
are found in the Authorised Daily Prayer Book on pp.
4, 5, and 6, were private prayers said in the secrecy of
the home (see Berachoth, 11b, 16b, 17a, 31a, and 60b;
likewise Jalkut Psalm ix. 9 ; and Tana de bê Elijahu § 21).
The new note struck by Jesus was his precept of secrecy
as the absolute rule of prayer. He wished his followers
to pray not " in the Synagogues and at the corners of
the streets," but in their " inner chamber." The precept of secrecy is set forth in an expression which is
borrowed from Isaiah xxvi. 20 : " Come, my people,
enter thou into thy inner chambers (LXX. uses the
same word as in the Sermon), and shut thy doors about
thee." This verse gives the keynote to the eschatological teaching of Jesus with reference to the works of
righteousness in the coming Kingdom. Prayer, as well
as almsgiving and fasting—if they are to be practised
at all—must be done only in secret. Isaiah insists on

the seclusion of the people of the Lord from His judgment on the world (see Isa. xxvi. 21). Likewise the members of the Messianic Kingdom are to separate themselves from the hypocrites and the godless when they pray to the Father in Heaven. At the outset of his career, Jesus undoubtedly frequented the Synagogues. He took part in the services, and, according to the Evangelists, impressed the people. Jesus was certainly conscious of the effect produced by his teaching, because he asked his disciples, " Who do the multitude say that I am ? " The question occurs in the three Synoptic Gospels. One might ask : What has the effect produced by the teaching of Jesus to do with prayer ? Jewish prayer in the age of Jesus, as also in subsequent times, consisted of three elements. First of all, there was the reading of the Law with its expositions ; this was the nucleus of public worship. Then there was praise of God, and finally, actual prayer for specific purposes. The first two elements—instruction and praise—were naturally uttered in such a manner as to enable the audience to follow. In the first century of the common era the people had no prayer-books, and therefore had to rely upon the public recitation of the service. The real prayers, asking God for His mercy and favour, were said silently (Tephillah be-lachash). Nevertheless, we are told that " Jesus was the first to enjoin clearly secret and silent prayer " (Cambridge Revised Version : Matthew, p. 31).

Jesus, by his own practice, illustrates these three aspects of Pharisaic worship. He can also be described as loving to stand and take part in public worship in the Synagogues, and on a hill, or at the side of a lake, where men could see him. He tried to impress his

followers. Otherwise, why should he inquire, " Who
do the multitudes say that I am ? " (Luke ix. 18). If
Jesus, in the Sermon on the Mount, said anything new,
it was that the old Jewish public worship should cease
and be replaced by private devotions in one's inner
chamber. Dr. Schmidt admits that " with reference to
Jesus' advice as to private prayer, the Church has paid
little or no attention to him, but has vied with the
heathen nations, both in regard to the publicity and
the length of the prescribed prayers (*Prophet of Nazareth*,
p. 314). We fail to understand Bishop Gore's reason
for saying that Jesus passed " no slight on ' common '
or public religious actions " (*The Sermon on the Mount*,
p. 120). It is not quite reasonable for the Bishop to
ask us to infer the attitude of Jesus from the practice of
Paul (1 Cor. xvi. 2). Paul never knew Jesus, and in all
his epistles we have no reference to the " Sermon on the
Mount." Probably, he never knew it, for in his day it
had not yet developed into the form now found in
Matthew's Gospel. The reference to 1 Corinthians has
no bearing on public religious actions, on the contrary
it says : " Let each one of you lay by him in store."
This refers to Paul's custom of setting aside contributions, destined for the Church in Jerusalem. The
Bishop gives a further proof in support of his contention
that Jesus in no wise condemned public religious actions,
by referring to Matthew (xviii. 19, 20), which says :—
" If two of you shall agree on earth about anything
that they ask, it shall be given them from my Father
who is in heaven. For where two or three are gathered
together in my name, I am in the midst of them." This
has nothing to do with public prayer as we understand
the term ; it refers to the " power of the keys," or

" binding and loosing," in connexion with discipline in the early Christian community (see Hastings' *D.B.*, iv. p. 31).

J. Weiss, Wellhausen, Loisy, and Dr. Carpenter do not attribute these verses to Jesus. Again, Dr. Carpenter says that in Matthew vi. 1–18 " we hear the voice of later ecclesiastical usage " (*The Synoptic Gospels*, pp. 94 and 345). As a last resort, Bishop Gore refers to the institution of the Eucharist as a proof that Jesus did not slight public worship. If Jesus instituted the Lord's Supper, it was a purely private family celebration, based on the Passover Night service, or perhaps on the Friday Eve home service known as the " Kiddush." Moreover, in view of Jesus' eschatological outlook, for he awaited the speedy consummation of the Messianic Kingdom, I find it hard to accept the view that he could have instituted the Eucharist as a new worship or even as a perpetual memorial of his death, for did he not promise to return speedily and inaugurate the Kingdom ? We cannot enter now into an investigation as to the origin of the rite. Professor Gardner holds that Paul was its author, having " turned a Pagan ceremony to Christian use in a moment of ecstasy under the influence of what he had seen of the Greek mysteries in Corinth " (see Hastings' *D.C.G.*, ii. p. 64). The fact remains that in the Sermon, Jesus is slighting all public religious acts— almsgiving and praying, as well as fasting. He was strongly opposed to *public* observances. His reason seems to be based on man's duty of imitating God. Just as God is in secret, so the disciple must serve God in secret.

We have already seen that Dr. Büchler considers the public fasts for rain as the historical background of the passages in Matthew dealing with the Pharisaic works of righteousness. He says that he " can recall no reference in early Rabbinical literature to people who prayed in the streets " (*The Journal of Theological Studies*, x. p. 266). The only instance considered by Dr. Büchler deals with public fasts for rain, which were undoubtedly held in the street or market-place. This seems almost sufficient reason for assuming that Matthew was referring to such an occasion, although in vv. 16–18 he does not say that the people who fast are parading their piety in " the streets or in the Synagogues." Worship in the streets or market-places was not, however, limited to these fast-days. There were vast assemblies of the people in the towns and villages known as Maamodoth. Maimonides says that the people gathered together for prayer on fast-days, and Maamodoth, in the streets or market-places (H. Tephillah xi. § 21 ; Megillah, 26a). The assemblies consisted of the laymen belonging to the twenty-four divisions of the entire Hebrew people (see Maimonides, Hilchoth Kelê Hammikdash vi. §§ 1, 2). It was quite impossible for all the members of the entire division of the people to go up to Jerusalem when their turn came. Instead of this, only a small deputation went to the Temple ; and the rest of those belonging to the division met together in the street or market-place, and there engaged in prayer (see Hamburger, *Real-Encycl.* ii. pp. 877–80). This is possibly the origin of Matthew's reference to praying in the streets. The Rabbis insisted on the duty of praying to God in an attitude which befits our relation to our Father in Heaven. We are to pray with devotion (Kavonoh); " for a little prayer with devotion is much better than many prayers without devotion." (Cf. Rosh Hashana iii. 8).

I

A few sayings of the Rabbis on the subject of prayer may prove interesting. "The prayer of the righteous is short" (Mechilta, Beshallach, ed. Weiss, p. 53*b*). "Prayer must be silent, lest the transgressors be put to shame" by hearing their sins mentioned in the prayer (Sota, 32*b*). To this day, prayers of supplication (Tachanun) are said silently. The Confession (Viddui) in the Amidah on the Day of Atonement is also said silently by the worshipper. The Midrash Yalkut has a fine passage based on Psalm iv. 4 :—"'Stand in awe and sin not, commune with your own heart upon your bed and be still. Selah.' God says, stand in awe and pray in the Synagogues and sin not, but, if it be impossible to go to the Synagogue, pray upon thy bed ; and if thou art unable to pray—then meditate in thine heart, as it is said : ' Commune with your own heart upon your bed.' " The *Testaments of the Twelve Patriarchs* contain several passages dealing with prayer. Thus :— "Ye see, therefore, my children, how great things patience worketh, and prayer with fasting. So ye, too, if ye follow after chastity and purity with patience, and prayer with fasting in humility of heart, the Lord will dwell among you, because He loveth chastity" (Test. Joseph x. 1 f.). Philo is fond of dwelling on the need of humility when men offer up prayers or sacrifices. "How can man comprehend the supreme power of God ? Let him, then, at once reject all vain and treacherous conceit, and, discarding haughtiness and pride, let him try to become pleasing to God, and to conciliate the merciful power of that Being who hates arrogance." (*On Those Who Offer Sacrifices*, § 2, M. ii., p. 252). "Men can bring themselves the most perfect completeness of virtue, and thereby they are counted as though they offered the most excellent of all sacrifices, honouring God their Saviour, with hymns and thanksgivings ; the former uttered by the voice, and the latter without the agency of tongue or mouth ; the worshippers making their invocation with their soul alone " (ibid. § 3, M. ii, p. 253). " The altar of God is the grateful soul of the wise man " (ibid. § v., M. ii. p. 255).

These passages are typical of Jewish teaching on divine worship. The mediaeval Jew did not lose his sense of the value of prayer. Bachya's *Duties of the Heart* is full of fine teaching on the spiritual life that is sustained by prayer.

The Sermon continues : " And in praying use not vain repetitions, as the heathens do : for they think that they shall be heard for their much speaking. Be not therefore like unto them : for your Father knoweth what things ye have need of, before ye ask Him " (vi. 7 and 8). It is generally assumed that the reference to the heathens is contained in the story of the scene on Mount Carmel, when the priests of Baal indulged in vain repetitions (see 1 Kings xviii. 26). Long before the time of Jesus, his namesake, Jesus the son of Sirach, had said " repeat not thy words in thy prayer " (Ecclus. vii. 14). The Rabbis also refer to the warning of Ecclesiastes (v. 2) : " Be not rash with thy mouth, and let not thine heart be hasty to utter anything before God ; for God is in heaven, and thou art upon earth ; therefore let thy words be few." The modern Christian commentaries disregard Jesus' reference to the heathen, and accuse the Pharisees of " vain repetitions in prayer." Thus the *Century Bible* speaks of " the long and magniloquent orations of Pharisees and the heathen " (Matthew, p. 157). The *Westminster New*

Testament illustrates the passage by quoting from the Talmud an isolated saying, without giving the source or the date of the teaching :—" Every one that multiplies prayer is heard." Then we are told " that such prayer, says Jesus, is heathenish " (Matthew, p. 64). The Talmud contains many sentences teaching the value of short prayers. It is exceedingly unjust to take an isolated saying of a Rabbi and make it represent the true Jewish spirit. In the case in point we will readily grant that a Rabbi said, " Every one who multiplies prayer is heard." Lightfoot is probably the authority relied on by the *Westminster New Testament.* He refers to T. J. Taanith, 67c. But this is only one opinion, and it is counterbalanced by the contrary statement, which enjoins that prayer is not to be said as a duty in a formal manner, but that we should make our prayer an entreaty before God (Aboth ii. 18). The Psalmist teaches us that God is near to all who call upon Him in truth (Psalm cxlv. 18). " When ye pray," says the Talmud, " know before whom ye pray " (Berachoth, 28b). Scripture declares, " Thou shalt love the Lord thy God with all thine heart " (Deut. vi. 5), implying that when we pray we should give all our heart to God, and not think of anything else (Tanchuma Ki Tabo § 1). The Talmud rules : " Any artifice used for attracting attention deprives prayer of all its value " (Joma, 19b). Rabbi Eliezer referred to the example of Moses when praying for the recovery of Miriam (Num. xii. 13). Only five words were used, " Lord, pray heal her now " (Sifrê § 105, p. 28b on Num. xii. 13 ; Berachoth, 34a).

Berachoth contains many references to prayer. On folio 32b, we read : "It was taught in the name of Rabbi Jochanan, 'If one prays with persistence, thinking that therefore God must hear his prayer, he hopes in vain,' as it is said ' wearisome prayer (lit. hope) maketh the heart sick ' '' (Prov. xiii. 12). When a Rabbi prolonged his prayers he was rebuked and reminded that he was neglecting the things of eternity, by praying for the things of the passing hour (Sabbath, 10*a*). There is a fine passage on prayer in Dr. M. Güdemann's *Jüdische Apologetik*, p. 166 ; his last quotation sums up the Pharisaic attitude towards prayer :—'' Whether one indulges in prolonged prayer or recites a few words, it matters very little, if only the heart be turned heavenward '' (Berachoth, 5*b*).

We are struck by the extraordinary contradiction between the teaching about prayer attributed in the Sermon on the Mount to Jesus and his actual practice, as recorded in the other parts of the Gospels. Sometimes he continued all night in prayer (Luke vi. 12). Was this not an instance of '' much speaking '' in prayer ? He himself used the same words again and again in Gethsemane (Matt. xxvi. 44 ; Mark xiv. 39). He publicly recited the customary prayers at meals (Luke xxii. 17 ; Mark xiv. 22 ; Matt. xxvi. 26 ; John vi. 11). In Luke (xi. 8) the habit of importunity in prayer is recommended. Jesus urges the need of persistence in asking God for what man needs. Repetition of prayers, even in the same form of words, was encouraged by him, both by example and by precept (Luke xviii. 1–8).

There is undoubtedly one point with regard to the method of prayer which is absolutely new in the teaching of the Gospels. Men had been taught by the Scribes and Pharisees to worship God and even to pray to Him as a Father ; now they are told in the New Testament

to pray to the Father in the name of Jesus the only son
(John xvi. 23, 24, 26). Anything asked in the name of
Jesus will be granted (John xiv. 13, 14). This is the
only condition. It has led to the worship of Jesus as a
divine person. Several times in Matthew, and once in
Mark, we are told that the people " worshipped " Jesus.
In no case did he reject the worship, or rebuke those
who offered it to him. This aspect of prayer and worship
is indeed, both new and un-Jewish.

The commentators like to refer to the repetition
of the *Shemoneh Esreh* (Eighteen Benedictions) as
proof that the Pharisees were fond of wordiness and
repetitions in prayer. They forget that, according to
the Didache (viii. 3), the Christian prayer substituted
in the place of the " Shemoneh Esreh," and known as
the " Lord's Prayer," was also repeated three times
every day. In the Book of Common Prayer of the
Church of England there are very many instances of
" wordiness and repetitions." To give but one instance,
the Litany or General Supplication, which must be said
at least three times every week, contains eight times
the prayer, " Good Lord, deliver us " ; again, " We
beseech Thee to hear us, good Lord," occurs twenty-
two times. The Jew need not feel ashamed of his
fiturgy. More ancient than that of the Church, it is
also in every respect more valuable as a means of
teaching the great facts of religion.

When we come to the so-called Lord's Prayer, which
follows on the section we are now considering, we shall
discuss the question of its originality. The Lord's
Prayer (Matt. vi. 9–15) is undoubtedly interpolated
between the sections dealing with praying and fasting.
The latter section (vv. 16–18) is as follows :—" More-

over, when ye fast, be not, as the hypocrites, of a sad countenance : for they disfigure their faces, that they may be seen of men to fast. Verily I say unto you, They have received their reward. But thou, when thou fastest, anoint thy head and wash thy face ; that thou be not seen of men to fast, but of thy Father who is in secret : and thy Father, who seeth in secret, shall recompense thee." Dr. David Smith, in the *Westminster New Testament* (Matthew, p. 66), sees in this direction of Jesus " really an abolition of the practice " of fasting. Again, the disciples are warned not to be like the Pharisees—" the hypocrites." They fasted twice in the week (Luke xviii. 12), on Monday and Thursday, and to deviate from this practice the early Christians fasted, also twice every week, but on different days—Wednesdays and Fridays (Didache viii. 1). Jesus, according to the Gospels, fasted forty days during the Temptation (Matt. iv. 1–11). The Church has perpetuated this by its Lenten fast lasting forty days. The Sermon on the Mount, as far as chapter vi. (1–18) is concerned, really seems to reflect later ecclesiastical customs, and just as charity and prayer were to be in secret, so fasting is to be a personal and private affair. This was not the intention of Jesus, who (Mark ii. 18–22) decreed that all fasts should be abolished now that he was about to inaugurate his Messianic Kingdom. This accords with the opinion of some of the Rabbis that all the fasts (except, of course, the Day of Atonement, the only fast prescribed by the Law : Leviticus xvi. 29) were not to be considered to be obligatory when there was peace for Israel (such as would obtain in the Messianic Kingdom). This is practically foretold by the prophet Zechariah (viii. 19) ; see Rosh Hashana, 18*b*.

Private fasts in expiation of one's sins were not encouraged by the Rabbis (Taanith, 11*a*). We have already noted the fact that the fast days brought some benefit to the poor, who received charity (especially food) to enable them to have a meal at the termination of the fast (Synhedrin, 35*a*). " The merit of the fast day is in the amount of charity given to the poor " (Berachoth, 6*b*). The ostentation of the Pharisees, when fasting, is assumed to be referred to in the words, " they make their faces unsightly " (v. 16), which, from the context, implies that the head was not anointed nor the face washed. It was only on the Day of Atonement that, in the time of Jesus, washing the body and anointing the head were prohibited; on all other fasts, before the destruction of the Second Temple (70 C.E.), only food was forbidden (Joma, 73*b* ff. ; Taanith i, 4 ff.).

It may be instructive to compare the fasts of the Synagogue with those of the Church. A fast is prescribed by the Church before the Communion is administered. The Catholic Church distinguishes between natural and moral fasts. The former signify total abstinence from all kinds of food and drink for a given period ; the latter mean such abstinence as is dictated by the bodily or mental dispositions peculiar to each individual. Some of the Church moralists justify the institution of the fast because it is an act of temperance. The Church has considerably more fast days than the Synagogue. The motive for fasting is also different. The Church has nothing corresponding with the Jewish Day of Atonement. The minor fasts in the Jewish Calendar are days of grief for national disaster. In the Church, the motive is summed up in one word— mortification. Even then the fasting is quite different from the total abstinence that obtains in the Synagogue. On a Church fast day one full meal is permitted during the twenty-four hours of the fast, and the meal is to be taken at midday. According to the moralists, D'Annibale and Noldin " good reason justifies one in taking a collation in the morning, dinner at noon, and the morning allowance (i.e. breakfast) in the evening, because the substance of fasting still remains intact " (see Noldin's *Summa Theologiæ Moralis*, n. 674). If such a passage were to be found in the Talmud, or in the codes of Maimonides and Karo, we should be gently reminded that the Pharisees indulged in " play-acting," and that they were rightly called hypocrites. Dr. Schmidt (*Prophet of Nazareth*, p. 315) acknowledges that " the larger branches of the Church have continued the custom (of fasting and public repentance), without the slightest regard to the warning of Jesus, while some of the Protestant denominations have abandoned the practice, but not without inventing new forms for the *public* display of contrition and sorrow for sin."

The phrase " they make their faces unsightly " (v. 16) is not found elsewhere in the Gospels or in the other books of the New Testament. Dr. Charles (*Testaments of the Twelve Patriarchs*, p. lxxix.) draws attention to this fact, and points out that the phrase has a parallel in the Testaments : " For this (the evil disposition) *makes the face unsightly* " (Zeb. viii. 6, and see also Jos. iii. 4). The author of the Sermon borrowed this expression from the *Testaments of the Twelve Patriarchs*. It is strange that this interesting parallel should have escaped the notice of Mr. Montefiore in his commentary (*S.G.*, p. 538). Such sources of the Sermon on the Mount, which can be traced in pre-Christian Jewish

literature, are just those which should be noticed in a
" Jewish " commentary on the Gospels. Mr. Montefiore's remarks : " So far as I know, the rule about
fasting is highly original. It is conceived on true prophetic lines " (S.G., p. 538) are hardly justified when
one considers the actual teaching and practice of Jesus,
to which we have already referred. Mr. Montefiore
might have pointed out that fasting in the Rabbinic
literature does not meet with entire approval (see
Taanith, 11a and 22b). Here again the Jew, orthodox or
liberal, has nothing to learn from the teaching of Jesus
as set forth in the Gospels, or as expounded by the
creeds and customs of the Church.

LITERATURE

On Prayer, see Maimonides, *Hilchoth Tephillah*; Bachya ibn
Chalwah, *Kad Hakkemach*, *sub voc.* " Tephillah "; Hamburger,
article, ' Gebet.' See also Jehuda Ha- Levi, *Kuzari*, iii., 5.
On Private Prayer, see Lazarus, *Ethik des Judenthums*, pp. 382-4,
409 and pp. 424–5. On the Religious Life of the Jew, see Dr.
Güdemann's *Das Judenthum* (1902) pp. 67 ff.

CHAPTER X

THE FATHERHOOD OF GOD IN JUDAISM AND CHRISTIANITY

THE Lord's Prayer (Matt. vi. 9–15, and Luke xi. 2–4), says Tertullian, is an " epitome of the Gospel." The parable of the " Prodigal Son " (Luke xv. 11–24) has also been called the " Gospel within the Gospel." I have shown in my essay, " The Grace of God," that this parable is derived from the writings of the Jew Philo. I am now about to show that the " Lord's Prayer " is likewise quite Jewish. True prayer, says Wellhausen, is a creation of the Jews, and so the Lord's Prayer follows Jewish examples. Professor Nestle denies that it is a composition *ex formulis Hebraeorum* (Hastings' *D.C.G.*, ii. p. 59). It may be as well to give here the entire prayer, and then to proceed to discuss its several petitions. The text is as follows : " After this manner therefore pray ye : Our Father who art in heaven, hallowed be thy name. Thy kingdom come. Thy will be done, as in heaven, so on earth. Give us this day our daily bread. And forgive us our debts, as we also have forgiven our debtors. And bring us not into temptation, but deliver us from the evil one. For if ye forgive men their trespasses, your heavenly Father will also forgive you. But if ye forgive not men their trespasses, neither will your Father forgive your trespasses " (Matt. vi. 9–15).

The prayer is found again in Luke. It is generally acknowledged that of the two accounts, in Matthew and Luke respectively, of the occasion when the prayer was given, Luke's is to be preferred as the more historical (*D.C.G.*, ii. p. 61). In Luke, it has no connexion with the Sermon on the Mount. It will be seen that it is also much shorter, and I venture to think that it is also earlier than the version found in Matthew. Professor Pfleiderer observes :—" The prayer which Jesus taught is simpler in the Lucan than in the Matthæan version " (*Primitive Christianity*, ii. p. 147). He goes on to show that Luke is more original (ibid. p. 148). Luke's version is as follows : " Father, hallowed be thy name. Thy kingdom come. Give us day by day our daily bread. And forgive us our sins ; for we ourselves also forgive every one that is indebted to us. And bring us not into temptation " (Luke xi. 2-4). The Didache (viii. 2) follows Matthew's recension, but omits the last two verses (14 and 15). This is an indication that these two verses, which are not in Luke, are a later addition by the Evangelist who wrote the First Gospel.

Johannes Weiss in his commentary on Matthew vi. 9, adds that the Lord's Prayer in Matthew is a " liturgical piece of the established Christian community." He thinks that as Matthew is writing for a Jewish-Christian flock, he naturally uses such prayers as resemble Jewish prayers (*N.T. Commentary*, p. 266).

Dr. Harnack believes that Luke's and Matthew's recensions are both based on an earlier form of the prayer (see Dr. Klein's *Der älteste Christliche Katechismus*, p. 257 ff.). This original prayer is assumed to have been worded thus : " Father, give us to-day the morrow's bread and forgive us our sins as we forgive every one that is indebted to us, and lead us not into temptation." In the margin of the Revised Version (Matt. vi. 14) we read, "many authorities, some ancient, but with variations, add—For thine is the Kingdom, and the power, and the glory, for ever. Amen." This addition is called the Doxology. Scholars are generally of opinion that this formed no part of the prayer, but originated in liturgical use. It occurs in the Didache, but its peculiar form there does not agree with any of the forms known to occur in the authorities for the text of Matthew (see *The New Testament in the Apostolic Fathers*, p. 28 f.). Dr. Klein sees in the Matthæan version a type of the seven-fold Jewish prayer (Birkath Shêba) that was in vogue before the destruction of the Temple. The first three paragraphs of the prayer (vv. 9 and 10) form the usual introduction (Shebach). Then follows the prayer for one's personal wants (Tephillah) containing three petitions (vv. 11–13). Finally there is the Doxology which represents the Thanksgiving (Hôdayah). Moreover the threefold form of prayer is retained in the Shemoneh Esreh (Eighteen Benedictions). For the reason why actual prayer must be preceded by praise of God, see Berachoth, 31a, where Solomon's example (1 Kings viii. 28) is laid down as the rule to be followed ; see also Berachoth, 32a.

We can now affirm that the Lord's Prayer is quite Jewish in structure. As regards its contents, we believe that the same result will be arrived at, when we have once seen how all the phrases and petitions are *borrowed* from Jewish sources. In the seventeenth century, Grotius, an eminent Christian scholar, expressed the view that the Prayer was a combination of Jewish prayers. It was also believed by other scholars that the author of the prayer had selected the first few words of different Jewish prayers, in the same way as the prayer " Habinêu " has been compiled (see the Authorised Daily Prayer Book, p. 55, and Berachoth, 29a).

The first verse begins :—" Our Father who art in heaven, hallowed be thy name." " Our Father in heaven " is acknowledged by Dr. Dalman (*Die Worte Jesu*, p. 152 ff.) to be quite Jewish. He says that " Jesus dictated the current Jewish expression ' Our Father in Heaven' (Abinu Shebbashamayim) to his disciples." There are one or two small points to be noted. Matthew has " Our Father who is in Heaven," whereas Luke has only " Father." If, as we think, Luke is more original, then Matthew has expanded. If, on the other hand, Matthew be the earlier Evangelist, then it is noteworthy that Luke has altered the text of the Sermon by saying merely " Father." In this case the explanation is simple. Luke writes for Gentiles, and purposely avoids all genuine Jewish phrases and terms. " Father " was the usual epithet for a Greek or Roman deity ; but to the Jew a little more was customary, e.g. " Our Father," or " Father in Heaven," or " Our Father who art in Heaven." This difference between the two Evangelists clearly proves that Matthew's account reveals the Jewish source of this phrase. Dr. Dalman gives many instances of " Our Father in Heaven " in Jewish literature. Dr. Bousset concurs with Dalman's conclusions, although he qualifies this agreement by insisting that Jesus added depth and intensity to the meaning of God's Fatherhood, e.g. in the Parable of the Prodigal Son, etc. (*Die Religion des Judentums*, p. 434).

We deny that the Fatherhood of God is expounded

by Jesus with more depth and intensity than by the great prophets and teachers of Israel who lived before the age of Jesus. In the " Grace of God " I have shown that the Jew need not turn to the parables of the Gospel to learn the great lesson of the Fatherhood of God. This lesson has been borrowed by the Gospels from the Old Testament and other Jewish writings (e.g. Ps. ciii. 13 ; Hos. xi. 1 ; Wisdom of Solomon xiv. 3 ; Ecclus. xxiii. 1). It is untrue to say that Christianity is " the religion which teaches the Fatherhood of God and the brotherhood of man. . . . No one up to Jesus' time had ever taught them with equal clearness and in equal purity, and with the same freedom from other and inconsistent teaching " (Dr. Hastings Rashdall's *Philosophy and Religion*, p. 153). Dr. Rashdall then denies that Judaism teaches these truths as fully as Christianity. Other eminent Christian theologians claim that Jesus revealed the Fatherhood of God, as though he brought a new revelation to men (see *The Expositor's Bible*, " Luke," p. 156 ; Dr. Sanday's article in Hastings' *D.B.*, ii. p. 208 ; and his remarks in *Outlines of the Life of Christ*, pp. 13, 14, on the transcendent idea of God current among the Jews in the age of Jesus). Dr. Bruce (*Enc. Bib.*, col. 2,441) writes " Jesus used the new name of Father in speaking of God." Bousset's *Faith of a Modern Protestant*, and Harnack's *Wesen des Christentums* follow this line of criticism.

" It seems probable," says Professor Votaw, " that Jesus constantly used the title ' Father,' as the First and Fourth Gospels record ; but that it has been largely suppressed or altered in the sources of the Second and Third Gospels, again for the reason that it was a characteristically Jewish designation " (Hastings' *D.B.*, v. p.

35). J. Weiss also believes that Jesus addressed God only as " Father " (cf. Luke xxiii. 34 and 46 ; John xi. 41 ; xii. 27–28 ; xvii. 1 ff.)., and that the words " our " and " in heaven " were added by Matthew in accordance with Jewish precedent (op. cit., p. 265). The *Encyclopædia Biblica* (col. 2,821) adds " the truth is that we may say of the Lord's Prayer—applying what Theodore Zahn lately wrote (Forschungen 6 [1900] 153) of the teaching of Jesus as a whole—that Jesus uttered things which were said almost literally by Jewish teachers before and after him. On the other hand, ' duo si faciunt idem, non est idem ' ; and even if for the separate parts, words and thoughts of the Lord's Prayer parallels can be adduced from Jewish sources, as a whole this prayer remains unique. Moreover, it is difficult to be certain of the exact age of the parallels adduced." This is an exceedingly fair statement and is free from the bias so often manifested in theological writings.

The fundamental passage for the designation of God as Father is Exodus iv. 22. It is not only in the Bible that the Fatherhood of God is enunciated. The Jewish liturgy uses the term again and again. Thus, the fourth and sixth benedictions in the Shemoneh Esreh, in both the Palestinian and the Babylonian recensions, have " Our Father " as a title, addressed to God. This also occurs in the fifth benediction in the Babylonian recension (*Jewish Quarterly Review*, x, 1898, pp. 654–9, and Dalman, op. cit., pp. 299 and 301). This prayer is generally acknowledged to be as early as the ministry of Jesus ; even though its final recension was somewhat later. If we remember that Matthew's Gospel was compiled after 70 C.E., and not finally edited, as we now have it, till 119 C.E., we contend that it is quite unfair to say that the Shemoneh Esreh is later than Matthew. As the Lord's Prayer is also found in Luke, we might point out that Professor Schmiedel fixes the date of the Third Gospel between 100 and 110 c.e. The Shemoneh Esreh, says Schürer, " must have virtually attained its present form about 70–100 c.e., and its groundwork may safely be regarded as considerably more ancient. This inference is confirmed by the definite statement in the Talmud (Berachoth, 28b) that Simon the cotton dealer at Jamnia, in the time of Gamaliel II, arranged the Shemoneh Esreh according to the proper order " (see Schürer, *The Jewish People in the time of Jesus Christ,* ii. 2, § 27). In any case, we see that the Shemoneh Esreh is certainly earlier than the First or Third Gospels ; and in questions of priority it is surely valid to urge that it may very probably have been used by Matthew or Luke, or by their editors.

It is of vital importance to enter into these details, because we are so often reminded—even by Mr. Montefiore (*S.G.*, pp. ciii.–cv., and *Jowett Lectures,* p. 85)— that the Gospel records are so much earlier than the Rabbinical parallels quoted to illustrate them. In one of the books issued by the " Institutum Judaicum " in Berlin in 1905, this point is dealt with at considerable length. The book is by Dr. Erich Bischoff and is entitled *Jesus und die Rabbinen ; Jesu Bergpredigt und Himmelreich in ihrer Unabhängigkeit vom Rabbinismus.* In other words, the author essays to demonstrate that the *entire* Sermon on the Mount and the Gospel teaching of the Messianic Kingdom, are both independent of Rabbinical teaching. Not only does he deny that Jesus owes a single thought to his Rabbinical contemporaries or predecessors, but he turns the table on his

K

opponents by suggesting that it is possible that the teaching of Jesus was utilized by later Rabbis (pp. 3 and 4). This is also Dr. Plummer's opinion. He adds: " So that the borrowing, if there is any, is on the side of the Jews, or may be so " (Hastings' *D.B.*, iii. p. 342). To return to Dr. Bischoff. He points out that Lightfoot, Scheidt, and other Christian scholars, such as Schöttgen, Vitringa, Otho, Tholuck, have asserted that the Lord's Prayer contained a few reminiscences of Rabbinical prayers. " They did not, however, decide the question of priority. Nevertheless, it has become the fashion to look upon this prayer as a more or less beautiful mosaic constructed out of existing Jewish prayers. Hamburger (*R.E. Suppl.* iii. p. 55) states ' Every sentence in this prayer is found in the prayers and sayings of the Jewish teachers in the Talmud ; consequently the entire (!) prayer has its origin in Jewish thought.' All the prayers and sayings quoted by Hamburger are, without exception, later in date than Jesus and the Gospel of Matthew. This fact has not prevented Wünsche from indulging in the same nonsense of speaking of Rabbinical sources of the Lord's Prayer " (p. 73).

Thus far Dr. Bischoff. In his remarks on the next page, he deals with Hamburger's parallels to the phrase : " Our Father in Heaven." Let Dr. Bischoff state his own case. Hamburger refers to Joma viii. 9, where we are told that Akiba (died 135 C.E.) exclaimed :— " Happy are ye, O Israel ; think before whom ye are purified and who purifies you ! Your Father in Heaven." In a note Dr. Bischoff assumes the truth of the tradition that Rabbi Akiba died at the age of 120 years, so that he was, at all events, a younger contemporary of Jesus. He also grants that Akiba might have said the passage in question in the year 55 C.E. He refuses, however, to believe that it was really said before the destruction of the Temple in 70 C.E. ; and prefers to fix the date as late as the Hadrianic persecution, which cost Akiba his life.

If we avoid both extremes and adopt the middle date of 70 C.E., we are still justified in using this saying as a parallel to the Sermon on the Mount, because the Gospels, which contain the Sermon, were unwritten in 70 C.E. Another passage adduced by Hamburger is also severely criticized by Dr. Bischoff. Rabbi Eliezer the Great (Dr. Bischoff does not discuss his date) said : " Since the destruction of the Temple . . . on whom shall we rely ? On our Father in Heaven " (T. B. Sota, 49a, b). Again we are told that the passage probably belongs to the Hadrianic persecution (133 C.E.). But Dr. Bischoff should first demonstrate that Rabbi Eliezer witnessed that event. He did not. Rabbi Eliezer died about 117 C.E. (see Graetz, *Geschichte der Juden*, iv. p. 50). Dr. Bischoff objects that all the parallels adduced by Hamburger or other Jewish writers are later than 70 C.E., and that these parallels are not prayers at all. He also points out that the texts in Joma viii. 9 ; and in T. J. Maaseroth 50c (quoted by Lightfoot, p. 121) have " your Father in Heaven," and not " our Father." The fact remains that Rabbi Eliezer spoke of " *our* Father in Heaven " before the Gospels were written. Dr. Bischoff then points out that in the Old Testament we do not find " our Father in Heaven." He grants that " Targum Jerushalmi " to Deuteronomy xxxii. 6, has " your Father in Heaven," but he objects to Lightfoot's reference to Isaiah lxiii. 16, and lxiv. 8 ; because " in Heaven " is not found in these two passages. He concludes by saying "Jesus is, as far as I know, the first who used this title in addressing God" (p. 75).

Dr. Bischoff would have a very difficult task to justify this last statement. In the first instance, he assumes that Matthew is not only more original, but also more correct than Luke. This point is not conclusively settled. Luke, as we have seen, says merely 'Father.' Mark, the oldest of the Gospels, also tells us that Jesus spoke of God as Abba (Father ; see Mark xiv. 36). Moreover, it is quite impossible to be sure of the exact wording of the original prayer—if there ever was one ; because neither Matthew nor Luke give us an original prayer. All the Evangelists wrote in Greek, which was unknown to Jesus, who spoke Aramaic.

The question now arises : Did Jesus ever utter this prayer ? There are indications that he did not. First of all, if it was his prayer, why do we find no trace of it in the oldest Gospel Mark, or in John, or in any of the Pauline epistles ? This negative proof may be considered to be of little value. There are other grounds for doubting its genuine character. Why pray for the coming of the Kingdom, if Jesus believed that he had already inaugurated it ? Why pray to be delivered from the evil one, when it was believed that Jesus had once for all overcome him in the temptation ? (Matt. iv. 1–11). From another point of view, we can well understand that the Prayer represents what Dr. Carpenter calls "the voice of later ecclesiastical usage" (*The Synoptic Gospels*, p. 94). Let us not forget that the earliest description of the public worship of the Christian Church speaks of "continuing stedfastly with one accord in the Temple" (Acts ii. 46). This clearly shows that the customary Jewish devotions were still adhered to by the early Christians. It was only later on, after the destruction of the Temple, that the Christian community separated from Judaism. Just as the fast days were transferred from Monday and Thursday to Wednesday and Friday (see Didache viii. 1), so we may suppose a new prayer (i.e. Lord's Prayer) was substituted in place of the official Tephillah (i.e. Shemoneh Esreh) recognized by the Jews. In fact, this is acknowledged by the Didache viii. 2 : " Do not pray as the hypocrites (i.e. Pharisees), but as the Lord commanded in his Gospel, " Our Father." Under the same influence of active opposition to Judaism and Jewish customs, we can account for the origin of the " Lord's Day " in place of the Jewish Sabbath.

Whether the term " Father " is borrowed or not, the fact is indisputable that the Jews, long before the birth of Jesus, used this term, and used it in its widest meaning as teaching the universal Fatherhood of the One God. We have already dealt with this subject in chapter VII, on " The Ideal Life in the Gospels and the Torah." It now remains to point out parallels to the actual words or phrases of the prayer. " Our Father " occurs in the liturgy in the well-known prayer Abinu Malkênu (T. B. Taanith, 25b)—for Biblical references see Deut. xxxii. 6 ; Is. lxiii. 16, and lxiv. 8 ; Jer. iii. 4 and 19 ; xxxi. 9 ; Mal. i. 6 ; and ii. 10. The words " in Heaven " can be compared with " But our God is in Heaven" (Ps. cxv. 3, and cf. Ps. ii. 4). " This attributive to the ' Father,' " says Hastings' D.B. (v. p. 35), " is a truly Old Testament and Jewish phrase, which Jesus quite surely adopted and employed." We agree. The entire phrase, " Our Father who art in Heaven," also occurs in the Jewish liturgy, see Achelis, *Bergpredigt*, p. 229, and Lightfoot, p. 120—for " your Father who is in Heaven," see Kaddish (*Authorised Daily Prayer Book*, p. 76). Lightfoot truly remarks : " This epithet of God (' The Father who is in Heaven ') was very well known among the Jews and very usual with them. . . . They were thoroughly instructed from their cradles to call God ' The Father in Heaven.' "

The next phrase of the prayer is " Hallowed be thy name." The best parallel to this is the opening phrase of the Kaddish (P. B. p. 75), " Magnified and hallowed be His name." The Kaddish is often referred to in Rabbinical writings as the praise " Let His great name be blessed " (see Berachoth, 3*a*, Siphrê Haazînu, § 306, p. 132*b*, and see Zunz, *Gottesdienstliche Vorträge*, p. 385). The opening phrase of the Kaddish is based on Ezekiel xxxviii. 23, " I will magnify myself, and sanctify myself, and I will make myself known in the eyes of many nations ; and they shall know that I am the Lord " (cf. xxxvi. 23). Another parallel to " Hallowed be thy name " is to be found in Psalm cxi. 9 : " Holy and reverend is His name." The ideal of Jewish life is summed up in the expression " Kiddush Ha-shem," *sanctification of God's name.* This implies absolute love and loyalty to God and His will. Isaiah (xxix. 23), foretells the return of Jacob to the old true faith ; and then " they shall sanctify my name ; yea, they shall sanctify the Holy One of Jacob." The third benediction of the Shemoneh Esreh is a " sanctification " of God's name, based on Isaiah vi. 3. An objection to quoting the Kaddish, as a parallel, is raised by Professor Nestle in Hastings' *D.C.G.* ii. p. 59, because it has " the national, eschatological, or Messianic element from beginning to end," whereas this element is "remarkably thrown into the background in the Lord's Prayer." Now the first half of the Kaddish is not prayer proper, but praise. It is, moreover, equally true of that part of the Lord's Prayer which deals with praise to say " that it is limited solely to the members of the Messianic Kingdom " (see Achelis, *Bergpredigt*, p. 233). " Our Father " refers only to the Father of the disciples of Jesus, who has revealed the Father to them (John xx. 17, and Luke xii. 32). This part of the prayer is also entirely eschatological, and prays for the coming of the Messianic Kingdom.

We believe that we have given a complete answer to the criticisms brought against the Jewish origin of the first petition of the Lord's Prayer. It may be as well to mention that our refutation of Dr. Bischoff's statements applies equally well to a remarkable brochure by Professor König, of Bonn, entitled *Talmud und Neues Testament*. We would finally draw attention to the Dean of Lichfield's new book, *The Gospel of the Kingdom*, in which the Sermon on the Mount is considered in the light of contemporary Jewish thought and ideals. The Dean admits that the Lord's Prayer is " framed generally on Jewish modes of thought and expression, which are themselves for the most part derived ultimately from the Old Testament : but none the less it constitutes a catholic model for all peoples and all time. The different clauses may be illustrated from the sayings of Jewish teachers, but the Prayer as a whole, in its spirit as in its proportion, entirely transcends anything which even the best of them had ever produced " (p. 161). We may return to this last criticism when we have considered the entire prayer. Nevertheless, the admissions of Dean Savage are a tremendous advance upon the negative position assumed by Professor König and Dr. Bischoff. Religion has nothing to lose by admitting the proved results of critical investigation.

LITERATURE

Schöttgen, *Horæ Hebraicæ*, with interesting parallels from Midrash and Zohar ; Taylor, *Sayings of the Jewish Fathers*, (pp. 176, 177) ; Wünsche, *Erläuterung der Evangelien* ; see also *Jewish Encyclopedia*, article ' Father' and Kohler, *Theologie*, chapter xl. For ' Shemoneh Esreh,' see J. Elbogen, *Geschichte des Achtzehn-Gebets ;* Zunz, *Gottesdienstliche Vorträge* (2nd ed.), pp. 380–2.

CHAPTER XI

THE KINGDOM OF GOD IN JEWISH AND CHRISTIAN
TEACHING

" THY Kingdom come " (Matt. vi. 10) is the second
petition of the Lord's Prayer. A parallel is furnished
again by the Kaddish—" May He establish His kingdom " (*Prayer Book*, p. 75). In the eleventh benediction of the Shemoneh Esreh, we find a further
parallel : " And reign over us, Thou alone." It has
often been pointed out that, according to Rabbinic
teaching, " every benediction to be valid must contain
not only the name of God, but must refer also to God's
Kingdom " (Berachoth, 40b). The general form of a
benediction is " Blessed art Thou, O Lord [our God],
King of the universe." This clearly implies the universal rule of God, based on the greatest of all facts—that
He is the only Lord, and also on the belief that He is our
God and Creator, and the Father, in whose image we
have been made. God's Kingdom on earth has not been
fully realized. The great obstacle is man's sin and pride
exhibited in preferring his own will to that of God.
The kingdom of pride (Malchuth Zadon) will be completely overthrown when the Messianic age dawns.
The proud (Zedim and Minim) oppose God's will as
revealed in the Law (cf. Matt. vii. 23), and by their sinful
arrogance hinder the development of universal peace and

justice on earth. The Zedim (arrogant) and the Minim (Antinomian Gnostics) are considered by Dr. Moriz Friedländer to be pre-Christian parties among the Jews (*Geschichte der jüdischen Apologetik*, p. 470 ff.). The question is often asked, What did the term "Kingdom of God" mean to the Jew of the age of Jesus? Modern writers give us to understand that the Pharisaic conception was materialistic, particularistic, and permeated by a political spirit.

This, for instance, is the deliberate opinion of Professor König (op. cit. p. 17), which, to an extent, is shared by Mr. Montefiore, who says that the Jewish conception in the days of Jesus of the Kingdom of God "included what we may loosely call a national and material element, and a religious and spiritual element, and that these two elements were closely welded and united together. . . . The Jews would be emancipated from their oppressors; they would be happy and prosperous for evermore. This does not sound a very religious conception, and it is often regarded and stigmatized as material and political and particularistic and national, with many other disagreeable adjectives. But it was never held by any decent teacher in this sort of artificial isolation. Happiness and prosperity, yes— these would indeed be marks of the Kingdom, but not these alone, we must add to them peace and justice and righteousness and the knowledge of God. These additions surely make a vast difference to the picture. . . . Far be it from me to deny that the particularistic note predominates . . . a Rabbi might have said that an enormous proportion of the heathen world would be annihilated at the Judgment, and that the rest (of the Gentiles) would acknowledge the truth and sovereignty of the God of Israel. . . . Undoubtedly, however, it did include a strong nationalistic element." (*Jowett Lectures*, p. 61 ff.). It should be pointed out that Mr. Montefiore and Professor König fail to give us any Jewish authorities for their views. There are genuine sources ready at hand to enable us to answer this question impartially and critically. The Jews never lost the hope that, in the future, they and other men would constitute one kingdom with God as the only eternal King (Zech. xiv. 9). This is what Josephus means when he speaks of the "Theocracy" as the proper title of the Hebrew State (*Contra Apionem*, ii. 165). Philo likewise speaks of the Kingdom of God which will regulate not only the lives of nations, but also the daily conduct of every individual. Daily should a man take upon himself the yoke of God's Kingdom and with Moses say, "Reign, then [O Lord], through eternity as King (Exod. xv. 18) over the suppliant soul, and never leave it for a moment free from thy governance ; for unbroken servitude under thee is better than freedom, yea better than a world-dominion" (*About the Planting of Noah*, § 53, M. i. p. 337 ; and see J. H. A. Hart's *The Hope of Catholick Judaism*, pp. 38, 39).

Josephus and Philo, however, do not stand alone in looking forward to a glorious golden age, when the ideal of the national kingdom will be replaced by the ideal of a divinely-governed universal Kingdom, in which the religious and spiritual elements will predominate, and transform the materialistic and particularistic elements until then supreme in the narrow kingdoms of men. To make good this statement we need reliable testimony. Where can we look for such evidence ? Surely in the Apocalyptic literature of the pre-Christian age. This literature is concerned with the revelation of the future, such as the defeat of sin and the victory of virtue, and the establishment of God's Kingdom. Then we have the Apocrypha, which represents both the Palestinian and Alexandrian teaching of the pre-Christian age. If we read the New Testament in the light of this Jewish literature which preceded it, and bear in mind the great fact that the Rabbinical literature in Talmud and Midrash represents a genuine historical development of Pharisaic Judaism, then we shall have sufficient valid material to enable us to reconstruct the world of ideas and aspirations which filled the heart and soul of the Jew of the first century C.E. This method of study has not been adopted by Mr. Montefiore in his treatment of the Synoptic Gospels. The result of his laborious compilation is disappointing in several respects, but his failure points out the way to a more critical study in the future. The question at issue is : What was the meaning of the Kingdom of God to a Pharisee in the time of Jesus ? We shall endeavour to answer this question by briefly indicating what the Kingdom of God meant to the writers of some of the more important books of the Apocalyptic and Apocryphal literature Then we shall consider the teaching in the Gospel and in the Talmud.

The *Book of Jubilees* (135–105 B.C.E.) is distinguished by the spirituality of its description of the Messianic Kingdom. The *Similitudes of Enoch* (chs. 37–71 written about 95–80 B.C.E.) speak of the Messianic judgment wl , n " unrighteousness will disappear as a shadow " fro :1 the earth (xlix. 2). In the *Psalms of Solomon* (70– ''' B.C.E.), God himself is to be the eternal King (xvii. The proud sinners *among the Jews* will

be driven from the inheritance usurped by them.   The
other nations will come to see the glory of God (xvii. 25
ff).   In the *Assumption of Moses* (7–30 c.e.), we have
the picture of the Messianic age in its religious aspect.
There is no mention of any victory over the heathen.
As a last reference (although we have by no means
referred to all the sources) we will mention the Messianic
expectation as exemplified by the oldest Jewish portions
of the *Sibylline Oracles* (c. 140 B.C.E.).   God will set
up an eternal Kingdom over all mankind, with Jerusalem
as its capital.   The Gentiles will accept God's law ; and
peace and quietness shall obtain (iii. 652–795).   In the
Apocrypha we find a few references to the Messianic age
and the Kingdom of God.   Thus Tobit (second century
B.C.E.) declares that many nations shall come from
afar to the name of God (xiii. 11).   That this is not the
reluctant homage of tributary people is shown by the
sequel, which speaks of " generations of generations "
(*ibid.*) praising God with songs of rejoicing.   In Sirach
(c. 180 B.C.E.), God is asked to send His fear on all
nations (xxxvi. 2).   This is sometimes taken as a sign of
Jewish narrowness.   But " God's fear " means religion
and it is rather a sign of the universal Jewish spirit to
pray on behalf of the heathens that the only true religion
may be theirs.   The prayer proceeds : " And let them
know Thee, as we also have known Thee " (ibid. xxxvi.
5).

Our final reference will be to the *Book of Wisdom*
(c. first century B.C.E.).   The princes of the Gentile world
are invited to honour wisdom (i.e. religion) that they
may enjoy the eternal kingdom (vi. 21).   Again " the
ways of those who are on the earth " (i.e. humanity) are
corrected by wisdom and find salvation by this means

(ix. 18). Is there a finer teaching than is set forth in that wonderful passage : " For thou lovest all things that are, and abhorrest none of the things which thou didst make ; for never wouldst thou have formed anything if thou didst hate it " (xi. 24) ? Is not God's Kingdom, as taught by this book, invested with an unparalleled universalism that need not fear comparison with anything in the Gospels—" Thy sovereignty over all maketh Thee to forbear all " ? (xii. 16). We see from these references how it would be possible to draw a picture of the Messianic Kingdom utterly unlike that presented by Mr. Montefiore or Professor König.

Let us inquire a little more deeply into this all-important matter by considering the views of yet another modern writer. Professor Gilbert contrasts the Jewish with the Christian ideal of the Kingdom. He says : " Jesus' conception of the Kingdom of Heaven was not developed out of that of the Scribes. It was the antithesis of that. . . . He put away as fundamentally evil . . . the ideal of his people. . . . Hence for him the kingdom in its fundamental idea was something to be realized from within, quietly and gradually, by spiritual means. The Scribes, on the contrary, looked for a kingdom to be realized from without in a spectacular and supernatural manner " (Hastings' *D.C.G.*, i. pp. 934, 935). Is this the truth ? Jesus did not, according to the Synoptics, abandon the belief that the Kingdom of Heaven was to come immediately through some dramatic, catastrophic exercise of the divine power ; nay, he claimed that he was to be the instrument to establish the Kingdom. He spoke in apocalyptic fashion of the Son of Man coming on the clouds. His coming would illuminate simultaneously all quarters of the Heavens like the lightning (Luke xvii. 24). Is this not rightly described as a realization of the Kingdom " from without in a spectacular and supernatural manner " ? We confess that we cannot reconcile the divergent views of the Gospels as to the Kingdom. Dr. J. E. Carpenter remarks : " Truly has the First Gospel been called a ' Gospel of contradictions ' " (*The Synoptic Gospels*, p. 363). This criticism applies equally well to the other Gospels. Thus, in one passage we are told that the Kingdom is at hand (i.e. not yet present) ; again, it seems to be implied that the Kingdom is already present (e.g. Matt. xi. 11, or Matt. xii. 28) in which the expelling of demons is offered as proof that the Kingdom has come. Then there was this difference, says Professor Gilbert, that Jesus taught that the Kingdom was to be realized from within, quietly and gradually, by spiritual means. Is this not totally at variance with the actual practice of Jesus ? The story of the entry into Jerusalem shows that Jesus consciously assumed the outward or public office of the Messianic King, based on the prophecy of Zechariah ix. 9 : " Behold, thy King cometh unto thee : he is just, and having salvation ; lowly, and riding upon an ass, even upon a colt the foal of an ass." The Gospel of Matthew (xxi. 7) has misunderstood this text and makes Jesus enter Jesusalem riding upon *two* animals—the ass and the colt. " His (public) entry (into Jerusalem) was connected with his consciousness of his Messianic mission . . . and planned in order to satisfy the expectations of many who were waiting for the coming of the Kingdom of God, ' the consolation of Israel,' and ' the redemption of Jerusalem ! ' " (Luke ii. 25, 38). This gave rise to Pilate's charge, " Art thou the King of the Jews ? " and supplied the Roman with the legal basis for his condemnation (see Hastings' *D.C.G.*, i. p. 520).

The disciples, who had been trained to understand the meaning of the Messianic Kingdom, thought that Jesus entered Jerusalem to set up a visible Messianic monarchy. They hailed him by crying, " Blessed is the Kingdom that cometh, the Kingdom of our father David " (Mark xi. 10). Thus the disciples and Jesus himself believed that the Messianic Kingdom was to be established with outward spectacular display. That Jesus also believed that his Kingdom was to be political and national—if it had been successfully established—is proved by his promise to his ' little flock ' : " Fear not, it is your Father's good pleasure to give you the kingdom " (Luke xii. 32). Again, he says to his disciples : " And I appoint unto you a Kingdom, even as my Father appointed unto me, that ye may eat and drink at my table in my Kingdom ; and ye shall sit on thrones judging the twelve tribes of Israel " (Luke xxii. 29 and 30 ; cf. Matt. xix. 28). When he saw that his dream of the Messianic Kingdom was not to be realized, he announced that he would come again and display his power (Matt. xxiv. 3, 27, 37) as judge with supreme judicial authority (John v. 22), and punish all his opponents (Matt. xiii. 41). I cannot enter into a very full discussion of Jewish thought in regard to the Kingdom of Heaven. A few disconnected sayings of the Rabbis must suffice. " The yoke of God's Kingdom is received by man when he admits the unity of God (T. B. Berachoth, 13*a*). This is surely " realized from within " and not " from without." Again, the Messianic age will witness the conversion of the ungodly nations and the establishment of God's Kingdom throughout the earth. It is not Messiah's Kingdom, but God's Kingdom which is to be established in the hearts of humanity. The Talmud adds that the only difference between the present course of the world and that of the Messianic age will be the abolition of persecution (Berachoth, 34*b*, Sabbath, 63*a* and 151*b*, and Pesachim, 68*a*).

It is quite true that the Pharisaic conception of the Kingdom of God is diametrically opposed to the Christian view. The former teaches that God's Kingdom— the rule of One Father and King—will be universal. This is to be brought about through Israel : " I will also give thee for a light to the Gentiles, that thou mayest be my salvation unto the end of the earth " (Isa. xlix. 6). The Christian teaching is quite different. It speaks of the redemption of fallen humanity cursed by God's law. This redemption must be made through God, and therefore He must send " His only begotten Son " into the world to die for the sins of men. Moreover, the fully realized Messianic Kingdom of the Christian religion is not a normal holy life here on earth, but a heavenly realm, to which admission is obtained by faith in Jesus. Opposed to this is the Jewish or Pharisaic belief that " the remnant of Jacob shall be in the midst of many peoples as dew from the Lord, as showers upon the grass ; that tarrieth not for man, nor waiteth for the sons of men " (Mic. v. 7). But, says Dr. König, " the Jewish idea of the Divine Kingdom is local—it is confined to Palestine or to Jerusalem " (op. cit. p. 19). " In the future," says the Midrash, "Jerusalem shall extend to the extremities of Palestine and Palestine shall cover the earth" (Yalkut on Isa. xlvi. 23 ; Sifrê Deut. i, 1. p. 65*a*). König finds the antithesis between Jewish and Christian theories of the Kingdom summed up in the Jewish and Christian attitude towards slavery (op. cit. pp. 17, 18).

L

Rabban Jochanan ben Zakkai denounces the Hebrew who, of his own accord, remains a slave, indicating thereby that he prefers the yoke of flesh and blood to the yoke of God's Kingdom (T. J. Kiddushin i, 2. 59d, T. B. Kiddushin, 22b, Tosephta Baba Kama, vii. 5). Opposed to this is the Christian view that ignores slavery and says : " Render therefore unto Cæsar the things that are Cæsar's " (Matt. xxii. 21, cf. Rom. xiii. 1 ff.).

Rabban Jochanan insisted on the right of freedom as the prerogative of every son of God. God's Kingdom cannot rest on the basis of human power overriding the will of God. God had once for all, through the history of Israel, broken the shackles of enslaved humanity, and thereby He had inaugurated His Divine Kingdom on earth (Exod. xix. 6). It is quite impossible to assert that Rabban Jochanan's teaching has been surpassed by the New Testament. It is, moreover, undeniable that Jesus did not condemn the institution of slavery. In fact, he seems to have considered it a necessary element in the coming Kingdom. There was to be but one Lord and Master, namely, Jesus himself ; all the rest were to be his bondsmen or slaves. This accounts for the supreme praise which is passed upon service marked by absolute submission (Mark x. 44). True it is that Paul preached : " There can be neither bond nor free . . . for ye are all one in Jesus " (Gal. iii. 28, cf. Col. iii. 11). But it must not be forgotten that it is only in Jesus (i.e. within the narrow confines of the Church), that the distinction between bondage and freedom is cancelled. We must leave, for the present, further consideration of this subject. Fuller information can be obtained from Dr. Schechter's *Aspects of Rabbinic Theology*, chapters v., vi., and vii, ; and from Dr. Kohler's *Systemat.*

Theologie des Judentums, pp. 250 ff. Neither of these eminent writers takes the Apocalyptic and Apocryphal writings into account.

Returning once more to the petition of the Lord's Prayer, " Thy Kingdom come," we believe that we have established its thoroughly Jewish origin. I imagine that the confirmation of this view on the part of the following non-Jewish authorities will be gladly welcomed. Professor Votaw admits that the prayer, " Thy Kingdom come " was in substance the prayer which for centuries Israel had addressed to God " (Hastings' *D.B.,* v. p. 36). Dr. Plummer agrees that this petition is the most Jewish of all the petitions (*Commentary on Matthew,* p. 98). Finally, Dr. Taylor rightly points out that the coming of the Kingdom, and the sanctifying of the Name are brought together in some passages of the Old Testament, thus : " And the Lord shall be King over all the earth ; in that day shall the Lord be one, and His Name one " (Zech. xiv. 9).

The next petition is : " Thy will be done, as in Heaven, so on earth." What better parallel than Psalm cxxxv. 6, could be suggested—" Whatsoever the Lord pleased, that hath he done in Heaven and on earth " ? Psalm cxv. 3, " But our God is in Heaven : He hath done whatsoever He pleased," is another suitable parallel. In the Rabbinic literature the following parallels are of interest. Rabban Gamaliel II. used to say, " Do God's will as if it were thy will, that He may do thy will as if it were His will " (Aboth ii. 4). Judah ben Tema said : " Be strong as a leopard, light as an eagle, fleet as a hart, and strong as a lion, to do the will of thy Father who is in Heaven " (ibid. v. 23). What is a short prayer ? Rabbi Eliezer said : " Do Thy will in Heaven above, and give satisfaction to them that fear Thee on earth beneath, and do what is good in Thine eyes : Blessed art Thou, O Lord, who hearest prayer " (Berachoth, 29*b* and Tosephta Berachoth, iii. 7). This is one among many equally beautiful and expressive prayers. Dr. Bischoff (op. cit. p. 77) points out that Rabbi Eliezer lived in the beginning of the second century C.E. This is somewhat misleading. He was a pupil of Rabban Jochanan ben Zakkai and was a recognized teacher before the destruction of the Temple (70 C.E.). He was a contemporary of Paul, Matthew and Luke. Dr. Bischoff then points out that even if this prayer be earlier than the Gospels, is it likely that Jesus would have adopted it, because Rabbi Eliezer recommended its use in the hour of danger, whilst Jesus wished his prayer to be adapted to all occasions ? We would urge in reply, that the " Lord's Prayer " was not originally intended to be a prayer for all occasions. According to Luke (xi. 1) it was given, in private, to the disciples only, in answer to the request of one of them for an exclusive form for their own use. It was originally a private prayer for the individual disciple only.

In commenting on the Lord's Prayer, Mr. Montefiore writes : " The brevity of the prayer and its conciseness are very striking. Jewish prayers tended to become too long ; repetitions were indulged in to a wearisome extent, and too many epithets and adjectives of praise were added on to the invocation of God. These tendencies were, however, not so marked in Jesus' time as later. But the Lord's Prayer, with its simple adequate invocation, ' Our Father,' and its few short petitions sets a fine example " (*S.G.*, p. 534). Is this a balanced judgment ? Have not the prayers of the Church tended to become too long ? We have seen that repetitions

are indulged in to a wearisome extent.   In the Church
hymn books do we not find many epithets and adjectives of praise added to the invocations of the Christian deity ?   Moreover, it would have been fair if Mr.
Montefiore had referred to the many brief prayers contained in the Jewish liturgy.   We admire the beauty
and brevity of the Lord's Prayer, but insist that this
Jewish prayer is matched by several other prayers equally
concise and valuable.   If it " sets a fine example," what
is to be said of the following prayer of the Rabbis ?
" The needs of Thy people Israel are many, but their
wisdom is little.   May it be Thy will, O Lord, our God,
to grant to each one his sustenance, and to every creature sufficient for its needs.   Blessed art Thou, O Lord,
who hearest prayer."   The Lord's Prayer asks only for
the needs of the disciples, whereas this Talmudic prayer
asks on behalf of *every* creature (Berachoth, 29*b*, and
Tosephta Berachoth, iii. 7).   In the Tosephta this fine
prayer contains twenty-five words.   The Lord's Prayer
excluding the Doxology, contains 87 words.   Another
prayer of one of the Rabbis began thus :—" Sovereign of
all worlds !   It is revealed and known before Thee that
our will is to do Thy will " (Berachoth, 17*a*).   There are
also twenty-five words in the original.

Some of these quotations may be criticized on the
score of belonging to a later age than that of Jesus.   We
have purposely chosen them, so as to meet the charge
brought by Mr. Montefiore against the lengthy Jewish
prayers *after* the age of Jesus.   It is well known that the
Scriptures contain many parallels to this petition of
the Lord's Prayer, e.g., " Teach me to do Thy will "
(Ps. cxliii. 10) and again, " I delight to do Thy will "
(Ps. xl. 8).   Dean Savage says : " It would seem, there-

fore, that Jesus, when he included this phrase in his prayer, purposely took over the expression from the contemporary religious phraseology. It appears here for the first time in his teaching. It will reappear at the close of the Sermon " (*The Gospel of the Kingdom*, p. 169). We cannot understand how Dr. Plummer can deny the existence of real parallels to the petition " Thy will be done " (*Commentary on Matthew*, p. 94). He even refers to Aboth v. 23, and also quotes from the *Testaments of the Twelve Patriarchs* the following illustration :—" The sun, moon and stars change not their order ; so do ye also change not the Law of God by the disorderliness of your doings " (Naphtali iii. 2).

To observe the Law is the Jewish way of doing the will of God. It is usually understood that the third petition of the Lord's Prayer—" Thy will be done "—is an explanation of the preceding petition, " Thy Kingdom come." It seems to imply that, where God's will is done, there God's kingdom is established. This is obviously the case in Heaven (Ps. xix. ; Neh. ix. 6), and when it will be done likewise on earth, then God's Kingdom has come. This is also the thought underlying the passage quoted from the *Testaments of the Twelve Patriarchs* as a parallel to the Lord's Prayer. For similar teaching see Ecclus. xvi. 26–28 ; xliii. 6 ff. ; Enoch ii. 1, and Psalms of Solomon xviii., last three verses. Another pre-Christian parallel occurs in the Apocrypha : " As may be the will in Heaven, so shall he do " (1 Macc. iii. 60). Here again the pre-Christian literature of the Jews teaches the same lesson as to God's Kingdom, and the duty of man to do God's will, as the so-called Lord's Prayer is said to enunciate. Jews

and Christians stand on common ground in praying
for God's Kingdom.

LITERATURE

See J. H. A. Hart, *The Hope of Catholick Judaism.* Dr.
Bousset, *Die Religion des Judentums* (2nd ed.), pp. 245 ff., who
gives references to literature by G. Dalman, Johannes Weiss,
and Volz ; and see also G. Hoennicke, *Das Judenchristentum*,
(pp. 44 ff.). For the Jewish standpoint see Hamburger, *R.E.*,
ii. pp. 770 ff. ; Jewish Encyclopedia vii. p. 502 f., and also the
article in *Monatsschrift* (1897) on *Messiaszeit und zukünftige
Welt*, by Dr. M. Löwy. For the views of the author of the Book
of Jubilees on the Messianic Kingdom (cf. above p. 140), see
Charles, *The Book of Jubilees*, pp. lxxxvii. 9, 10 and 150.

CHAPTER XII

THE third petition of the Lord's Prayer according to Matthew's recension, which we considered in the last chapter, is missing in Luke. No authority can be claimed for the variant reading in Luke (xi. 2, 3), according to which, instead of " Hallowed be Thy name," or " Thy Kingdom come," we read " Thy holy spirit come upon us and cleanse us." Luke has a special doctrinal interest in the Holy Spirit, and it is in keeping with this characteristic of the Third Gospel that this reading is found here and not in Matthew's version of the Prayer (see Dr. Plummer's *Luke*, p. 295 *n*). It is hardly necessary to point out that the term " holy spirit " occurs in the Psalms (li. 11). Dr. Denny (Hastings' *D.C.G.*, i. p. 736) holds that " the holy spirit is connected with the Messianic age and with the preparations for the coming of the Messiah." There seems to be good reason for agreeing with this statement. The prophet Joel (ii. 28) foretells the outpouring of the Divine Spirit upon all flesh, as a sign of the Messianic glory. According to the Talmud, the holy spirit in a man will enable him in the Messianic age to bring the dead back to life (Aboda Zara, 20*b*; and see Ezek. xxxvii. 14). The gift of the holy spirit is only bestowed on the repentant (Isa. xxix. 24 ; Mal. iii. 3 ; M. Sota ix. 15). Baptism symbolized the work of repentance (Ezek. xxxvi. 25–27 ; 1 Sam. vii. 6 ; and Tana de bê Elijahu (ed. Friedmann), p. 72 ; and see Dr. Klein, op. cit. p. 264).

Once again we can see how the Gospels have borrowed the entire framework of the Messianic conception from the Pharisaic Judaism, out of which Christianity grew. The Gospels speak also of repentance, and baptism which was connected with the inward process of conversion. There is also the gift of the holy spirit accompanied by the power of working miracles. The Messianic leader in the Gospel story applies to himself the words of Isaiah, " The *spirit* of the Lord God is upon me " (lxi. 1).

The fourth petition is a prayer for the personal needs of the individual. " Give us this day our daily bread." A good parallel is found in Proverbs (xxx. 8) : " Give me neither poverty nor riches, feed me with the food that is needful for me." The last few words of this quotation mean literally " the bread of my portion." The Greek word for " daily " ($\epsilon\pi\iota o\acute{\upsilon}\sigma\iota o\varsigma$) in the Lord's Prayer occurs in Matthew and Luke in this connexion only. Bishop Lightfoot shows that this word $\epsilon\pi\iota o\acute{\upsilon}\sigma\iota o\varsigma$ means for the coming day or the morrow (*On a Fresh Revision of the N.T.*, Appendix, pp. 195–234). This is supported by the statement of Jerome (on Matt. vi. 11), " I found in the *Gospel according to the Hebrews*, the word Mahar (i.e. for the morrow), so that the sense of the petition is : Give us to-day our bread for to-morrow." If this be the meaning we can suggest a contrast. The Talmud says : " The man who has bread in his basket (for to-day) and asks, What shall I do for to-morrow's bread ?—belongs to the people of little

faith " (Sota, 48b). " God who maketh the day, pro-
videth also its sustenance," says the Mechilta (Beshallach, ed. Weiss, p. 56b). Reverting to the usual interpretation according to Matthew's text, " Give us this
day our daily bread," Dr. Taylor thinks that this petition
contains an allusion to the giving of the Manna (Exod.
xvi. 4) : " Behold I will rain bread from heaven for you,
and the people shall go out and gather a day's portion
every day." The last words were interpreted by the
Rabbis as follows. Rabbi Joshua said : " A day's
portion every day " meant that a man should gather on
one day for the next day, as on Friday for Saturday.
Rabbi Eliezer ha-Modai (of Modaim) said it meant that
a man should not gather on one day for the next day,
because it is said (" debar yom beyomo ") " the portion
for each day on its day " (Mechilta in loc.). (For Dr.
Taylor's theory see *Sayings of the Jewish Fathers*, pp.
125 ff.) Dr. Klein follows Dr. Taylor, but also refers
to the parallel case in Beza, 16a in which Rabbi Joshua's
attitude was anticipated by Shammai, whilst Hillel's
rule was adopted by Rabbi Eliezer (op. cit. pp. 259 ff.).
It is gratifying to see that Dr. Bischoff (op. cit. p. 78)
admits the possibility of Jesus having had Proverbs
xxx. 8 (" feed me with the bread of my portion ") in
mind, when he bade his disciples pray for their daily
bread. Hillel recited Psalm lxviii. 19 : " Blessed be the
Lord day by day," when he partook of his daily fare.
Dr. Klein (op. cit. p. 260) thinks that the differences of
opinion and custom between Hillel and Shammai were
reflected by Matthew and Luke respectively. Matthew
writes : " Give us this day our daily bread " ; Luke has :
" Give us this day our bread for the coming day " (xi.
3). This latter version is manifestly in direct contra-

diction to Matthew (vi. 34) : " Be not anxious for the
morrow."

Another parallel to Matthew's version is given by
Dr. Taylor, namely, Isaiah xxxiii. 16 : " His bread
shall be given him ; his water shall be sure." Naturally,
in the " Grace after Meals " we thank God for the food
" wherewith He feedeth and sustaineth us continually
every day " (*Prayer Book*, p. 280). We note that Mr.
Montefiore fails to suggest any Biblical or Rabbinic
parallel to this petition. The Prayer continues : " And
forgive us our debts, as we also have forgiven our debtors "
(Matt. vi. 12). The Greek word for debt ($\dot{o}\phi\epsilon\acute{\iota}\lambda\eta\mu a$)
is probably a literal translation of the Aramaic " Choba,"
which not only means " debt ", but also " sin " (for
references see Levy, Targum—Wörterbuch, pp. 240–241).
The connexion between the two meanings " debt " and
" sin " is easily seen. When a man sins he immediately
owes a debt, i.e. reparation, to God. " Debts " in
Matthew is replaced by " sins " in Luke, which was
undoubtedly the original sense. This is substantiated
by the explanatory addition given by Matthew who
speaks of " trespasses " (14, 15). The Shemoneh
Esreh, in the sixth Benediction, offers a good parallel—
" Forgive us our Father for we have sinned, pardon our
trespasses " (*Prayer Book*, p. 46). A condition is laid
down as the *sine qua non* of obtaining pardon. There
is no question in the " Lord's Prayer " of the Cross, or
Vicarious Atonement, or of Faith in Jesus (Matt. ix. 2
and Acts x. 43), but only the duty of forgiving others.
The Rabbis point out that it is just as necessary for a
man to meet his obligations as between man and man,
as it is to discharge his debts to God (Shekalim iii. 2).
" Forgive thy neighbour," says Ben Sirach, " the hurt

that he hath done unto thee, so shall thy sins be pardoned when thou prayest " (xxviii. 2, and see the following verses). " God says to the transgressor," according to the Talmud, " thy sins against Me are forgiven thee, but go to thy creditor and ask his pardon also " (Rosh Hashana, 17b).

Both Dr. Bischoff (op. cit. p. 79) and Dean Savage (op. cit. p. 175) point out that in the Talmudic parallels, including the passage we have just quoted, the reference is to wrong done, and not to wrong suffered by the suppliant ; whereas in the Lord's Prayer it is forgiveness for injury received which is enjoined. In the passage we quoted from Ecclesiasticus, forgiveness is also demanded for the injury received. This is equally true of the following Talmudic passage : " All who are forbearing and forgiving and do not insist on their rights will be forgiven their sins " (Joma, 23a, and see Taanith, 25b, and Megilla, 28a). The petition may be connected with Mark xi. 25 : " And whensoever ye stand praying, forgive, if ye have aught against any one, that your Father also who is in heaven may forgive you your trespasses." We note that the reference here is to wrong done, not to wrong suffered by the suppliant. We have already met with this teaching in the earlier part of the Sermon on the Mount (Matt. v. 23 ff., and see chapter V. on " The New Law of the Gospel *versus* the Old Law ").

We will not repeat the parallels given in connexion with Matthew (v. 23), but we wish to draw attention to the following passage in the *Testaments of the Twelve Patriarchs*—" Love each one his brother, and put hatred away from your heart ; love one another in deed, and in word, and in the inclination of the soul. . . .

Love ye therefore one another from the heart ; and if a man sin against thee, cast forth the poison of hate and speak peaceably to him, and in thy soul hold not guile ; and if he confess and repent, forgive him (see Matt. xviii. 15). But if he deny it, do not be angry with him, lest he catch the poison from thee and take to swearing and so thou sin doubly, but if he be shameless and persistent in his wrong-doing, even so forgive him from the heart and leave to God the judgment " (Test. Gad ch. vi.). This passage and the following extracts : " Have therefore compassion in your hearts, my children, because even as a man doeth to his neighbour, even so also will the Lord do to him " (Test. Zeb. v. 3, cf. viii. 1, 2) ; " and if any man seeketh to do evil unto you, do well unto him, and pray for him and ye shall be redeemed of the Lord from all evil " (Test. Jos. xviii. 2) are considerably more than a century earlier than the teaching of Jesus and in no wise does the teaching of the Gospel excel, or even at times equal, the high moral tone of this remarkable Jewish book.

The lesson of forgiveness is purer and higher in the *Testaments of the Twelve Patriarchs* than in the Gospels. The " Testaments " teach forgiveness even if the opponent is shameless and persists in his wrong-doing—the Gospels say that if he refuse to hear, let him be excommunicated—" let him be unto thee as the Gentile and the Publican " (Matt. xviii. 15–17). The sixth petition of the Lord's Prayer—" And bring us not into temptation, but deliver us from the evil one " (Matt. vi. 13) is found in Luke in an abbreviated form : " And bring us not into temptation " (xi. 4). We are inclined to consider Luke's version earlier than Matthew's expansion which is merely explanatory. This petition

is again quite Jewish, and occurs in the Hebrew Prayer
book : " O lead us not into the power of sin. . . . or
of temptation " (p. 7). We have seen that Dr. Taylor
connects the fourth petition, " Give us this day our
daily bread " with the Manna (Exod. xvi. 4). In connexion with the Manna the words " that I may tempt
them " occur and seem to suggest the sixth petition
which we are now considering (see *Sayings of the Jewish
Fathers*, pp. 125 and 127). Dr. Taylor adds several
Talmudic prayers containing the petition, " deliver us
from temptation " (ibid. pp. 128–130).

Considerable discussion has arisen as to whether the
last word of the petition, " the evil one," is masculine, or
whether it is merely neuter, and means " evil." " But
a consideration of New Testament usage leaves little or
no real doubt that here, as elsewhere, it is masculine "
(*The Gospel of the Kingdom*, p. 179). This is seen in the
parable of the sower (Matt. xiii. 19) : " the evil one cometh
and snatcheth away that which has been sown." In the
parallel accounts in Mark and Luke, the " Evil One " is
replaced by " Satan " and " the Devil " respectively.
John frequently speaks of the " Evil One " as a personal
being (1 John iv. 3, and v. 18). Dean Savage comes to
the conclusion that in the Lord's Prayer, the Evil One is
a personal being and is the active adversary of the " sons
of the Kingdom " (see, however, Preuschen, *Hand-
wörterbuch zum N. T.*, p. 947, and Achelis, *Bergpredigt*.
pp. 288–289). Dean Savage (op. cit. p. 180) admits a
similarity between this petition and certain prayers
found in Berachoth. He denies any direct connexion
between the two. " It does, however, serve to emphasize
the fact that the Prayer which Jesus gave was moulded
on the lines of Jewish religious thought, and that it was

based upon the stage of development which had been already reached under the Old Covenant." In addition to the parallel which undoubtedly exists to the petition in the Jewish Prayer Book, we find in Sirach the lesson enunciated that man has free will and can overcome the evil inclination called in Hebrew "Yezer Hara'" (see xv. 11–17). "Put thy trust in God and He will help thee" (ii. 6). God is the deliverer in temptation (xxxiii. 1). The Greek word for temptation in Sirach is the same word as is used in the Lord's Prayer.

It would be an interesting study to inquire into the problem of temptation from the Jewish as well as the Christian standpoint. In the Lord's Prayer, it is clearly seen that the Devil is the author of man's temptation; whereas in the Jewish prayer (*Daily Prayer Book*, p. 7) the evil inclination within man's heart is the source of all evil. This Jewish view is ultimately based on Genesis viii. 21, which says, " for the imagination of man's *heart* is evil from his youth," and on Genesis vi. 5, which teaches that " every imagination of the thought of man's *heart* is only evil." Throughout the whole of Jewish theology the Devil plays a comparatively little part compared with that assigned to him in Christian theology. Already in the Talmud, the Devil, or Satan, is identified with the " Yezer Hara," or evil inclination *within* man (Baba Bathra, 16a). This evil inclination must not be conceived as having an independent existence outside man's heart, nor is it a power at war with God. Schechter observes : " As is so often the case in Jewish theology, the Rabbis, consciously or unconsciously, managed to steer between the dangerous courses (*Aspects of Rabbinic Theology*, p. 264). On the other hand, the Devil, or Satan, in Christian theology, is a power at war with God. He is the prince of this world (John xiv. 30). D. F. Strauss rightly urges that the entire conception of the Christian personal Messiah and his kingdom is as inseparable from the belief in a personal Devil with his Satanic kingdom, as the belief in the North Pole is inseparable from the belief in a South Pole (quoted by Dr. Kohler, op. cit., pp. 146 and 147). If, as Judaism teaches, there is no real personal devil—then there is no need for Jesus to overcome or to attempt to overcome the non-existent. If the Devil is only the personification of the evil principle, then the " Messiah-idea " is sufficient to overcome this " devil-idea." It must not be forgotten that one of the most noteworthy features of the Old Testament theology is the rare reference made to Satan. There is no express mention in the Hebrew Scriptures of Satan as a personal spirit of evil, who is the enemy of God and His Kingdom.

This, however, is the view of Satan, or the Devil, in the New Testament and is entirely novel and un-Jewish. " The complete revelation of Satan as the malignant author of evil was reserved for the time when, with the advent of Jesus' kingdom, the minds of God's people were prepared, without risk of idolatry, or of the mischievous dualism of such a religion as that of Zoroaster, to recognize in the serpent of Eden and in the Satan (of the Old Testament) . . ., the great adversary of God and man, whose power is to be feared and his temptations resolutely resisted ; but from whose dark dominion the Son of God had come to deliver mankind " (Hastings' *D.C.G.*, ii. p. 570). This is the modern Christian view. Jewish theology taught that every man can and must overcome his own evil desire (" Yezer Hara ") as Scripture teaches : " Sin coucheth at the door : unto

thee shall be its desire, and thou shalt rule over it "
(Gen. iv. 7, cf. Siphrê, Deut. vi. 6 § 33, p.74a). Philo knows
nothing of a personal Devil who is the prince of this
world. Pharisaic Judaism is certainly not the source
whence the Gospels derived their theory of Satan.
The earliest identification of Satan with the serpent in
the Garden of Eden is to be found in the New Testament.
Mr. Montefiore says that " Yezer Hara " is sometimes
" half-personified and regarded as a power of evil as
much outside man as within him " (S.G., p. 535).
This is not borne out by the general opinion of the
Talmudists. Dr. Schechter says (op. cit. p. 258) : " That
generally speaking the heart and the ' Yezer Hara ' are
interchangeable terms " (see also Lazarus, Ethik des
Judentums, p. 270). One or two passages will make
this point quite clear. " Who is mighty ? He that
subdues his ' Yezer ' " (Aboth iv. 2). " Two ways hath
God given to the sons of men, and two inclinations "
(Testaments of the Twelve Partriarchs, Asher i. 3).
" For there are two ways of good and evil, and with
these are the two inclinations in our breasts discriminat-
ing them (ibid. 5 and see the note on p. 162 by Dr. Charles
in his edition of the Testaments). This book teaches
us that God looks on the inclination of a man (Gad v. 3)
who has the power to choose good or evil. In the
Sibylline Oracles, the seat of evil is also placed in the
heart (iii. 548). Moral evil is due to the pleasure of the
heart in the evil inclination.

We need not discuss at length the Doxology ; it is no
longer doubted by the critics that this was not a part of
the prayer, as it originally stood in Matthew. The form
found in the Didache (viii. 2 ; x. 5) is the oldest version.
This form ultimately developed into the full expression :

M

" For Thine is the Kingdom, and the power, and the glory for ever, Amen." The original source of the doxology is 1 Chronicles xxix. 11: " Thine, O Lord, is the greatness, and the power, and the glory . . . Thine is the Kingdom." Doxologies are by no means uncommon in Jewish literature. In the Psalms we find at the end of each of the first four books a benediction, and the last book concludes with a psalm which is a doxology. In the Temple the people did not use " Amen " as a response, but said " Blessed be His name, whose glorious Kingdom is for ever and ever." (See Mishna in Joma, 35b and 39a; Taanith, 16b, Berachoth, 63b, and Sota, 40b.) This old Jewish doxology speaks of the Name and the Kingdom just as in the Lord's Prayer. The Doxology adopted by the Church is also used in the Synagogue, (see p. 67, *Daily Prayer Book*) ; it is also customary to say it at the conclusion of the Hymn of Glory (ibid. p. 78 ; see Baer's *Abodath Jisrael*, p. 251). The Lord's Prayer is followed by two verses which are quite out of place : " For if ye forgive men their trespasses, your Heavenly Father will also forgive you. But if ye forgive not men their trespasses, neither will your Father forgive your trespasses " (Matt. vi. 14 and 15). The verses are probably inserted as a comment on the fifth petition : " Forgive us, as we have forgiven." I have already given several parallels and there is no need to add to them.

The Jews instinctively rejected the whole scheme of the Messianic Kingdom as expounded by Jesus. They denied the dualism—God and the Devil—which formed its background. They refused to accept Jesus as the only son of God, and denied the need of a saviour to overthrow the Devil. This attitude is clearly proved by the abuse heaped on the Jews in the Gospels. They

are told : " Ye are of your father the devil " (John viii.
44). The Lord's Prayer is, as we have seen, lacking in
originality. There is not a single idea or expression
which cannot be found in pre-Christian literature of
Israel. In the course of transmission the only addition
has been the Doxology, which, like the rest of the prayer,
has been borrowed from Jewish sources. We entirely
fail to understand the readiness of Mr. Montefiore " to
allow to Jesus any ' originality ' . . . which his disciples
would like to claim for him " (S.G., p. 536). The fact
that the sources of the Lord's Prayer are the Old Testament, and the pre-Christian Apocalyptic and Apocryphal
literature of the Jews, forces the impartial critic to deny
any originality to the author of this prayer. Dr. Charles
admits that the parallels in " thought and diction "
between passages in the *Testaments of the Twelve
Patriarchs* and passages in the Synoptic Gospels are
too close for us to believe that Jesus was not acquainted
with this early Jewish book. The same conclusion is
forced on us by comparing, say, passages in Ecclesiasticus and the Gospels. We are not disposed to surrender
the title to originality which undoubtedly belongs to
the Jewish literature. We can well understand how the
Jew, Philo, so well used by New Testament writers, was
believed by the early Church to have been a Christian.

Mr. Montefiore (ibid. p. 536) says of the author of the
Lord's Prayer : " Whoever put it together chose with
fine religious feeling and insight." He admits that " it
is not original in its ideas," but he insists that " it is
original in the choice of ideas and in their grouping."
It would interest him very much to hear that even in
" the choice of ideas, and in the grouping " there is no
more originality than in its ideas. We follow Dr. Klein

(op. cit. pp. 268–9) in tracing the original source of the
Lord's Prayer. We are not about to select a parallel
here and there from the vast Rabbinical literature, but
we shall show how the Lord's Prayer grew out of the
thirty-sixth chapter of Ezekiel (verses 23–31). V. 23 :
"And I will sanctify my great name," became "Sanctified
(or hallowed) be thy name" (Matt. vi. 9). V. 24 :
"And I will take you from among the nations, and
gather you out of all the countries" represents the
divinely promised result of the establishment of God's
Kingdom on earth. This is expressed in the Lord's
Prayer by the second petition, "Thy Kingdom come"
(Matt. vi. 10). Vv. 25–27 : "And I will sprinkle clean
water upon you and ye shall be clean . . . a new spirit
will I put within you. . . . And I will put my spirit
within you," is exactly paralleled by the Lucan variation : "Thy holy spirit come upon us and cleanse us."
V. 26 : "And I will take away the stony heart out of
your flesh," corresponds to the petition, "Deliver us
from the evil one." Here we see the marked difference
between the old Jewish and the new Christian conception
of the source of sin and temptation. The "stony
heart" is within man and there is no "evil one" outside
man. To return to Ezekiel, verse 28 : "Ye shall be
my people, and I will be your God"—then, indeed, shall
we realize the third petition of the prayer, "Thy will be
done, as in heaven, so on earth" (Matt. vi. 10). The
blessing promised in vv. 29, 30 : "And I will call for the
corn and will multiply it, lay no famine upon you. And I
will multiply the fruit of the tree, and the increase of the
field . . ." reappears in the petition : "Give us this
day our daily bread" (Matt. vi. 11). Finally in v. 31 :
"Then shall ye remember your evil ways and your doings

that were not good ; and ye shall loathe yourselves in your own sight for your iniquities and your abominations," we have the same thought as is expressed by the petition : "And forgive us our debts " (i.e. sins) (Matthew vi. 12).

It is to be hoped that a frank avowal will be made by scholars in the future that the Lord's Prayer is merely an adaptation of these nine verses of Ezekiel. This should finally settle the question as to the originality of the Lord's Prayer. It is taken, we have seen, from the Old Testament, and therefore can lay no claim whatsoever to originality.

LITERATURE

'Demonology' in *Jewish Encyclopedia* (New Testament Demonology), vol. iv. p. 519, and see Bibliography at end of article. On 'Satan,' see Maimonides, *Moreh Nebuchim*, iii. 22. On 'Yezer Hara,' see *Jewish Encyclopedia, sub voc.*, and Lazarus *Ethik des Judenthums,* Porter's essays in *Yale Biblical and Semitic Studies*, and Conybeare's article on 'Demonology of the New Testament,' *J.Q.R.* viii., July and October 1896, pp. 263 f.

NOTE

The variant reading (Luke xi. 2, 3) referred to above (p. 152) is discussed by Zahn, *Geschichte d. neut. Kanons*, ii. p. 471 ; see also Texts and Studies I. 3, *The Lord's Prayer in the Early Church* (1891) pp. 25 ff.

CHAPTER XIII

THE UNJEWISH ASCETICISM IN THE GOSPELS

I NOW proceed to consider a long passage in Matthew (vi. 19–34) discouraging worldly anxiety and recommending renunciation. This passage is rightly considered by many modern authorities to be an interpolation. Professor Votaw admits that " nearly all of those scholars who regard the Sermon in the First Gospel as a composite production in whole or in part, look upon this section (Matt. vi. 19–34) as extraneous to the original discourse, being brought in here from some other historical connexion " (Hastings' *D. B.*, v. p. 39). There are two arguments against its present position ; the subject matter of the section is remote from the theme of the preceding section ; and secondly, the material of verses 19–34 of this sixth chapter of Matthew is found scattered in Luke, none of it appearing in his discourse vi. (20–49), which is parallel to the earlier part of the Sermon on the Mount. Votaw admits that there is an abrupt transition between Matthew vi. 18, and vi. 19 ; he thinks that this abruptness may be due to the fact that we have only extracts or a digest of the historical Sermon. The reader will easily detect its inconsistency with the flow of the argument in the Sermon. Moreover, it is placed in Luke in another connexion. It is self-evident that the Lord's Prayer was intended by Matthew to mark the dividing line between the two main divisions of his account of the Sermon. As we have already seen, the first half discussed the relation of the New Law of the Messianic Kingdom to the Old Law of Israel. In the second half of the Sermon, the conduct of the Members of the Kingdom is discussed ; first as towards God (Matt. vi. 19–34), and then as towards the brethren of the Kingdom (vii. 1–27). The keynote will vary ; at one time we shall see the lesson of sacrifice set before the disciples, at another we shall find prudence recommended.

The first principle laid down is the need of avoiding all material cares and ambitions. This is admirably summed up in the term asceticism. For the different forms taken by the ascetic life in Christian antiquity see Duchesne's *Christian Worship*, E.T., pp. 419 ff. We must not lose sight of the underlying thought that accompanied the varied practices of the early Church— namely, the belief in the " Parousia " or early return of Jesus, when he would establish his new Kingdom (see Matt. xxiv. 3 ; 1 Cor. vi. 2 ff., and xv. 23). The time was short and before one could prepare for the coming of the Kingdom, it might suddenly arrive. Under such conditions, we can easily understand the motive that prompted such teaching as the following section of the Sermon (Matt. vi. 19–21) : " Lay not up for yourselves treasures upon earth, where moth and rust doth consume, and where thieves break through and steal ; but lay up for yourselves treasures in heaven, where neither moth nor rust doth consume, and where thieves do not break through and steal ; for where thy treasure is, there will thy heart be also." The parallel in Luke is somewhat different. " Sell that ye have, and give alms ;

make for yourselves purses which wax not old, a treasure in the heavens that faileth not, where no thief draweth near, neither moth destroyeth. For where your treasure is, there will your heart be also " (xii. 33, 34). The following story of the proselyte Monobazus, King of Adiabene, a contemporary of Jesus, is given by Schöttgen as a parallel to these verses of the Sermon (19–21). Dr. Bischoff (op. cit. p. 85) objects that the King's conversion to Judaism took place in 36 C.E.—two or three years after the death of Jesus. Further, that Monobazus became king in 61 C.E. Consequently, he argues, the narrative we are about to give is unjustly described as a parallel.

Admitting the accuracy of these dates, do we know that Jesus ever uttered this part of the Sermon ? It is hardly consistent with serious criticism to speak of the authenticity of the " Sermon on the Mount." Which recension of the Sermon is *more* authentic, and which recension is less authentic ? The very title is, as we have seen, open to question. Luke's " Sermon in the Plain " is probably more correct than Matthew's " Sermon on the Mount." The mountain itself is in all probability a fiction, intended to serve as a pendant to Sinai, the scene of the Revelation of the Old Law. In speaking of the authenticity of the Gospels, it is interesting to note that, as early as the middle of the second century, Marcion and the Gnostics charged the *Jews* with having corrupted the text of the Gospels. Marcion rejected the Gospel account of the Parousia as being part of the Jewish corruption of the Gospels(see Hastings' *D.B.*, iii. p. 680). Is it not possible that the editor of the Gospel of Matthew as well as the editor of the Gospel of Luke had heard of the unprecedented bounty of the

proselyte king ? Now for the story. In a time of dire
distress due to famine, Monobazus distributed all his
wealth to the poor. He was reproached by his relatives,
who said : " Thy fathers gathered treasures, but thou
hast squandered them." He replied : " My fathers laid
up treasures upon earth ; but I lay up treasures in
heaven. . . . My fathers gathered them into a place
over which the hand of man hath power ; I have laid
them in a place over which the hand of man hath no
power. My fathers gathered that which bears no fruit ;
I have gathered that which yields fruit. My fathers
gathered Mammon (wealth) : I have gathered souls.
. . . My fathers gathered for this world ; I have gathered
for the world to come " (T. J. Peah i, 1. 15b ; Baba
Bathra, 11a ; Tosephta Peah, iv. 18 ; and Pesikta
Rabbati, xxv.). Two expressions, " Mammon " and
" treasures in heaven " are common to the Sermon on
the Mount and the Rabbinic narrative. Mammon in
Aramaic means gain as well as money. Wealth used
for a bad purpose is called in the Targum " Mammon of
wickedness " (Hab. ii. 9), which is not to be confused with the New Testament " Mammon of unrighteousness " (Luke xvi. 9). In Luke (xvi. 13) Mammon is
personified and opposed to God. This leads at once to
the New Testament view of wealth as part of the Evil One,
who is ever at war with God. This is quite opposed to
Jewish teaching. Wealth *per se* is neither good nor
evil. It is bestowed on man by God, and like all Divine
gifts can be used or abused. Proverbs iii. 9, has the
fine exhortation, " Honour the Lord with thy substance,"
which is translated by the Targum : " Honour the Lord
with thy Mammon." The Rabbis knew the seductive
attraction that wealth exercises, and we are warned that

there are people to whom money is more precious than life itself (Berachoth, 61*b*). In the Gospel money is considered to be tainted. This is the reason why it is called " the Mammon of unrighteousness " (Luke xvi. 9 and 11). This term also occurs, according to Dr. Charles, in Enoch lxiii. 10, but it is probably a post-Christian interpolation (see Hastings' *D.B.*, iii. p. 224). In Jesus' mind it was quite impossible for a man at one and the same time to serve two masters, God and Mammon (Matt. vi. 24).

We shall return to this verse ; meanwhile it will be necessary to try to account for the marked antipathy displayed by Jesus and the Gospels to wealth. Before, however, we set out to do this, we will briefly consider the term " treasure in heaven," which is common to the Gospels and Rabbinic literature. We have already met with its use in the Mishna : " the heavenly capital " which remains for ever (Peah i. 1). For Old Testament usage see Hastings' *D.B.*, iv., *sub voc.* ' Treasure.' Long before the time of Jesus, a Jew had said : " Work righteousness, therefore, my children, upon earth that ye may have it as a treasure in heaven " (Test. Levi xiii. 5, and cf. Test. Naph. viii. 5). In the Slavonic Enoch we find the passage : " He who increases his lamp before the face of the Lord, the Lord increases greatly his treasure in the heavenly Kingdom " (xlv. 2 cf. lix. 1–4). The interesting point in this last parallel is the combination of man's lamp with heavenly treasure. In the Sermon on the Mount the verse after 21 (which speaks of heavenly treasure) refers also to the " lamp." A good parallel occurs also in Buddhist literature—" Let the wise man do righteousness ; a treasure that others share not, where no thief can steal ; a treasure which passes not away (*Buddhist and Christian Gospels;* ed. Anesaki, p. 83). We cannot enter into a prolonged discussion as to whether the Gospels have been influenced by the Buddhist literature. There are very striking parallels which suggest direct borrowing. The subject has been ably discussed by Professor von Hase, *Neutestamentliche Parallelen zu Buddhistischen Quellen,* and by Seydel, *Das Evangelium Jesu in seinen Verhältnissen zur Buddha-Sage.* In the stimulating book of Albert Schweitzer, entitled *The Quest of the Historical Jesus,* the question of Buddhistic parallels is discussed (pp. 290–2) and the view expressed that no success has attended, or seems likely to attend, the attempt to apply Buddhist ideas to the explanation of the thoughts of Jesus. This judgment is somewhat partial, because Schweitzer has only considered the case as it was presented by Seydel in his earliest book, which I have mentioned. But Seydel's other books on the same subject, *Buddha und Christus* and *Die Buddha-Legende und das Leben Jesu nach den Evangelien* have not been criticized by Schweitzer. He also ignores the fascinating book of Pfleiderer, *Das Christusbild des urchristlichen Glaubens* (1903) and Van den Bergh van Eysinga, *Indische Einflüsse auf evangelische Erzählungen,* 1904.

Why did Jesus and the Gospels (especially Luke) attack wealth as something necessarily unrighteous ? Here is a new standpoint utterly at variance with the Jewish and Rabbinic teaching. The question may be stated in another form :   How are we to account for the ascetic spirit to be found not only in the Gospel, but in its living commentary—the Church ? This question suggests another : Why has Judaism persistently rejected asceticism, in spite of occasional attempts to intro-

duce some aspects of ascetic life ?   Israel is a people
alone in the world, unlike all other nations.   The terribly inhuman persecutions inflicted on the Jew during
thousands of years have made it impossible for him to
seek of his own free will suffering or poverty.   There was
enough misery in his life to make him seize every possible
occasion for forgetting his suffering.   He naturally re-
joiced whenever the opportunity arose.   Moreover, his
religion bade him " rejoice in God," and " serve God
with joy."   Did not God Himself see that everything
which He had made was very good ? (Gen. i. 31).
There was nothing evil in God's world—even death itself
was a blessing in disguise.   We should consecrate everything to the service of God and man.   Philo asks :
" Have you great abundance ?   Share it with others,
for the beauty of riches is not in the purse, but in the
power it gives one to succour those who are in need "
(*On Joseph* § 24, M. ii., p. 61).   Jesus, on the other
hand, teaches that riches have no beauty.   The rich
man is accursed, and shall not enter God's Kingdom.
" Lay not up for yourselves treasures upon earth," he
cries.   The *summum bonum* of the Gospels is the new
kingdom that Jesus will establish.   " Anything which
will enable a believer in Jesus to reach this goal is to be
considered as one of the goods of life worthy of man's
appreciation."   Whatever, on the other hand, hinders
a believer from entering the Kingdom is considered to
be an evil, and as such to be renounced (see Lemme,
Christliche Ethik, p. 432).

   This affords a clue which may enable us to answer the
question why wealth is considered by Jesus to be evil
and therefore something to be renounced.   It was felt
that sin was more easily indulged in by the man of means

who could purchase not only luxuries, but with his wealth could ruin others as well as himself. Was not the rich man feared ? Did he not count for more than the poor man ? Did not the rich exploit the poor ? " Woe to the rich " had been an old cry that is re-echoed in the Gospels (Luke vi. 24). Thus we see that there was something to be said against the dangers of wealth. But Jesus goes much farther. He denies the right to possess wealth. His command is, " Lay not up treasure." Wealth is evil and must be renounced. Where did this doctrine arise ? Some scholars (e.g. Dr. Kohler) would see in the Essenes the source whence Jesus derived his ascetic teaching. Philo says that the Essenes were celibates who lived together in community houses, sharing all things in common. An authentic account of the Essenes is set forth in Philo's treatise *Quod Omnis Probus Liber*, written about 20 C.E. Eusebius has preserved a fragment of Philo's *Apology for the Jews* which supplements the information given by Philo in the treatise just quoted. Josephus also describes the sect which he calls *Esseni*, although he sometimes uses the name *Essaei* which occurs in Philo. The Essenes practised voluntary poverty and were indifferent to money or worldly things. (Josephus, *Wars*, ii. viii. 3 and *Antiquities*, xviii. i. 5). Christian scholars are ready to admit that John the Baptist may have been influenced by the Essenes, but they deny that Jesus derived his teaching from this sect, which in so many ways deviated from the orthodox Judaism of the first century. Clement of Alexandria (Strom. iii. 6) claims that Jesus was the founder, as well as the chief example of the ascetic life.

If Jesus did not derive his ascetic teaching from the

Essenes, we must try to account for it in some other manner. We have already seen that Jesus preached his Gospel to the poor. In the Beatitudes, the poor are promised happiness in the coming Kingdom. The present order of values will be reversed. Dives, the rich man, and Lazarus, the poor man, will exchange rôles in the Kingdom of Heaven (Luke xvi. 19–31) ; Lazarus will be happy and prosperous, whilst Dives will be wretched in hell. Shall we be wrong in attributing the antipathy of Jesus to wealth to the fact that he and his followers were in abject poverty ? Celsus makes a point of attacking Christianity because it was a creed of the poorest of the poor (Origen c. *Cels.* ii. 1). The first Christians were called Ebionites, i.e. the poor (Epiphanius, *Haer.* xxxi. 2), because of their poverty. Dr. Lambert points out that " the Ebionites, as we meet them in later Church history, resemble the Essenes in taking an ascetic view of life and regarding voluntary poverty as a thing of merit and a means of preparing for the Messianic Kingdom." (Hastings' *D.C.G.*, i. p. 506). Whether the teaching of Jesus gave rise to the asceticism of the Ebionites, or whether the Gospel derived its ascetic teaching from the Essenes, the fact remains that poverty in the Gospels is considered to be a passport to the Heavenly Kingdom, whilst riches are the way to perdition. We have already spoken of the apocalyptic nature of the Kingdom of God which Jesus believed he was about to inaugurate. We stated that it had for its background a dualism—God and the Devil. This dualism led to the thought that matter is opposed to spirit, producing the antithesis of wealth and poverty. The things of the flesh (e.g. wealth) must be renounced in order to develop the life of the spirit. The new Kingdom was to see the overthrow of the Devil and his allies (wealth, luxury, and life's attractions). The new teaching of Jesus says : " If any man would come after me, let him deny himself" (Matt. xvi. 24).

This is the refrain which continually recurs. A man must surrender all his possessions to follow Jesus (Matt xix. 21) ; he must even renounce the closest family ties. This is no mere figurative expression. A man, in order to become a disciple, must renounce father and mother, wife and children (Matt. x. 37, Luke xiv. 26). Again we are told : " Whosoever . . . that renounceth not all that he hath, he cannot be my disciple " (Luke xiv. 33). Jesus declares with the greatest possible clearness that every earthly blessing must be sacrificed in order to obtain, through him, the higher blessing of his Kingdom. It is quite easy to give other examples of this ascetic spirit. Jesus denies a disciple permission to bid farewell to his relatives (Luke ix. 62). The opposite course was pursued by Elijah when he called Elisha to follow him. Jesus even denies his own mother and brothers, and refuses to see them or speak with them (Mark iii. 33). All this and much more of Jesus' ascetic teaching is foreign to Jewish religious thought and practice. The doctrine of self-mutilation (Matt. xix. 12)—" There are eunuchs which have made themselves eunuchs for the sake of the Kingdom of Heaven "—is an abomination according to the Mosaic Law (Deut. xxiii. 1 ; cf. Lev. xxii. 23 ff.).

Let it not be urged that all this is not to be taken literally. It *was* taken literally by the Church. Celibacy arose in imitation of the example of Jesus. During the middle ages, as well as in the first four centuries of Christianity, the dominant note was asceticism. The horrible example of the famous Church Father, Origen, who literally emasculated himself for the sake of the Kingdom of Heaven, was not an isolated instance of the ascetic spirit that has always permeated Christian life. The ascetic imitation of Jesus realized by Francis of Assisi is another famous example (see Professor von Walter's *Franz von Assisi und die Nachahmung Christi*). This mediæval saint wrote a series of rules for the monks who joined his order. He cites the verses Matt. xix. 21 ; xvi. 24 ; and also the following two passages : " If a man cometh unto me and hateth not his own father, and mother, and wife, and children, and brethren, and sisters, yea, and his own life also, he cannot be my disciple " (Luke xiv. 26) ; also " And every one that hath left houses, or brethren, or sisters, or father, or mother, or children, or lands, for my sake, shall receive a hundred-fold and shall inherit eternal life " (Matt. xix. 29). Many ancient authorities include *wife* in the verse just quoted (see Luke xviii. 29). All these verses were taken quite literally, and unless one was prepared to follow these laws of the " higher life " he could not be received as a member of the Franciscan brotherhood (von Walter, op. cit. p. 41).

How utterly different is the rule of life laid down by the Jewish mediæval moralists, e.g. Bachja ibn Chalwah in his *Kad Hakkemach, sub voc.* ' Wealth.' He begins by quoting Proverbs (xxiii. 4, 5) : " Weary not thyself to be rich. . . . Wilt thou set thine eyes upon that which is not ? for riches certainly make themselves wings." Wealth is bestowed by God's providence. The poor of to-day may be the rich of the morrow, and *vice-versa.* Solomon says, " A good name is rather to be chosen than great riches, and loving favour rather than silver and gold. The rich and poor meet together ; the Lord is the maker of them all " (Prov. xxii. 1, 2). Every good (such as wealth or strength) can produce harm if abused. Wealth has only been bestowed on men in order to enable them to do deeds of mercy. " Gold," says the Midrash, " was made for God's sanctuary and service." Charity is also a highway leading to God. " The crown of the wise is their riches, but the folly of fools is only folly " (ibid. xiv. 24). This verse was applied to the wise and foolish use of wealth respectively. Thus far Rabbi Bachja. The Scriptures warn men that wealth has its perils, and that it ill becomes a man to fix his thoughts wholly on that which he must leave behind, when death summons him hence (see Psalm xlix). Jeremiah utters the grave warning : " Let not the wise man glory in his wisdom, neither let the mighty man glory in his might, let not the rich man glory in his riches ; but let him that glorieth glory in this, that he understandeth and knoweth me, that I am the Lord who doeth lovingkindness, judgment and righteousness in the earth ; for in these things I delight, saith the Lord " (ix. 23, 24). Wisdom, strength and wealth are not the highest ideals of life, but love, justice and righteousness.

We cannot account for Dr. Harnack's verdict : "Asceticism has no place in the Gospel at all " (*What is Christianity?* p. 88). Surely the passages we have quoted are sufficient evidence that Jesus taught asceticism as the ideal rule of life. Dean Savage justifies the ascetic teaching inculcated by Jesus in his Sermon by suggesting that " the anticipation of the Messianic Kingdom of God amongst the Jews had become more and more materialistic. . . . The hopes of the people were set upon an exaggerated material prosperity of plenty,

N

and in regard to this, the selfishness of their exclusivism
ran riot. More particularly their imagination centred
itself on the idea of eating and drinking at a royal feast
from which all other nations should be excluded, when
the Messiah's kingdom was established " (op. cit. p.
194). The authority of Edersheim's *Life and Times* is
relied on by the learned author, who also quotes " Haga-
dath Megilla " f. 102–2 as one of the sources whence
he drew his picture of the Jewish conception of the
Messianic banquet.

Has the Dean seen this book ? We should like to know
a little more about it. The argument is that the Jewish
materialistic conception of the Messianic Kingdom had
to be counteracted by this new ascetic teaching of Jesus.
We certainly admit the force of the argument, but are
the facts as to the Jewish conception in accordance with
the Dean's interpretation ? Granting, for the sake of
argument, that the Jews in the first century really
believed in a great Messianic banquet, in which the " selfishness of their imagination ran riot " by thinking that
" all other nations should be excluded." Well, this
conception was also, unfortunately, shared by Jesus and
his followers ; and there is as much need to correct the
gross materialistic conception of the Messianic Kingdom
as recorded in the Gospels, as there is to correct the conception of the Messianic banquet in the Haggadic stories
of the Midrash. The Dean admits (op. cit. p. 194,
note 3) that the idea of a literal prosperity and refection
lingered on even among Christians (see Iren. v. 35, ed.
Harvey). It is surely well-known that the new Kingdom was spoken of in the Gospels as a banquet. Jesus
teaches : " I say unto you, that many shall come from
the east and the west and shall recline (at the banquet)

with Abraham, and Isaac, and Jacob, in the Kingdom of Heaven, but the sons of the Kingdom (i.e. the Jews), shall be cast forth into the outer darkness ; there shall be the weeping and gnashing of teeth " (Matt. viii. 11, 12). The parables of the Marriage of the King's Son (Matt. xxii. 2–14) and the Great Supper (Luke xiv. 16–24) supply us with sufficient evidence that in the Gospels the Kingdom is likened to a banquet (see also Luke xiii. 29 ; xxii. 30 ; Rev. iii. 20 ; xix. 9). Jesus even promises to drink wine in the new Kingdom (Matt. xxvi. 29). Thus we see that not only is a materialistic conception of the Kingdom found in the Gospel, but, as it excludes the Jews, " The sons of the Kingdom," we cannot deny that " exclusiveness " is one of its characteristics.

We are somewhat surprised, however, that the Jewish references to the Messianic banquet are taken in their literal sense (see Berachoth, 17a, " In the world to come there is no bodily enjoyment "). They are Haggadoth, and must be interpreted as allegories or parables. Maimonides says that the Messianic banquet is an allusion to the spiritual joys of the intellect (Commentary on Mishna Synhedrin x. (Chelek) 1).

The Sermon on the Mount teaches that the earthly treasures are destroyed by moth and rust. The reference to the moth may be paralleled by the words of Isaiah : " For the moth shall eat them up like a garment " (li. 8). The reference to " rust " may be paralleled by Malachi iii. 11 : " I will rebuke the devourer . . . and he shall not destroy the fruits of your ground." The Septuagint translates " devourer " by the same Greek word which occurs in the Sermon, although it is here rendered by " rust." " Where thy treasure is, there will thy heart be also " (Matt. vi. 21) is probably a proverb.

The meaning is that if our treasure is on earth, our heart will also be there. This is probably suggested by Psalm lxii. 10 : " If riches increase, set not your heart thereon," or by Job xxxi. 24 : " If I have made gold my hope, and have said to the fine gold, Thou art my confidence." Ben Sirach says : " Blessed is the rich that is found without blemish, and that goeth not after gold. . . . Who hath had the power to transgress and hath not transgressed ? and to do evil, and hath not done it ? his treasure (or goods) shall be made sure " (Ecclus. xxxi. 8, 10, 11). This represents the Jewish attitude towards wealth, which brings untold blessings if rightly used. The Gospel looks upon wealth as tainted, the Jewish Scriptures declare that gold and silver belong to God (Hag. ii. 8). The Midrash gives God the title of " The Rich One of the Universe " (Deut. Rabba ii. 4, see L. Dukes, *Zur Rabbinischen Spruchkunde*, p. 41). This title may possibly be due to an homiletical interpretation of Proverbs xviii. 23, " ' The poor (man) useth intreaties : but the rich (God) answereth roughly.' Moses, the poor man, besought God, who possesses all, for permission to cross the Jordan, but God hearkened not unto him " (Deut. iii. 23–26). The wealth praised by the Rabbis was not superfluity of money, but contentment. " Who is rich ? He who is satisfied with his lot " (Aboth iv. 1). The pursuit of wisdom, truth, and righteousness was more esteemed than the pursuit of Mammon. Nevertheless, there was no genuine desire to renounce money, or to refuse to utilize it in a good and proper manner. Herein Judaism rejects the Gospel teaching. Christianity regards a great many sins as deadly—the sin of wealth is one of the number. This has no parallel in Judaism. Christianity is not of the world—Judaism is of the world. "Prepare thyself in the ante-chamber (this world) before thou goest into the Audience Hall" (the future world) is the quaint dictum of the Rabbis (Aboth iv. 21). The abiding worth of Judaism is its teaching that man should live naturally the *best* life, which is the holy life, the unselfish life, the full life for God and humanity. Judaism is not "a religion," it is life.

LITERATURE

F. C. Conybeare's article on ' Essenes ' in Hastings' *D.B.*, i. pp. 767 ff., especially p. 772 for Bibliography. On ' Asceticism,' see Bacher, *Agada der Tannaiten*, i. pp. 164, 264 ; ii. 74 ; and see index, *sub voc.*, Schechter, *Some Aspects of Rabbinic Theology*, pp. 277-8. Lazarus, *Ethik des Judenthums*, 272 ff., and Reinach, *Orpheus*, E.T., pp. 56, 57, and index, *sub voc.* On ' Heavenly Treasure ' see note of Dr. Charles, *Testaments of the Twelve Patriarchs*, p. 52. (His Talmudic references need revision.) For the latest view on the economic teaching of Jesus, see Professor Kirn, *Die Sittliche Forderungen Jesu*, in the sixth series of *Biblische Zeit und Streitfragen*, p. 34 f.

NOTE

The N. T. word θησαυρός, treasure (Matt. vi. 19), occurs in the Midrash in an Aramaic transliteration, see Krauss, *Griechische und Lateinische Lehnwörter im Talmud*, ii. p. 587. Of course θησαυρός is very common in LXX.

CHAPTER XIV

"HAVE NO CARE," THE NEW LAW OF THE GOSPEL

THE Sermon on the Mount resumes the discourse about purity of purpose or single-mindedness in serving God. The transition from the ascetic teaching about earthly treasures is somewhat abrupt and immediately suggests an interpolation. The text in Matthew (vi. 22–23) is as follows : " The lamp of the body is the eye ; if therefore thine eye be single, thy whole body shall be full of light. But if thine eye be evil, thy whole body shall be full of darkness. If therefore the light that is in thee be darkness, how great is the darkness ! " Luke (xi. 34–36) connects the parallel saying with another address ; but his context is less appropriate than Matthew's. Jewish literature abounds in the expressions " a good eye," and " an evil eye," which are used to designate the opposite characteristics of generosity and envy. The following sayings will illustrate the ordinary use of these terms : " He that gives a gift should give with a beautiful eye " (T. J. Baba Bathra iv. 11. 14*d*; cf. T. B. Sabbath, 74*a*). " There are four dispositions in almsgivers. He who desires to give, but that others should not give, his eye is evil towards the things of others ; he who desires that others should give, but will not give himself, his eye is evil towards his own," etc. (Aboth v. 16). Rabban Jochanan ben Zakkai, who lived and taught long before

the Synoptic Gospels were written, said to his disciples :
" Go forth and see which is the good way to which a man
should cleave ? " One answer was : " A good eye," and
in reply to his further question as to which was the evil
way which a man should avoid, one of the disciples
answered " an evil eye " (Aboth ii. 13, 14). The " good
eye " and " evil eye " also occur in the Old Testament ;
" He that hath a good (i.e. bountiful) eye shall be blessed,
for he giveth of his bread to the poor " (Prov. xxii. 9).
" Eat not the bread of him that hath an evil eye, neither
desire thou his dainties ; . . . eat and drink, saith he
to thee ; but his heart is not with thee " (ibid. xxiii.
6 and 7 ; and see Taylor, op. cit. p. 35).

In the Sermon the lesson is enforced that if man has his
eye " single " like his heart, and he is only absorbed by
the thought of the heavenly treasures, then his whole
personality will be endowed with perfect light. If, on
the other hand, a man's eye be evil (i.e. not single)—
because he cares for the varied treasures of this world—
his vision is blurred and his mind and soul will be full of
darkness. We have a good parallel to this last thought
in Proverbs xxviii. 22 : " He that hath an evil eye
hasteth after riches." According to Philo, " the intelli-
gence is to the soul. what the eye is to the body " On
the Creation of the World, 17, M. i., p. 12). Professor
Pfleiderer (Primitive Christianity, E.T., ii. p. 327) thinks
that Matthew is not referring to the physical eye, but to
the inner light (the ethico-religious sense of truth). If
this be so, it would be finely paralleled by Proverbs xx.
27 : " The spirit of man is the lamp of the Lord." This
leads to the idea of every man having within him a source
of spiritual light, corresponding with the eye, the external
organ of vision. If this organ be sound and normal, the

body will be fully illumined. Whatever light is enjoyed by the body is due to the eye. When the eye has good vision, all the members of the body move as though they were actually endowed with sight. If the eye be evil, then the opposite result ensues. The body is given over to darkness and the limbs grope along, because there is no light visible to the body. There may be also a reference in the Sermon to Job (xviii. 5, 6) which describes the blindness of the sinner : " The light of the wicked shall be put out . . . the light shall be dark . . . and his lamp beside him shall be put out." See, also, Proverbs xiii. 9.

We find the whole lesson of this part of the Sermon briefly given by Philo : " It is as impossible that the love of the world can co-exist with the love of God, as for light and darkness to co-exist at the same time with one another " (Fragments : John of Damascus, 370 B., M. ii. p. 649). Professor Jülicher (ii. p. 101) insists that the " evil eye " does not refer to a physical defect, but simply means the eye, that sees all things from the point of view of envy or greed. The " single eye " means, that it sees everything as it really is, without any evil thought or selfish wish. God, says the prophet, has " eyes too pure to behold evil " (Hab. i. 13). The good man who is naturally endowed with single-mindedness cannot see evil, because his eye is single. Evil means darkness, and it is not natural for the " single " eye to behold the darkness. Ben Sirach tells us to " glorify the Lord with a good eye " (Ecclus. xxxv. 8). The *Testaments of the Twelve Patriarchs* also speak of " walking in singleness of eye " (Test. Issachar iii. 4 ; the Greek has the same word as Matthew). In the same Testament, we read the following interesting passage :—

" The single-minded man coveteth not gold,
  He over-reacheth not his neighbour,
  He longeth not after manifold dainties,
  He delighteth not in varied apparel.
  He doth not desire to live a long life,
  But only waiteth for the will of God.
  And the spirits of deceit have no power against him,
  For he looketh not on the beauty of women.
  There is no envy in his thoughts,
  Nor worry with insatiable desire in his mind,
  For he walketh in singleness of soul,
  And beholdeth all things in uprightness of heart,
  Shunning eyes made evil through the error of the world
  Lest he should see the perversion of any of the commandments
    of the Lord " (iv. 2–6).

This fine piece can hold its own when compared with any passage in the Gospels. There can be little doubt that Jesus or the Evangelists had read the Testaments, and we have already seen that other parts of the Sermon have been influenced by the lofty ethics of this pre-Christian book. Another passage in the Testaments teaches, " The good man hath not an eye full of darkness, for he hath mercy on all, even though they be sinners and conspire to harm him." (Test. Benjamin iv. 2, 3, see Dr. Charles' note on pp. 106, 107 of his edition of the Testaments.)

The next verse in the Sermon connects the subject of the single eye with the duty of serving God with undivided loyalty : " No man can serve two masters : for either he will hate the one and love the other ; or else he will hold to one and despise the other. Ye cannot serve God and Mammon." (Matt. vi. 24 ; see also Luke xvi. 13.) There is a good parallel in the Testaments :—
" He who serves two opposite passions cannot serve God, for the passions blind his soul and he goes about by day as though it were night." (Test. Judah, xviii. 6.)

Here we have another instance of the close similarity in thought between the Testaments and the Gospels. Just as it is impossible for a slave to serve two masters so is it impossible for a man to serve God and Mammon at the same time. The Jewish moralists point out that man's deepest love of God need not necessarily involve the hatred of wealth. One can serve God through one's wealth. This teaching is denied by Jesus, whose standpoint was conditioned by his apocalyptic belief in the dualism of God and the Evil One. He tolerated no compromise and demanded, as we have seen, complete renunciation. If a man, he says, would love God, then he must hate the world and all it contains. The Testaments also warn us not to allow ourselves to become the slaves of money :—" The love of money leadeth to idolatry, because, when led astray through money, men name as gods those who are not gods, and it causeth him who hath it, to fall into madness " (Test. Judah xix. 1).

This, however, is something quite different from the Gospel teaching, which demands absolute renunciation. This idea will be worked out more fully in the next section of the Sermon (verses 25–34) : " Therefore I say unto you, be not anxious for your life, what ye shall eat or what ye shall drink ; nor yet for your body, what ye shall put on. Is not the life more than the food, and the body than the raiment ? Behold the birds of the heaven, that they sow not, neither do they reap, nor gather into barns ; and your heavenly Father feedeth them. Are not ye of much more value than they ? And which of you, by being anxious, can add one cubit unto his stature ? And why are ye anxious concerning raiment ? Consider the lilies of the field, how they grow ; they toil not, neither do they spin ; yet I say unto you, that even Solomon in all his glory was not arrayed like one of these.   But if God doth so clothe the grass of the field, which to-day is, and to-morrow is cast into the oven, shall he not much more clothe you, O ye of little faith ?   Be not therefore anxious, saying, what shall we eat ? or what shall we drink ? or wherewithal shall we be clothed ?   For after all these things do the Gentiles seek ; for your heavenly Father knoweth that ye have need of all these things.   But seek ye first his Kingdom and his righteousness ; and all these things shall be added unto you.   Be not therefore anxious for the morrow ; for the morrow will be anxious for itself. Sufficient unto the day is the evil thereof."

A similar poetical passage occurs in Luke (xii. 22– 31), where it follows on the parable of the Foolish Rich Man (xii. 16–21).   Luke's context seems in this case more original than Matthew's.   Jesus, according to Luke, was asked to settle a dispute between two brothers regarding an inheritance.   He refused to do this, and instead gave a discourse about earthly cares, which he illustrated by the parable of the foolish rich man who was surprised by death in the midst of his race after wealth.   Then follows the illustration of the ravens, which have neither barn nor storehouse, but are fed by God.   The question is also asked by Jesus, " Who can add a cubit unto his stature ? "   Professor Pfleiderer sees in all this the lesson taught by the preceding parable, and comes to the conclusion that the report of Luke, as compared with that of Matthew, is more original (op. cit. ii. p. 152).   Not only must the disciple of Jesus avoid wealth, but he must not even have a care for the material needs of ordinary daily life.   Not only should he be heedless as to what he will eat, or wear, but he is not to attempt to obtain these bare necessities of life. Jesus had only one concern—the coming Kingdom— " Seek ye first his Kingdom and his righteousness, and all these things shall be added to you " (Matt. vi. 33). This absolute faith in Providence, unaccompanied by *any* effort on man's part, is not Jewish doctrine. Man is placed on earth to labour : " in the sweat of thy face shalt thou eat bread " (Gen. iii. 19 and ii. 15). The argument in the Sermon is hardly satisfactory ; because birds have to gather their food, if they would not starve. If, again, man is to imitate the lilies of the field, he would go naked, because lilies do not wear raiment.

Mr. Montefiore, in commenting on this long section, fails to refer to a single parallel either in the Old Testament or in any of the pre-Christian writings of the Jews. His comment at the end of the section is noteworthy : " What is remarkable about the sayings of the Gospels is that they are often applicable to wholly alien conditions, and true even without that belief in the end of the world which underlies so many of them—no surer mark of their genius and first-classness. The same may be said of much in the Prophets and the Psalms " (*S.G.*, p. 545). Does Mr. Montefiore think that this section of the Sermon is really applicable to-day in our modern life ? Is there to be no care for the smallest details of daily life, no anxiety for the simplest needs of earthly existence, such as food or clothing ? Are we to leave all to God and to sit with our hands folded, only thinking of the coming Kingdom or praying for its advent ? Again we must point out that Jesus gave a new law of life for the short period that was to intervene before the Messianic Kingdom was established. He was an enthusiastic teacher of a new morality which was to obtain in the coming new age. Professor Pfleiderer points out " that any one who seeks to make eschatological enthusiasm a permanent authority and standard of social ethics is acting no more wisely than one who should attempt to warm his hearth and cook his dinner with the flames of a volcano " (op. cit. ii. p. 447).

The Church and the Christian world at large have not invariably followed this new teaching of Jesus as to wealth and the care for the daily needs of life. We have already referred to the communistic experiment of the first Christians at Jerusalem (Acts iv. 32–35). This arose, as we have seen, in consequence of the belief that Jesus was about to return to establish his kingdom. It was probably also due to the literal interpretation of Jesus' two commands : " Seek ye first the Kingdom of God and his righteousness, and all these things shall be added unto you " (Matt. vi. 33) ; and " Lay not up for yourselves treasures upon earth " (ibid. vi. 19).

Returning to the Sermon, we will follow verse by verse, or if necessary groups of verses, and adduce parallels to illustrate or contrast the teaching of Jesus. " Be not anxious for your life, what ye shall eat or what ye shall drink ; nor yet for your body, what ye shall put on. Is not the life more than the food and the body more than the raiment ? " (verse 25). The prophetic promise : " Thou wilt keep him in perfect peace whose mind is stayed on thee, because he trusteth in thee " (Isa. xxvi. 3) represents the Old Testament teaching as to how a man should meet the impending danger or the pressing cares of life. Trust in God is essential, but this does not mean a careless life. Man cannot, in spite of Jesus' teaching, live his life like the flowers and the birds. " Six days shalt thou labour and do all thy work" (Exod. xx. 9) is the Divine command. Philo speaks of the ideal wealth of life as follows : " Men who have a desire for the gifts of Nature rather than for those of vain opinion, devoting themselves to frugality, and simplicity, and temperance, will have a great abundance and means for all kinds of delicate living without pursuing them with pain and diligence, for wealth will come to those who know how to use it in a befitting manner. . . . For as to those men for whom that genuine wealth is stored up in Heaven, which has been derived from constant practice in wisdom and holiness, on them is bestowed the wealth which consists of money upon earth ; since the treasure houses, by the providence and care of God, are kept continually full ; because the impulses of the mind, and the labour of the hands, are not hindered in any way, so as to prevent the successful attainment of these objects which are constantly pursued with zeal " (*On Rewards and Punishments*, § 17, M. ii. pp. 424, 425). The same lesson is enforced by the Old Testament : " O fear the Lord, ye his saints, for there is no want to them that fear him . . . they that seek the Lord shall not want any good thing " (Ps. xxxiv. 9, 10). But let us fully realize that idleness or lack of interest will never lead to the fear or love of God. The teaching of the Gospels invariably goes to extremes. It says, " be not anxious for your life." Have *no* care. The Pharisaic doctrines strive after the more practical, if less ideal, golden mean. " Be not anxious *overmuch* " (2 Esdras ii. 27) is the moderate and possible teaching of the Rabbis. They never attempt to crush out human and natural habits, but endeavour to curb and refine them. They do not say, it is better " not to marry," " not to lay up treasure," but these and similar ways of men are carefully regulated and utilized for the good of humanity.

The next verse of the Sermon reads : "Behold the birds of the heaven, that they sow not, neither do they reap, nor gather into barns ; and your heavenly Father feedeth them. Are ye not of much more value than they" (v. 26). Nothing can surpass the beauty of the Psalmist's description of the Divine bounty :—"The eyes of all wait upon thee ; and Thou givest them their food in its due season. Thou openest thine hand, and satisfiest the desire of every living thing" (cxlv. 15, 16). The "birds of the heaven" is a marked Hebraism (cf. Gen. ii. 19), and the Scriptures assure us that the birds have their meat from God (Ps. lxxix. 2, and civ. 11, 12). Job argues that man is higher than the fowls of the heaven (xxxv. 11) ; see also Psalm viii. which has influenced so profoundly the teaching of Jesus. Can there be any reasonable doubt that Job's question, "ask the fowls and they shall tell thee" (xii. 7), was in the mind of the writer of this section of the Sermon (verse 26) which we now are considering? The appeal to Nature is not confined to the Old Testament. In a Baraitha of the early part of the second century we read that Rabbi Simeon, the son of Elazar, said :—"Never have I seen a gazelle spreading out figs to dry, or a lion carrying a burden, or a fox that had a workshop. Yet they are nourished without anxiety or trouble. They were only created to serve me ; but I was created to serve my Creator. If then these creatures which were only created to serve me receive their proper nourishment without anxiety or trouble, should I not, with much greater reason, expect to receive my daily bread without anxious care or hard toil, since I have been created to

serve my Creator ?   This would have been the case, had
I not polluted my works and impaired my rights to be
sustained by God " (T. B. Kiddushin, 82b, and T. J.
Kiddushin, iv. 11, 66d ; cf. Tosephta Kiddushin, v. 15).
This form of saying was also used by Jesus on several
occasions : e.g., " How much is a man of more value than
a sheep ? " (Matt. xii. 12, and cf. x. 31).   The Sermon
proceeds to point out that anxious care is unavailing
and unnecessary.

We need not discuss whether the modern theory of
education as to the value of physical exercises as a means
to development is unjustifiable, just because the teaching of the Sermon declares it to be impossible for a man
to add to his stature.   It may be objected that this is
not the correct meaning of the text.   Although adopted
by the Revised Version, we should note that in the margin, " age " is given as an alternative translation.   The
text would then be : " And which of you by being anxious
can add one cubit to his age ? "   The word (in Greek,
$\dot{\eta}\lambda\iota\kappa\iota\alpha$) means stature in Luke (ii. 52 and xix. 3).   There
is, however, nothing incongruous in applying a term of
measurement to age ;   it occurs in Psalm xxxix. 5 :
" Behold, Thou hast made my days as handbreadths."
We have already quoted from the *Testaments of the
Twelve Patriarchs* about the single-minded man who
" doth not desire to live a long life, but only waiteth for
the will of God " (Issachar iv. 3).   It is just as well to
remind the reader that Field (*Notes on Translation of the
New Testament*, pp. 6, 7), and Preuschen consider
" stature " to be the proper meaning.   If " age " be the
correct word, the saying is still unaccountable ;   for it
is not true that it is impossible to add to the length of
life by taking care.   Many " deceitful men," in conse-

"HAVE NO CARE" 193

quence of not taking care, do not " live out half their days " (Psalm lv. 23). If carelessness in many cases shortens life, carefulness may, in some cases, prolong life. If this be not admitted, the entire science of medicine must be regarded as quite futile. The next three verses continue the argument : " And why are ye anxious concerning raiment ? Consider the lilies of the field, how they grow ; they toil not, neither do they spin, yet I say unto you that even Solomon in all his glory was not arrayed like one of these. But if God doth so clothe the grass of the field which to-day is, and to-morrow is cast into the oven, shall he not much more clothe you, O ye of little faith ? " (28–30). The same principle that God, who cares for the lowliest of his works, will assuredly care for the noblest, which was applied in v. 26, is employed again in these verses.

The Greek for " consider " in verse 28, is found nowhere else in the New Testament, but is frequently used in the Septuagint (e.g. Gen. xxiv. 21). " Lilies of the field " is another Hebraism (see Song of Songs, ii. 16 ; iv. 5 ; vi. 2, 3, and Ps. ciii. 15). So also is the expression " Solomon in all his glory " (see 2 Chron. ix. 15 ff. ; 1 Esdras i. 5 ; cf. Tosephta Taanith, iv. 13).

Jonah was rebuked by God for only having pity on the gourd for which he had not laboured, and which he had not made to grow ; which came up in a night and perished in a night, and for not having any pity on Nineveh the great city with many inhabitants and much cattle (Jonah iv. 10, 11). Here again the principle is implied that human life is of infinitely greater value than the life of lower forms of creation. If Jonah was justified in feeling pity for a gourd, how much more should he have felt pity for the men, women and chil-

o

dren of Nineveh ? The same lesson is enforced in the following Rabbinic tradition :—" Elijah asked Rabbi Nehorai, Why had God created in his world tiny insects and worms ? He replied, " When human beings (Habberioth) sin, He looks on the lower forms of creation and says : ' If I sustain these tiny useless creatures, how much more must I preserve human beings who are useful.' " (T. J. Berachoth ix. 3. 13c.)

" Ye of little faith " has aleady been paralleled. It occurs several times in Rabbinic writings :—" He who prays with a loud voice is counted among those who are of little faith " (Berachoth, 24b, see also Mechilta, ed. Weiss, p. 59a). The word for " barn " in the Greek text of Matthew (vi. 26) is ἀποθήκη, which is the same word used by the Septuagint for the Old Testament " granary " in Jeremiah l. 26. The Greek has been borrowed by the Rabbis and occurs in Talmud (e.g. Sabbath, 50a, Jer. Nedarim ix. 4, 41c) and in Midrash (e.g. Exodus Rabba, xxx. 14). The Sermon continues :—" Be not therefore anxious, saying, what shall we eat ? or, what shall we drink ? or, wherewithal shall we be clothed ? For after all these things do the Gentiles seek ; for your heavenly Father knoweth that ye have need of all these things." The Rabbis would not rebuke a person who asked with anxious thought for his wife and children, " What shall we eat to-day ? " They did not approve the conduct of people who having sufficient for to-day, began to question whether the morrow would find them lacking their daily bread (Sota, 48b). We have already met the passage, " Your Father knoweth that ye have need of all these things " in almost identical words : " Your Father knoweth what things ye have need of, before ye ask Him " (Matt. vi. 8). That trust in God must go with reasonable forethought, is Jewish teaching. Jesus says : Only trust in God and do not have any anxiety for the things of life. God knows what you require, He will provide what is necessary.

As a parallel to this verse of Matthew, we submit the following Old Testament passages : Ps. ciii. (13, 14) : " Like as a father hath compassion on his children, so the Lord hath compassion on them that fear Him. For He knoweth our frame ; He remembereth that we are dust." (In the next verse of this Psalm man is compared with the flower of the field and the grass. The lilies of the field and the grass were also used by Matthew in this section.) One more parallel will suffice : " The Lord is good . . . He knoweth them that trust in Him " (Nahum i. 7). It seems that the verse of the Psalmist, " Cast thy burden (or according to the Septuagint ' anxiety ') upon the Lord for He will nourish thee " (lv. 22) forms the basis of this section of the Sermon. Are we not justified in thinking that Matthew was influenced by the Septuagint and read in this verse of the Psalms, a precept telling man to cast all *anxiety* upon God, for He would, in return, nourish him ? We have seen other instances of the Septuagint influence on the Sermon on the Mount.

Since Jesus did not know Greek, but recited the Psalms in Hebrew or Aramaic, it is clearly seen that this idea of casting anxiety on God, who will feed and support us, entirely due to the Septuagint, could not have originated with Jesus. His reading of the Psalm would have led to the teaching that man should commit his ways (as in Psalm xxxvii. 5) and also his works to God (Prov. xvi. 3). This is expressed in Psalm lv. 22 : " Cast thy burden upon the Lord and He shall sustain thee." The Hebrew metaphor is that of rolling a burden upon the shoulders of some one else (see Rosh Hashana, 26b). God will hold us erect if, bearing our daily burden, we ask Him for his help. This is evident if we read the second half of the verse : " He shall never suffer the righteous to stumble," i.e., He upholds all who seek his support. (See Delitzsch's *Psalms*, ii. p. 188, which point out that the Septuagint version of this verse of the Psalms is used in 1 Peter v. 7.) There is, however, nothing in the Psalms or any other book of the Old Testament which teaches us to have no care, but we are reminded to trust in God alone, for He is mighty to save.

LITERATURE

On ' evil eye,' see Hamburger, R. E. ii. p. 82, and Taylor, *Sayings of the Jewish Fathers*, p. 35. On ' Singlemindedness' see Hamburger, *Geist der Hagada*, article ' Aufrichtigkeit,' pp. 129, ff. On ' Divine Providence,' see Kohler, *Theologie*, chapters xxvi. and xxviii., and *Jewish Encyclopedia*, article ' Providence.' Philo's fragments on Providence are translated in Bohn's, *Philo*, iv. pp. 222 f. For further literature, see *Bibliography* given by Kohler, op. cit. p. 355.

CHAPTER XV

WHO WERE THE "LOVERS OF MONEY" IN THE FIRST CENTURY?

ACCORDING to the Sermon on the Mount (Matt. vi. 32) the disciples were to lead a life free of all worldly care and anxiety. They were not to ask—What shall we eat or drink, " for after all these things do the Gentiles seek." We find almost the same words in the parallel passage in Luke xii. 30. In Matthew's recension of the Sermon the Gentiles are mentioned three times as a warning to the disciples not to follow the heathen errors. It is remarkable that modern commentators upon the New Testament attribute to the unfortunate Pharisees even those special faults of the Gentiles which Jesus condemned. The commentators lay themselves open to the charge of actually disbelieving Jesus, who said that the Gentiles were guilty of these particular failings. This is ignored and the Pharisees are burdened with the acknowledged vices of the heathen. Little wonder that the Pharisee is believed to be the son of the Devil (John viii. 44), if not the very Devil. I have already noted the fact that the heathen habit of indulging in vain repetitions of prayers (Matt. vi. 7), condemned by Jesus, has been held to be a Pharisaic sin. Dr. Plummer in his commentary on Matthew, p. 106, holds the view " that Jesus warns his hearers against another vice which was common among the Pharisees, that of avarice." The only authority quoted to support this charge is Luke xvi. 14 : " And the Pharisees who were lovers of money heard all these things ; and they scoffed at him." The preceding verses of this chapter in Luke contain the parable of the Unjust Steward, and a few verses dealing with the right use of money.

Now, there is considerable doubt among most modern critics as to whether this parable is authentic. If it be genuine, then the Pharisees did well to deride such teaching as it contains. To praise an unjust steward for his sharp practice would not commend itself to their moral judgment. They would not even advise their followers to be " wise as serpents " (Matt. x. 16). In all probability, however, the entire section preceding the verse in which the Pharisees are termed " lovers of money," is not authentic. The whole of it is peculiar to Luke. It belongs to the single tradition, and is therefore less authenticated than the double or triple traditions (see *Enc. Bib.* col. 1,792). Luke's antipathy to wealth has been pointed out, and we submit that he associated his aversion of money with his hatred of the Pharisees and labelled them " lovers of money," i.e. lovers of that which is evil. In the Sermon on the Mount and in Luke's parallel, the heathens, and not the Pharisees, are accused of indulging in anxious care for mundane things. Avarice, according to Luke and Matthew, is a Gentile vice. Luke then improves this, by calling the Pharisees, the enemies of the Gospel, " lovers of money." This Evangelist is not an exact scientific historian. He allows himself the privilege of altering the traditions to suit his purpose. We must remember that he is writing for the Gentiles. Why should they alone be described as loving covetousness? He will mend matters by dragging in the wicked Pharisees and they shall be described also as "lovers of money." Let us illustrate this case by another example. Whereas Mark (viii. 15) reports Jesus as saying, "beware of the leaven of the Pharisees and the leaven of Herod"; Matthew (xvi. 6) says that the words were: "Beware of the leaven of the Pharisees and Sadducees"; Luke gets rid of the Sadducees and of Herod and merely says, "beware of the leaven of the Pharisees, which is hypocrisy" (xii. 1). This example will suffice to show how Luke manages to manipulate his Gospel sources.

Did he find anything in the various traditions referring to "lovers of money"? Possibly he did; but perchance it was the Herodians, or, better still, the Sadducees, who were branded. What interest was it for the Gentile readers of Luke to be told about these classes of people who no longer lived when he wrote his Gospel? What could be more natural than to refer to the Pharisees, who rejected the new teaching of Jesus and his apostles? Dr. Plummer knows even more than Luke about the Pharisees. He adds " they were often wealthy, and believed their wealth to be a reward for their zeal in keeping the Law. They regarded themselves as conspicuous evidence of the connexion between righteousness and riches." Johannes Weiss (op. cit. pp. 239 and 450) says practically the same thing. It is very difficult to disprove such statements. It would be quite useless merely to deny the truth of this caricature. We should be told that the Gospels say that the Pharisees " loved money " (Luke xvi. 14), and " devoured widows' houses " (Mark xii. 40). We shall endeavour to consider this question in the light of historical research and criticism. We regret that Mr. Montefiore is so ready to admit, without any critical investigation, " that it was the bad Pharisees and Rabbis who were attacked by Jesus " (*S.G.*, p. 295). It would have been advisable for Mr. Montefiore, in writing for Jewish readers, to have discussed the date of the Talmudic passages referring to the " bad Pharisees," and to have determined whether they were condemned by Jesus. To say that " The Assumption of Moses," according to some scholars, " alludes to Pharisees who are pretenders and hypocrites, and eat the property of the poor " (ibid.) is most unfortunate. Would it not have been of the deepest interest to the Jewish reader to learn the more authoritative opinion of Dr. Charles, who is clearly of opinion that " The Assumption of Moses " does not attack the Pharisees as Mr. Montefiore suggests ? I shall return to this point.

The reference to Josephus given by Mr. Montefiore seems also quite inadequate. The subject is of vital importance, as we really ought to know whether the Gospel accounts of the Pharisees are just and accurate, or prejudiced and untrue. The modern Jew, liberal or orthodox, is a lineal descendant of the Pharisees of New Testament times, and their honour and reputation are not to be lightly attacked. Mr. Montefiore is satisfied that " there was doubtless some material to attack " (*S.G.*, p. 295). After considering the available evidence, we shall draw our own conclusions.

As against Dr. Plummer, we might quote Dr. Hastings' *Dictionary of Christ and the Gospels* (i. p. 467), which states : " The Pharisees were not characterized by luxurious living." We have already noted the fact that in this standard work the Pharisees do not meet

with very much sympathy. If, then, they are not
described as being given to luxurious living, we may
believe that this opinion is as good as the opposite view
held by Dr. Plummer. In the same Dictionary we are
informed that it was the " Sadducees who were in com-
fortable circumstances " (vol. ii. p. 549). I quite agree
with this statement. It will not be disputed by any
impartial student that the Pharisees preached the keeping of the Law, and the coming world of bliss (Olam
Habba) as the reward of obedience. Dr. Hastings'
Dictionary admits that the " Rabbis taught their disciples to seek first after heaven and its righteousness, to
look past the present legal life to a future world of grace
and bliss " (vol. ii. p. 352). They did not " believe
their wealth to be a reward for their zeal in keeping
the law " ; because as a class they were mostly poor.
The wealth of the nation was in the hands of the aristo-
cracy (the Sadducees), and also in the hands of the
middle class, known as the " people of the land " (Ammê
Ha-aretz), who did not belong to the Pharisaic party,
because they found it too irksome to observe, among
other laws, the tithe laws connected with the produce
of their lands. The mass of the people were very poor.
This brief statement, so totally different from the
ordinary theory as to the economic condition of the
people of Palestine, in the first and second centuries
C.E., is based on the latest researches of Dr. Büchler
(see *Der Galiläische 'Am ha'-Areş des Zweiten Jahrhun-
derts*, and also see Mr. Montefiore's summary of Dr.
Büchler's theory in *S.G.*, p. lxxvi.).

Josephus offers some evidence which we shall now
consider. In point of time, he is earlier than Luke,
whose view we are criticizing. I have elsewhere drawn

attention (see *Grace of God*, p. 11) to the fact that Luke used Josephus, who writes: "If any one should ask them (i.e. the Pharisees) which of the two things they would choose to part with, their lives or their religious observances—they would readily prefer to suffer anything whatsoever, rather than a dissolution of any of their sacred customs" (*Antiquities*, xvi., ii. 3). Again he adds: "Now, for the Pharisees, they live meanly, and despise delicacies in diet, and they follow the government of reason. . . . They also believe that souls have an immortal vigour in them and that hereafter there will be rewards or punishments, according as they have lived virtuously or viciously in this life ; on account of which doctrines they are able greatly to persuade the body of the people " (ibid. xviii. 1, 3). The mass of the people were Pharisees. They suffered terribly at the hands of the cruel tax-collectors. Where was the opportunity for becoming rich when Herod's grinding taxation pressed so heavily on the bulk of the people ? According to Dr. Sanday (*Sacred Sites of the Gospels*, p. 15) there were two and a half million inhabitants in the land. Herod's annual income was £400,000 (*Antiq.* xvii. xi. 4). Moreover, his costly undertakings in connexion with the Temple, palaces, roads, baths, etc., were separate items for taxation. The brigandage and disorder due to the misgovernment under the Herods also helped to impoverish the mass of the people.

We can then appreciate the early saying in the Ethics of the Fathers: "Let the poor be as the children of thy house " (i. 5). The poverty and misery of the Pharisees are referred to in the *Psalms of Solomon* (iv. and v.), in *The Assumption of Moses* (c. vii.), and also in the Talmud (for references see especially the fine article on " Kleidernot " by Dr. Krauss in his *Talmudische Archäologie*, i., pp. 134, 135). The fact that the Rabbis, who gave their services as teachers and advisers gratuitously, were forced to engage in some secular profession or trade to earn their daily bread should enable the reader to disbelieve Luke's accusation that they were " lovers of money." We saw that Jesus wished his followers to renounce all their wealth, and not to serve Mammon. Was it not quite natural for Luke, who was such a follower, to look upon the Pharisees and the Rabbis who refused to obey the new law of renunciation as " lovers of money ? " I fully appreciate the line of argument that Luke followed, but was it true or just ? Mr. Montefiore says of the Scribes who " devour widows' houses " (Mark xii. 40) " it is perhaps implied that they acquired an authority over women, and let themselves be richly paid for their advice." This statement is unsupported by the slightest proof. We find that Mr. Montefiore has merely repeated the comment of J. Weiss (op. cit. p. 176), who also offers no proof. Hillel's poverty and Nahum of Gimzo's lack of every luxury (Joma, 35*b*, and Taanith, 21*a*) were not the exception but rather the general rule. Rabbi Chanina ben Dosa was so poor that he and his family had to subsist for an entire week on a measure (kab) of carobs (Berachoth, 17*b*). He did not even possess anything to dedicate to the Temple (Ecclesiastes Rabba i. 1). His rejection of the title of prophet (Berachoth, 34*b*, cf. ibid. Mishna, v. 5), in spite of the miracles performed by him, is a characteristic of the Pharaisic teachers. What could be clearer than Josephus' statement ? " The Sadducees are able to persuade none

204 SOURCES OF SERMON ON THE MOUNT

but the rich . . . but the Pharisees have the multitude on their side " (ibid. xiii. x. 6). The poor cried for relief (*Psalms of Solomon* iv.), and the Rabbis tried to help them in their distress.

The special laws for the relief of the poor which Rabban Gamaliel introduced are referred to by Dr. Hoennicke in *Das Judenchristentum*, p. 50. If, then, according to Josephus, the Sadducees were the rich people who loved luxury and ease, we have his evidence opposed to Luke. Is there further evidence on either side? We are, fortunately, able to answer this question in the affirmative. We have a vivid description of the injustice and avarice of the Sadducees in *The Assumption of Moses*, which was written, according to Dr. Charles, somewhere between 4 B.C.E. and 30 C.E. In other words, we have here a document contemporary with the life of Jesus, and consequently of first-class importance in determining the thought and customs of the Jews in Palestine. Dr. Charles also decides that this book was originally written in Hebrew by a Pharisee. The views of Schürer (*History*, ii. 3 ; 73–83) and of Dr. Clemen in Kautzsch's *Die Apokryphen und Pseudepigraphen des Alten Testaments*, ii. p. 315, as to the Pharisees being the object of attack in chapter vii., have been controverted by Dr. Charles, who says : " Our author pours the most scathing invective on his religious and political opponents, the Sadducees, whom (in chapter vii.) he describes in terms that frequently recall the anti-Saducean Psalms of Solomon. Through some inexplicable misapprehension, Schürer and others have regarded this chapter as a description of the Pharisees " (*Enc. Bib.* i. col. 236). Thus far Dr. Charles. I have already pointed out that Mr. Montefiore follows the erroneous interpretation advocated by Schürer.

The seventh chapter of *The Assumption of Moses* is as follows : " And in the time of these [events] scornful and impious men will rule, saying that they are just. And these will conceal the wrath of their minds, being treacherous men, self-pleasers, dissemblers in all their own affairs and lovers of banquets at every hour of the day, gluttons, gourmands . . . devourers of the goods of the poor, saying that they do so on the ground of their justice, but (in reality) to destroy them, complainers, deceitful, concealing themselves lest they should be recognized, impious, filled with lawlessness and iniquity from sunrise to sunset. Saying : ' We shall have feastings and luxury, eating and drinking, yea we shall drink our fill, we shall be as princes.' And though their hands and their minds touch unclean things, yet their mouth will speak great things, and they will say furthermore, ' Do not touch me lest thou shouldst pollute me in the place where I stand,' " (cf. Ps. Sol. viii. 13, for this combination of inward impurity and outward holiness).

Here again we have another picture of the grasping selfishness of the Sadducees. They were utterly indifferent to the religious ideals of Israel. Their only thought was to enjoy life. They had no patriotic sentiment ; a Roman régime was as good as, or even better than, a Jewish government. As supporters of the antinational ruling party, they knew that they could rob the poor with impunity. Finally, let us see if the Gospels throw any further light on our problem. The general poverty of the great mass of the people is attested by the stories of the miraculous feeding of 5,000 poor hungry people (Matt. xiv. 15–21 ; Mark vi. 34–44). Whenever Jesus came to the house of a Pharisee, he was received with a friendly welcome. Luxury was not indulged in, and Jesus even rebukes his host for not providing the costly ointment (Luke vii. 46 ; see Geiger's *Jüd. Zeitschrift für Wissenschaft und Leben*, vi. pp. 105 ff.). We do not deny that there may have been a few wealthy Pharisees. They formed the exception, and not the rule. Didon (*Life of Christ*), Mosheim, and Wetstein hold that in the parables of Dives and Lazarus (Luke xvi. 19–31), the rich man is a Sadducee. The Gospels do not say that the rich young ruler was a Pharisee. In all probability he was a Sadducee, because he is described as being clothed in purple, implying that he was a ruler. Political office was avoided by the Pharisees, who concentrated all their efforts on the religious side of Israel's mission in the world.

In the Apocryphal " Gospel according to the Hebrews," Jesus says to the rich young ruler who declined to abandon all his wealth : " How sayest thou, I have done the law and the prophets ? since it is written in the Law, ' Thou shalt love thy neighbour as thyself ' ; and behold, many of thy brethren, the sons of Abraham, are covered with filth and are dying with hunger, while thy house is full of many good things and nothing at all goes out of it to them." The poverty of the many is contrasted with the wealth of the single individual. The evidence, then, of Josephus, *The Assumption of Moses*, and the New Testament is conclusive. The Pharisees were not "lovers of money." The New Testament labels this class " tax-collectors." This is also admitted by Mr. Glover in his book, *The Conflict of Religions in the Early Roman Empire*, to which I referred in a former chapter. He writes : " Of the grosser class of sinners, he (Jesus) was tolerant to a point that

amazed his contemporaries. . . . He had apparently
no anger for the woman taken in adultery ; and he was
the ' friend of publicans and sinners '—even eating
with them. The explanation lies partly in Jesus' instinct for reality and truth. Sensualist and money-
lover were at least occupied with a sort of reality ;
pleasure and money in their way are real, and the pursuit of them brings a man, sooner or later, into contact
with realities genuine enough. Whatever illusions publican and harlot might have, the world saw to it that
they did not keep them long. The danger for such
people was that they might be disillusioned overmuch.
But the Pharisee lied with himself " (p. 124). I will
not discuss the point whether the Pharisee lied with
himself, but I will only lay stress on the verdict of Mr.
Glover that the " money-lover " was not the Pharisee.
This will enable the reader to estimate at its true value
the charge brought by Dr. Plummer against the so-
called " money-loving " Pharisees.

In 1862, Geiger pointed out that Jesus stood on Pharisaic ground and in his work as a reformer he followed
the lines of his great predecessor Hillel (*Jüd. Zeitschrift
für Wissenschaft und Leben*, ii. p. 37). It would be well
for modern Christian theologians to bear this fact in
mind in criticizing the Pharisees. It is a sign of the
better times in store for the advancement of historical
study to find that Mr. J. H. A. Hart protests against the
wholesale condemnation of all the Scribes and Pharisees
as hypocrites (see *Journal of Theological Studies*, vol.
xi. p. 40). I hope I have dealt quite fairly with the
available evidence. I accept the historical testimony
of the Gospels if it is not contradicted by itself or by
authorities equally valid. This is my standpoint.

The Sermon continues : " But seek ye first his Kingdom and his righteousness, and all these things shall be
added unto you " (vi. 33). Holtzmann (*in loc.*) thinks
that the parallel in Luke (xii. 31), " Howbeit seek ye
his Kingdom and these things shall be added unto you "
is more original than Matthew's version. " Seek ye
first," which Matthew has, seems to indicate an expansion of Luke's text, and at the same time a justification
of those disciples, who care for the material things of
life. This is not the only instance in which Matthew
weakens the ascetic spirit of the teaching attributed to
Jesus. Thus Luke's (xiv. 33) saying : " Whosoever
renounceth not all that he hath cannot be my disciple "
is omitted by Matthew. In the Sermon (vi. 33) Matthew
softens the original rigorism of Luke's parallel text, and
in the words of Pfleiderer, " already points in the
direction of those ' counsels of evangelical perfection '
which facilitated in Church morality the compromise
between the high-pitched ideal and the actual conditions
of social life " (op. cit. ii. p. 48). I suggest that the
phrase " seek God's Kingdom " was based on the
famous saying of Amos (v. 4) : " Seek me and ye shall
live " (cf. ibid. v. 14). Philo also has, " To follow
God, and to find refuge with him is eternal life " (*On
Fugitives*, 15, M. i. p. 557). Johannes Weiss (op. cit. p.
275) believes that Matthew has also expanded Luke's
" Seek the Kingdom of God " into " Seek first the
Kingdom of God and his righteousness." He holds that
the addition of " and his righteousness " is intended to
explain what is meant by the " Kingdom of God."
There is, Weiss thinks, a further implication that this
righteousness is to be taken in the Pauline sense of
" the righteousness of God through faith in Jesus "
(Rom. iii. 22).

This would undoubtedly be something quite new to the Jew. His monotheism meant perfect confidence in God without any intermediary. To seek God by seeking good was the message of the prophets, and was re-echoed by Scribe and Rabbi in every age. Josephus tells us that " the Jewish nation prefers righteousness to glory " (*Antiq.* xvi. v. 4). This righteousness is desired by the real seekers after God. " Quicken me in thy righteousness," said the Psalmist (cxix. 40), and his cry is constantly repeated by all who seek God's rule on earth. I am also inclined to believe that the words : " And all these things shall be added unto you " in the Sermon have been adopted from 1 Kings (iii. 13) : " And I have also given thee that which thou hast not asked, both riches and honour."

The last verse of Matt. (vi.) : " Be not therefore anxious for the morrow, for the morrow will be anxious for itself. Sufficient unto the day is the evil thereof " is a repetition of the previous teaching in verse 25 of this chapter. The Talmud records Ben Sirach's saying : " Let not grief (or anxiety) enter into thine heart for many strong men have been destroyed thereby " (Synhedrin, 100b). The Rabbis certainly taught " that man should not be anxious for the morrow." This saying is to be found also in Synhedrin, 100b : " Do not be anxious for the need of the morrow, for thou knowest not what a day may bring forth." This was quite in accord with Hillel's practice of daily thanking God for his providence and not having any anxiety as to the next day (Beza, 16a). " Sufficient unto the day is the evil thereof " (v. 34) was probably a proverb current among the Pharisees.

A good Talmudic parallel is afforded by the following

Haggada : " The Holy One, blessed be He, said unto Moses : Say to Israel, ' I was with you in this bondage, and I will be with you in the bondage of other king-doms.' Moses replied, ' Lord of the Universe ! Suffi-cient is the trouble in its hour ! ' " (Berachoth, 9*b*), mean-ing that it is foolish for man to seek evil and trouble ; enough when he is confronted by misfortune.

In 1903, Grenfell and Hunt discovered at Behnesa, the ancient Oxyrhyncus, in Egypt, a papyrus Gospel fragment. The date of the handwriting is about 250 C.E , and it contains a parallel version to part of the Sermon on the Mount. The following version is given by Grenfell and Hunt on p. 40. " [Take no thought] from morning until even, nor from evening until morn-ing, either for your food what ye shall eat, or for your raiment what ye shall put on. Ye are far better than the lilies, which grow but spin not. Having one gar-ment, what do ye [lack ?]. . . . Who could add to your stature ? He himself will give you your garment. His disciples say unto him, when wilt thou be mani-fested to us, and when shall we see thee ? He saith, when ye shall be stripped and not be ashamed."

The last paragraph may refer to Genesis iii. 7, and means that as in the Paradise of Eden our first parents were lacking raiment in their period of innocence, so likewise when the disciples become innocent they shall behold the Parousia (or Second Coming), when the world will be stripped of its garb of sin. It is possible that Gnostic influence has been at work in the com-position of this Gospel Fragment. It is interesting in preserving the reading " who could add to your stature," which I have already discussed (p. 192).

LITERATURE

For 'Life under the Herods,' see *Encyclopædia Biblica*, cols. 2,027 ff. For 'Carob' as special food of the poor, see *Enc. Bib.*, col. 1,574. For '*Poverty*' in Rabbinical literature, see Hamburger, *Geist der Haggada*, (Leipzig, 1857, pp. 123 ff.) *sub voc.* 'Armuth'. On the position of the poor in the New Testament, see articles 'Alms,' 'Community of Goods' in *Enc. Bib.* vol. i. and also see vol. ii., article 'Gospels,' § 110, on Ebionite passages in Luke. On the 'Denunciation of the Sadducean Priesthood' in the *Assumption of Moses*, see Büchler, *Die Priester und der Cultus*, pp. 77 ff. On the 'Pharisees of the New Testament,' see Freimann's article in Monatsschrift liv., pp. 703 f.

CHAPTER XVI

SOME PROVERBS—JEWISH AND CHRISTIAN—IN THE GOSPELS

WE must now turn our attention to the seventh chapter
of Matthew, which forms the conclusion of the Sermon
on the Mount. There are 29 verses ; of these the first
14 contain a loose series of sententious logia or aphorisms
which has no connexion with the preceding part of the
Sermon. In the finale of the Sermon, from v. 16 (second
half of the verse) to 27, we have a warning against
spurious forms of discipleship. The last two verses
(28, 29) do not belong to the Sermon.

We shall begin by considering the first five verses.
It would be possible to illustrate the aphorisms contained in them from non-Jewish literature. We shall
confine ourselves, however, to the Jewish parallels.
The first verse says : " Judge not, that ye be not
judged." It is not surprising to read in Dr. Plummer's
commentary upon this verse (p. 110) that : " It is possible that here again, as perhaps in Matthew vi. (19–34),
Jesus is selecting a fault for condemnation, because it
was common among Pharisaic professors of righteousness." Naturally, every conceivable vice and every
possible human weakness *must* be attributed to the
Pharisees. Bishop Gore, in his exposition of this section, adds : " Manifestly, what is in Jesus' mind is the

temper and character of the Pharisee. The Pharisee was in his way a strict religionist, a strict observer of religion. But you may almost say that the Pharisee tested progress in religion by the capacity to condemn other people " (p. 164). It would occupy too much space to mention all the other commentaries giving the same view. Johannes Weiss (op. cit. p. 274) cannot quite resist the temptation to attack the Pharisees. He writes : " We do not know whether Jesus was referring here to the Pharisees." It is, however, quite possible that this precept, " do not judge " was intended to be a rule of conduct that was to apply to the circle of disciples. It might be urged that Jesus was telling them that they are to abstain from all kinds of judgment. Just as they were not to resist evil (Matt. v. 39), so they were to abstain from passing judgment upon the actions or motives of their brethren. They were not to condemn their evil brother. Are we to assume that the precept refers to the exercise of legal authority ? Dr. Percy Gardner says : " ' They are not to judge.' This phrase seems to forbid any sitting in judgment on crime, such as being a member of a law court, perhaps even taking part in any execution of a legal sentence against a convicted malefactor " (*Exploratio Evangelica*, p. 197). We will not decide whether this is the right meaning. Tholuck has a similar interpretation, which seems to be supported by the parallel passage in Luke (vi. 37) :—
" And judge not and ye shall not be judged ; and condemn not and ye shall not be condemned ; release, and ye shall be released." In Luke, the " beam and mote " saying (vi. 41–42) stands in a slightly different connexion to Matthew's arrangement (vii. 3–5). In Luke, the command " judge not " (vi. 37) is separated from this

saying by the verses which speak particularly of generous giving, of blind leaders of the blind, and of the
disciple not being above his master. It has been suggested that the " beam and mote " saying comes in at
this point, because censoriousness is a natural fault of
young disciples. Is there a reference to Paul's attempt
to set his authority over that of the apostles who were
the disciples of Jesus ? We have already seen how in
the Sermon the disciples are commanded to agree with
their adversaries (Matt. v. 25), and even to love their
enemies and to pray for those who persecute them (ibid.
v. 44). We also saw that these precepts have not been
adopted in civilized life. The Church has never attempted to carry out these heroic commands. Jesus
said : " Judge not, that ye be not judged." We offer
as a contrast the much earlier saying recorded in the
Mishna. Joshua, the son of Perachyah said: " Judge
all men in the scale of merit " (Aboth. i. 6, and cf.
Shebuoth, 30a).

In our opinion this Pharisaic teaching is infinitely
superior to that of the Gospel. In the first instance, it
is impossible to carry out literally the Gospel injunction.
Man will always pass judgment on his fellows. Again,
the Gospel saying is inferior because it is negative,
whilst the Rabbinical saying is positive, universal, and
based on the ultimate human principle of love. Why
does the Gospel tell a man not to judge his fellow, because if he should disobey, he will be judged by God.
This sanction of fear is absent from the Rabbinical saying. The dictum : " Judge all men in the scale of
merit " has been expanded into the teaching, " He
who judges his neighbour in the scale of merit, will himself be judged in the scale of merit " (Sabbath, 127b).

The negative saying of the Sermon is, as Loisy truly points out (*Les Évangiles Synoptiques*, p. 621), a kind of inversion of the " Lex talionis," which Jesus is said to have condemned (Matt. v. 38). Dean Savage follows the same line as Dr. Plummer in describing the Pharisees as censorious. He says : " Even of their fellow-countrymen, partakers as they were of the same divine covenant, they could contemptuously sneer. . . . Even to Hillel is attributed the saying, ' No boor is a sinfearer ; nor is the vulgar (Am Ha-aretz) pious.' " This point is also discussed in a similar manner by Dr. König (op. cit. p. 25).

How is it possible to infer from Hillel's saying, that the Am Ha-aretz (i.e. one who refused to obey the laws of the tithe) cannot be a Chasid or saint, that the Pharisees were censorious ? I cannot follow this line of argument. When the Dean has quite mastered the meaning of Hillel's great saying, he will, I venture to think, reconsider his judgment. The Am Ha-aretz belonged to a class entirely different to that in which the Chasid was reckoned. One would hardly expect a person who is colour-blind to appreciate the beauties of a sunset as seen from the Lakes of Switzerland. Would an unmusical person enjoy Bach's fugues or Beethoven's symphonies ? In like manner, the Am Ha-aretz could not appreciate, nay, he did not wish to appreciate, the spiritual delights experienced by the Saint.

Dr. Büchler points out that the meaning of " Chasid " is not merely pious, it refers rather to the highest religious life or saintliness. The Chasidim or Saints performed various rites and ceremonies which were unknown to the ordinary Jew of the day, e.g. they spent some time preparing for prayer, so as to concentrate their

mind on their devotions (Berachoth v. 1, and see Dr.
Büchler, D.G. A.h.A. p. 20, n. 1). It was also the " censorious " Hillel who said "judge not thy neighbour
until thou art come unto his place " (Aboth ii. 5). It
cannot be said that Jesus observed the rule of " judge
not." His frequent attacks on the Pharisees, and his
impassioned condemnation of his fellow countrymen
betoken a censorious note in his own character. We
will refrain from any harsh criticism, and prefer to judge
in the scale of merit. We cannot do better than remember the old Rabbinic adage : " He who condemns others,
sees in them his own faults " (Kiddushin, 70a). This
also seems to be the meaning of the following verse in
Romans (ii. 1) : " for wherein thou judgest another, thou
condemnest thyself ; for thou that judgest dost practise
the same things." The next verse (2) in the Sermon
says, " For with what judgment ye judge, ye shall be
judged : And with what measure ye mete, it shall be
measured unto you." This does not really justify the
preceding verse, " judge not." Would it be a moral
teaching to let a man believe that merely by never
judging his fellows, he will escape the final judgment
of life ? There are several Jewish parallels to the second
verse of this seventh chapter of Matthew. These parallels are mostly earlier than the Gospels. I suggest
that the saying in verse (2) was adopted from the following passage of the *Testaments of the Twelve Patriarchs* :
" Have therefore compassion in your hearts, my children, because even as a man doeth to his neighbour,
even so also will the Lord do to him " (Test. Zebulun
v. 3). In the same Testament we read :—" Have,
therefore, yourselves also, my children, compassion
towards every man with mercy, that the Lord also may

have compassion and mercy upon you. Because also in the last days God will send his compassion on the earth and wheresoever he findeth bowels of mercy he dwelleth in him. For in the degree in which a man hath compassion upon his neighbours, in the same degree hath the Lord compassion also upon him " (ibid. viii. 1–3, cf. Sifrê, Deut. § 96, 93*b* and Sabbath, 151*b*). In the Talmud we have the sayings : " With the measure with which a man measures, so will it be measured to him " (Mishna Sota i, 7, and see Sota, 8*b*), and " Do not reproach thy fellow with thine own blemish " (B. Mezia, 59*b*). They are good parallels, and apart from the fact that they teach the same lesson as the Sermon on the Mount, the first quotation is exactly the same as the saying attributed to Jesus. It is undoubtedly correct to assume that Jesus or the Evangelist was quoting here (v. 2) a current popular saying. This also applies to the next three verses (3–5) : " And why beholdest thou the mote that is in thy brother's eye, but considereth not the beam that is in thine own eye ? Or how wilt thou say to thy brother, let me cast out the mote out of thine eye ; and lo, the beam is in thine own eye ? Thou hypocrite, cast out first the beam out of thine own eye ; and then shalt thou see clearly to cast out the mote out of thy brother's eye."

Wünsche gives as a parallel the following Talmudic passage : Rabbi Tarphon (a contemporary of Matthew and Luke) said : " I wonder if there be a man in this generation that will allow himself to be reproved. If some one says to his fellow, Cast out the mote out of thine eye, he will retort, Cast out the beam out of thine own eye " (Erachin, 16*b*). The same proverb also occurs in Baba Bathra, 15*b*.

Mr. Montefiore has an excellent comment on these few verses : " Jesus does not condemn *all* kinds of tit for tat, and here is a case in which he says that God Himself will act upon that principle " (*S.G.* p. 546). He also says that the ideas in these verses " are much the same as those also found in Rabbinic literature " (ibid. p. 547). Bischoff (op. cit. p. 89) objects to the quotation from the Mishna Sota about " measure for measure," because it was added, he says, by the compiler of the Mishna, Rabbi Jehuda the Prince, about 200 C.E. It was not, however, said for the first time by Rabbi Jehuda. Rabbi Meir, a contemporary of Luke and Matthew, who taught in the second decade of the second century C.E., is reported to have made use of the proverb. Thus the Talmud (Sota, 8*b*) states :— Rabbi Meir said : " Whence can it be proved that ' with the same measure with which a man measures, so shall it be measured to him ? ' " Such a method of quoting this expression clearly implies that Rabbi Meir was merely using a well-known proverb. Bischoff admits this, and thus answers his own objection as to the validity of using this parallel. Dalman also acknowledges the parallel between the Talmud and the Gospel in this instance.

I venture to suggest that the first two verses were originally intended to prohibit all kinds of judging, whether private or public. They contain part of the new teaching, and go beyond the old teaching of the Jews, who were not commanded to abstain from the right to pass judgment upon the actions and characters of their neighbours. The next three verses are, as we have seen, well-known proverbs teaching men not to be censorious in their judgments. They have no real connexion with the preceding verses, which prohibit judgment in every case, except to modify the impossible precept " Judge not." We have noted in dealing with divorce (Mark x. 2–12) how one report of Jesus' teaching is in no wise qualified, and how again elsewhere there is a modified form of the original teaching, which was found to be impracticable without some qualification or exception (Matt. v. 31, 32). The next verse (6) is as follows : " Give not that which is holy unto the dogs, neither cast your pearls before the swine, lest haply they trample them under their feet, and turn and rend you." I readily admit that this is one of the few original sayings to be found in the Sermon on the Mount. I cannot adduce any parallel from Philo, Josephus, the Talmud, or the Hellenistic Apocryphal literature. It is surprising that Mr. Montefiore should assert, " there seems little doubt that the dogs and the pigs are opprobrious Jewish appellations for the heathen " (op. cit. p. 547). Mr. Montefiore does not appear to be usually very anxious to refer the fine sayings of Jesus to the Rabbis, but as soon as a harsh statement is attributed to Jesus, Mr. Montefiore will not allow him to have been its author. I challenge the statement that " dogs and pigs are opprobrious Jewish appellations for the heathen." Although this verse has no parallel in the Gospels, Jesus, on another occasion, refers to the heathens as " dogs," or " little dogs " (Matt. xv. 26, and Mark vii. 27). Mr. Montefiore, who is so ready to admit the originality of so much of the teaching attributed to Jesus, might with perfect truth have reckoned this saying as one of the original elements in the Gospel teaching. Dr. Martineau speaks of this sentence as " an ebullition of scorn and insult " (*The Seat of Autho-*

rity in Religion, 5th ed., p. 658, quoted in *S.G.*, p. 547).
Again, Mr. Montefiore in his commentary (Mark vii. 27)
remarks that " dog " was " a frequent term of abuse
and contempt used by Jews about Gentiles " (*S.G.*, p.
178). There is, indeed, no Jewish or Rabbinical foundation for this opinion. Dr. Cheyne says that " in later
times the Gentiles were called dogs (Nidda, 77*a*, Baba
Kama, 49*a*) ; but the Talmudic use has no Biblical
authority ; Mark vii. 27 surely does not express what
may be called Biblical doctrine " (*Enc. Bib.* col. 1, 125).
We are grateful to Dr. Cheyne for his admission that
the Old Testament does not employ the term " dog " as
an opprobrious appellation for the heathen. Dr. Cheyne
is, however, quite mistaken in thinking that the Talmud
makes use of this term of abuse. The references to the
Talmud given by Dr. Cheyne are not quite correct.
There is no passage Nidda, 77*a* ; 73*a* is the last page
of this book. Nidda, 77*a* is due probably to a printer's
error, and we suggest that Nidda, 17*a* was the reference
intended by Dr. Cheyne. If this be so, we find that
there is no reference on this folio to " dog " as a term
of abuse. The other reference, Baba Kama, 49*a*, is
equally unfortunate ; it does not use " dog " as a designation of the heathen. On the other hand, there is
positive evidence that " dog " was a frequent term of
abuse and contempt used by Jesus in the Gospels and
by the other New Testament writings. In the Second
Epistle General of Peter, the heretics who were opponents of the Church are attacked and condemned : " It
has happened unto them according to the true proverb,
The dog turning to his own vomit again, and the sow
that had washed to wallowing in the mire " (ii. 22, cf.
Rev. xxii. 15). In Paul's epistle to the Philippians he

writes : " Beware of the dogs, beware of the evil workers " (iii. 2). Whether Paul refers here to the heathen or to his opponents the Judaizing Christians (as Dr. Hoennicke, op. cit., p. 145 believes) is quite immaterial. The fact is established that Christians, and not Jews, used " dog " as a term of abuse. It also occurs in the Didache, where Jesus' use of the term, as recorded in the Gospels, is quoted. The Didache lays down the rule : " Let no one eat or drink of your holy things (i.e. the Eucharist) except those baptized into the name of the Lord, for in regard to this the Lord hath said : ' Give not that which is holy to the dogs ' " (ix. 5). The " dogs " clearly refer not only to the heathens but also to the Jews (see Holtzmann, *Hand-Commentar*, p. 123).

Bishop Gore follows the usual interpretation of Matthew vii. 6, by saying that it teaches " reserve in communicating religious privileges and religious truths. . . . The Church would explain herself in apologies and dissipate misconceptions, but it was not her way to press her innermost truths upon the indifferent " (op. cit. p. 174).

The efforts of the present Bishop of London and his followers in pressing Christianity upon the poor, ignorant Jews who have sought a refuge from persecution in this land of freedom are not in harmony with this teaching of Jesus, according to Bishop Gore's explanation. The following parallels from Rabbinical writings illustrate this modern interpretation of this very troublesome text. Hillel's predecessor, Abtalyon, said : " Ye sages, be heedful of your words, lest ye incur the penalty of exile, and be exiled to a place of evil waters, and the disciples who come after you drink thereof and die, and the Heavenly Name be profaned " (Aboth i. 11). Hillel said : " When people gather in, then thou must scatter, and when people scatter, then must thou gather in. When thou seest that the Law of God is precious to Israel and all rejoice therein, then shalt thou scatter " (thy instruction), as it is said, " There is he that scattereth, and increaseth yet more " (Prov. xi. 24). When thou seest that the Law is forgotten in Israel and all are not concerned therewith, then shalt thou gather in, as it is said, " It is time for the Lord to work, for they have made void thy Law " (Ps. cxix. 126 ; Tosephta Berachoth, vii. 24 ; and cf. Berachoth, 63*a*).

Dr. Bischoff informs us (op. cit. p. 91) that the earliest reference in Jewish literature to the expression " Cast not your pearls before the swine " is to be found in Gabirol's Mibchar Happenenim (*The Choice of Pearls*), chapter i. This interesting fact was discussed sixty years ago by Leopold Dukes in the *Literaturblatt des Orients*, 1850, pp. 440, 459. Gabirol found this Gospel saying in the Arabic literature. It occurs in Algazali. The Gospel use of the term " dog and swine," as appellations for the heathens, discloses the spirit of exclusiveness that characterized the teaching of Jesus. His kingdom was not for all humanity, only for his followers who had faith in him. His new teaching—the Gospel of the Kingdom—was not proclaimed to all, but was given intentionally in the form of parables, so that only the immediate circle of disciples should comprehend ; whilst to those without—the people at large— " all things are done in parables ; that seeing they may see, and not perceive ; and hearing, they may hear, and not understand ; lest haply they should repent and it should be forgiven them " (Mark iv. 11, 12, and Matt. xiii. 11, 13) Wellhausen explains Matthew vii. 6,

" Give not that which is holy," as referring to the " King-dom " or " Gospel teaching." The " dogs " are, of course, the heathens, in accordance with Matthew x. 5 : " Go not into any way of the Gentiles, and enter not into any city of the Samaritans." Jesus had no mis-sion for the heathen world. The Church in the first century followed his teaching, but Paul rejected it. He—a Pharisee of the Pharisees—knew only too well that Jesus had no new Gospel for Israel. The message of Jesus was only for the heathen nations, who were gradually to be weaned from idolatry to the belief in an eternal God. Paul felt that it was an impossible task to lead the heathen straight to God. He accord-ingly taught the mediatorship of Jesus, who, on the analogy of the heathen mythology of the Romans and Greeks, became the only son of God, sent to redeem the world at the cost of his life (see *Enc. Bib.*, col. 3,628 ; and Pfleiderer's *Primitive Christianity*, i. ch. xv.).

One of the latest views as to the meaning of " dogs and swine " in the Sermon on the Mount is that of Dr. Friedrich Spitta (*Jesus und die Heidenmission*, p. 53). His theory is that verse 6 of Matthew vii. should be fol-lowed by v. 13 : " Enter ye in by the narrow way " ; and the sense given by this combination is, that the disciples should avoid false prophets and teachers. We fail to see the cogency of this interpretation, as in the latter part of chapter vii. we find a caution against false prophets (v. 15). It is hardly likely that this subject would be repeated in the same section of the chapter. Again, Dr. Spitta ignores Matthew xv. 26 : " It is not meet to take the children's bread and cast it to the dogs." Jesus clearly implies that the Jews were the " children " and the Gentiles were the " dogs."

The remarkable manner in which the Rev. David Smith, in Dr. Hastings' *D.C.G.*, plays with Rabbinical quotations is instructive. Sometimes he gives a Latin version, at other times the English translation of the Hebrew original. His remarks in explaining " dog " in Mark vii. 27, merit our best attention. He writes : " He (i.e. Jesus) was not speaking after the heartless and insolent manner of the Rabbis, who branded the Gentiles as ' dogs ' (cf. Megill. Ex. xii. 6) ; ' An holy convocation to you ; to you, not to dogs ; to you, not to strangers ' " (*D.C.G.*, ii. p. 447). The writer would be surprised to learn that there is no such book as " Megillah Exodus." He is clearly quoting second-hand or third-hand information. Mechilta is the name of the book in which this Rabbinic quotation is found. We would also like to point out that, as in the second clause, " to you, not to strangers," the Gentiles are referred to ; in the first clause, " to you—not to dogs," a totally different meaning is conveyed. It refers to actual dogs in a literal sense. This interpretation is in harmony with the text of Exodus xii. 16 (not xii. 6, as Mr. Smith writes), and xxii. 31. " Dog " occurs twice in Exodus, xi. 7 and xxii. 31. In each case it refers to the animal, and cannot possibly be interpreted as a term meaning Gentiles, as we have already seen that Dr. Cheyne admits that there is no biblical use of " dog " as a term of abuse. Mr. Smith gives another reference : " Pirk. Eliez. 29." It will surely be admitted that it is hardly fair to quote the Pirke de Rabbi Eliezer as a Rabbinic book contemporary with the Gospels, or with the latest books of the New Testament. Zunz (*Gottesdienstliche Vorträge*, p. 289) fixes the eighth century c.e. as the earliest date of its composition. Mr. Smith speaks several times of " R. Hillel." This, also, is an error. Hillel is never called " Rabbi." We will leave the statement of Mr. Smith, and only add one remark: In future, when Christian scholars speak of the " heartless and insolent manner of the Rabbis," we fervently hope that the original writings of these Rabbis will be studied and quoted. Not only should we judge in the scale of merit, but also in the scale of truth.

LITERATURE

In addition to the Commentaries on the Gospels, for ' Proverbs in the Gospels,' see Jülicher, *Die Gleichnisreden Jesu* (1910). A good collection of Rabbinic proverbs is to be found in G. Levi, *Parabeln, Legenden und Gedanken aus Talmud und Midrasch* (ed. Seligman). Dukes, *Blumenlese* and *Zur Rabbinischen Spruchkunde* will be found useful.

NOTE TO PAGE 219

The expression ' dogs and swine' occurs also in the *Fragments of an Uncanonical Gospel* from Oxyrhynchus, ed. Grenfell and Hunt (1908) p. 17, in the conversation in the Temple between Jesus and the High Priest. The expression is used by Jesus. On the non-Jewish origin of the term see Heinrici, *Bergpredigt* p. 82 f. and see also Clemen, *Religionsgeschichtliche Erklärung des N.T.* p. 37.

NOTE TO PAGE 223

D. H. Müller (op. cit. p. 46) has suggested that originally Matthew vi., 19–24, was followed by Matthew vii., 7–13. His argument is based on the parallelism that is to be found in these two sections.

CHAPTER XVII

THE JEWISH ORIGIN OF THE GOLDEN RULE

THE next section of the Sermon on the Mount (Matt. vii. 7–11) deals with encouragement to prayer. Dr. Spitta (op. cit. p. 52) suggests that this part of the Sermon has been misplaced. He argues that it belongs to the fifth chapter of Matthew, because the next verse of this section (Matt. vii. 12) has its parallel in Luke vi. 31, which is part of the paragraph dealing with the new law of loving one's enemies (27–38). Consequently the preceding verses in Matthew vii. (7–11) should follow verse 42 in the fifth chapter of that book, because verses 39–42 in this chapter correspond to Luke vi. 29, 30. This seems to be confirmed by the fact that the verb αἰτεῖν (to ask) occurs in Matthew vii. 7 and also in v. 42. Thus far Dr. Spitta. The theory is most suggestive and would restore the connexion which is now lacking in the seventh chapter of Matthew.

The main idea underlying the teaching in Matthew vii. 7–11, is that the Heavenly Father never disappoints his children. We have met with this lesson in an earlier part of the Sermon (Matt. vi. 8). The text (vii. 7–11) is as follows : " Ask, and it shall be given you ; seek, and ye shall find ; knock, and it shall be opened unto you : for every one that asketh receiveth ; and he that seeketh findeth ; and to him that knocketh it shall be opened.

Or what man is there of you, who, if his son shall ask him for a loaf, will give him a stone ; or if he shall ask for a fish, will give him a serpent ? If ye then, being evil, know how to give good gifts unto your children, how much more shall your Father who is in heaven give good things to them that ask him ? " In Luke xi. 9–13, a somewhat different text is to be found. Instead of Matthew's " good things " (v. 11), Luke has " holy Spirit " (v. 13). I am inclined to believe that Matthew's text is in this instance earlier than Luke's.

Commentators speak of a " rough resemblance " between the things contrasted, namely, a loaf and a stone, a fish and a serpent, or according to Luke (xi. 12) between an egg and a scorpion. I fail to see the least resemblance. If a child is old enough to ask for bread, fish, or an egg, he will have sufficient common sense to recognize in the stone, serpent, or scorpion something useless and harmful. Every child knows by instinct that his parents will never give him what he cannot eat. Likewise men know by instinct that the gifts of God are for their benefit. The Rabbis teach the same lesson : " Whatever God does is entirely good " (Berachoth, 6ob). " God never deals harshly with his creatures," i.e. Jew and Gentile (Aboda Zara, 3a). That God is as merciful as man is repeatedly emphasized by the Scriptures: " As a father pitieth his children, so the Lord pitieth them that fear him " (Ps. ciii. 13). Another parallel is given by Ecclesiasticus (xviii. 13), which contrasts human sympathy, which is limited with Divine mercy, which is infinite : " The mercy of a man is upon his neighbour, but the mercy of the Lord is upon all flesh." The Jew who wrote 2 Esdras (often called 4 Ezra) entreats divine pity for the many called, of whom only a few will be chosen. He is assured that God's mercy and love exceed that of man : " For thou comest far short that thou shouldst be able to love my creature more than I " (viii. 47). This is earlier than the Gospels. It is also the teaching in the passage of the Sermon which we are now considering. But we have not found in the Gospels any teaching as to the loving Fatherhood of God excelling the comforting assurance of Isaiah : " But Zion said, God hath forsaken me, and the Lord hath forgotten me. Can a woman forget her sucking child, that she should not have compassion on the son of her womb ? yea, these may forget, yet will I not forget thee " (xlix. 14, 15).

Philo speaks of God being towards the world, what parents are to their children. God is the Father (*On Providence*, Mangey ii. p. 635). In his treatise on the Special Laws, he refers again to the analogy that exists between our parents on earth and our Father in Heaven (*Honouring Parents*, § 1. Tauchnitz ed. of Philo v. p. 55). Let us turn our attention to the first verse of our passage in the Sermon. The injunction to pray is thrice repeated, " ask—seek—knock," in order to emphasize the duty of prayer. Jesus promises his disciples that their prayers shall be answered by God. " Ask and it shall be given "—there is no qualification. This verse is somewhat contrary to the earlier teaching in the Sermon (Matt. vi. 7, 8) where the Gentile custom of persistent prayer is deprecated. It is a hopeless task to attempt to reconcile the contradictions of the Gospels.

This section of the Sermon does not meet with the approval of Mr. Montefiore. He writes : " Doubtless Jesus assigned to prayer a higher power than we can assign it to-day. . . . One can, let us hope, have faith, and yet not have this wholesale belief in the efficacy of unrestricted prayer " (*S.G.*, p. 549). We will now suggest a few parallels to this part of the Sermon.

Matthew's " fish and serpent " and Luke's " egg and scorpion " (xi. 12) were probably derived from the current Greek proverb : " For a perch a scorpion " (see Jülicher, op. cit. ii. p. 39). " Ask and it shall be given " seems to recall, " Ask thy father and he will shew thee " (Deut. xxxii. 7). Another parallel is, " Ask of me, and I will give thee " (Ps. ii. 8).

The next phrase in the Sermon, " seek, and ye shall find " has probably been borrowed from Proverbs (viii. 17) : " And those that seek me diligently shall find me " ; or from Jeremiah (xxix. 13) : " And ye shall seek me, and find me." Isaiah has also a similar passage : " Seek ye the Lord while he may be found " (lv. 6), see also 1 Chronicles xxviii. 9 and 2 Chronicles xv. 2. The next expression, " Knock, and it shall be opened unto you " may be paralleled by the sweet words in the Song of Songs (v. 2) : " It is the voice of my beloved that knocketh (saying), open to me." The " bread and stone " phrase does not occur in the Old Testament. An interesting passage in Seneca may be the source of this strange expression. Fabius Verrucosus used to compare a benefit conferred by a harsh man in an offensive manner to a stone loaf (*panem lapidosum*) which a hungry man is forced to receive, but which he cannot eat (*de Beneficiis*, ii. 7).

There can be no doubt that the authors of the New Testament made good use not only of the Jewish writings, but also borrowed freely from the Stoic literature. Seneca was born before the Christian Era and died in 65 C.E. The chapter on the Stoics in Mr. Glover's *Conflict of Religions in the Early Roman Empire*, will repay reading. The best modern literature on the ethics and theology of the Stoics is given by Mr. Glover in the footnotes of this chapter. We will just add a few passages, not mentioned by Mr. Glover, to illustrate our contention that the writings of Seneca were used by the New Testament authors. Thus, " God is no respecter of nations, ranks, or conditions, but all, barbarian and Roman, bond and free, are alike under his all-seeing Providence " (*de Beneficiis*, iii. 18). This has been used by Paul who says : " there can be neither Jew nor Greek, neither bond nor free, neither male nor female, for ye are all one in Jesus " (Gal. iii. 28). Again, " God dwells not in temples of wood and stone, nor wants the ministrations of human hands " (Ep. 95). Did Luke copy this when he wrote : " Howbeit the Most High dwelleth not in houses made with hands " (Acts vii. 48) ? Finally " The Holy Spirit resides within us " (Ep. 46), reappears in Luke's famous saying : " the Kingdom of God is within you " (xvii. 21).

Now to pass to the consideration of the most famous verse of the entire Sermon : "All things therefore whatsoever ye would that men should do unto you, even so do ye also unto them : for this is the Law and the Prophets " (Matt. vii. 12). Luke's parallel is slightly different : " And as ye would that men should do to you, do ye also to them likewise " (vi. 31). The position in which Luke places this verse is most instructive. He is speaking of the Law of Love and explaining how it should be carried out (see vv. 27–30). He then gives the ' Golden Rule ', and continues his interpretation of the Law of Love. In other words, the Golden Rule is an interpretation or paraphrase (Targum) of the Old Testament Law of Love, found in Leviticus (xix. 18) : " love thy neigh-

bour as thyself." Such a Targum is the negative form
in Tobit (iv. 15) : " And what thou thyself hatest, do
to no man." This is identical with the expression of
Hillel (Sabbath, 31*a*) : " What is hateful to thee, do not
to thy neighbour." This negative rule is still preserved
in the Targum pseudo-Jonathan ben Uzziel, who also
has the positive form of Onkelos (Lev. xix. 18) : " A
man should show love to his fellow by not doing to him
what he dislikes when done to himself."

Matthew's words after the Rule, stating its source,
" for this is the Law, and the Prophets " are naturally
omitted by Luke. The " Law " and the " Prophets "
would not appeal to his Gentile readers. Matthew's
preservation of these words is, however, of great interest,
because it establishes the fact that the Golden Rule was
quite Jewish—it *was* " the Law and the Prophets."
Many critics believe that this verse (12) formed the true
end of Matthew's Sermon on the Mount. Mr. Montefiore holds that " the Golden Rule sums up all the demands and injunctions of the Sermon. . . . The close
Rabbinic parallel, which in this case goes back to Hillel,
and is therefore earlier than Jesus, is put in a negative
form . . . if an undoubtedly authentic saying of Hillel
were to be discovered in the positive form, every Jewish
writer would, I fancy, be rather pleased, while every
Christian writer would, I fancy, be rather sorry " (*S.G.*,
p. 550).

In 1909, before Mr. Montefiore's commentary on the
Synoptic Gospels was published, I had issued my pamph-
let, *The Law of Love in the Old and New Testaments.*
In chapter v. of this pamphlet, I dealt with the Golden
Rule. I pointed out that the Golden Rule is Jewish
and has not only a negative form, but also a positive

form. The origin of Hillel's and Jesus' versions of the Golden Rule is the *positive* commandment of Leviticus xix. 18 : " Love thy neighbour as thyself." This is the source of several forms of the Golden Rule to be found in Jewish literature. Thus, Rabbi Elazar ben Arach said, " Let thy neighbour's honour be as dear to thee as thine own " (Aboth ii. 15). In *Aboth de Rabbi Nathan* this saying is expanded : " Just as a man sees to his own honour and reputation, so let him see to his neighbour's, and just as he does not like an evil report to be spread concerning his own character, so let him desire not to spread an evil report concerning his neighbour " (chap. xv. p. 60, ed. Schechter). This is interesting, because we have the positive and negative forms combined. Another Rabbi paraphrased the Mosaic law of love in this wise : Let the property (Mammon) of thy neighbour be as dear to thee as thine own (Aboth ii. 17). This is also positive. Again, just as a man looks [with a good eye] upon his own home so let him look upon the home of his neighbour (Aboth de Rabbi Nathan, xvi. p. 62).

In addition to these positive forms of the Golden Rule, there is another one considerably earlier than Jesus : " Consider thy neighbour's liking by thine own " (Ecclus. xxxi. 15). This disposes of the following passage in the *Encyclopædia Biblica*, col. 2,444 : " Analogies [to the Golden Rule of Matthew vii. 12] can be found in other religions, but with this difference, that, whilst in the teaching of Jesus the rule assumes a positive form, in *all* other known instances it is given negatively. The negative confines us to the region of justice ; the positive takes us into the region of generosity ; for we wish more than we can claim, or than the average man is willing to do to others." Johannes Weiss (p. 275) adds that Jesus' saying surpasses the Jewish principle, which is only negative. Weiss only refers to Hillel's use of the negative form of the Rule, and following him, Mr. Montefiore, too, ignores the several positive forms to be found in Jewish literature of the pre-Christian age. The story of Hillel is well known, but very rarely is full justice done to its meaning. The heathen who came to Hillel and asked to be taught the *whole* law in the minute or two during which he was able to stand on one foot was not doing that which he would like to have suffered at the hands of some one else. Judaism is a simple system of ethics and not an intricate compendium of philosophy or theology. Hillel had to meet the case of this heathen, who needed a summary of Jewish teaching best calculated to bring home to him the unworthy attitude he had adopted. What could be more practical than the negative form of the Golden Rule, " What is hateful to thee to suffer at the hands of another, do not do to thy fellow man " ? (Sabbath, 31*a*). Eusebius has preserved a similar form of the rule used by Philo : " Moreover, it is ordained in the Laws themselves that no one shall do to his neighbour what he would be unwilling to have done to himself " (*Preparation of the Gospel*, viii. 7. 6). It also occurs in the Letter of Aristeas (ed. Thackeray, p. 39). This interesting document was written by a Jew, according to Wendland, between 96 and 63 B.C.E., about a century before Jesus' ministry. J. Weiss and Mr. Montefiore fail to speak of the use of the negative form of the Golden Rule by the New Testament and the Early Church. In the Western text of Acts xv. 20, 29 we have the reading : " And whatsoever they do not wish to be done to them, not to do that to others " ; " And whatsoever ye do not wish to be done to yourselves, do not ye to another " (see Holtzmann, *Hand-Commentar* i. p. 125 and Knowling's note *in loc.* in *Expos. Greek Testament*). In Paul's Epistle to the Romans we read : " For he that loveth his neighbour hath fulfilled the law. For this, Thou shalt not commit adultery, Thou shalt not kill, Thou shalt not steal, Thou shalt not covet, and if there be any other commandment, it is summed up in this word, namely, Thou shalt love thy neighbour as thyself. Love worketh *no* ill to his neighbour : love therefore is the fulfilment of the law " (xiii. 8–10). This is an excellent example of the Rabbinical method of interpreting the precept of love. Paul, like Hillel, prefers the negative paraphrase. This preference is shared also by the Didache i. 2 : " And all things whatsoever thou wouldst not have done to thee, neither do thou unto another." Other examples are Const. Apost. vii. 1 ; Clement of Alexandria, Strom. ii. 23 and 139 ; and Tertullian, adv. Marc. iv. 16.

In all these instances we find the negative form and not the exceptional positive form found in Ben Sirach and the Gospels. The negative form also occurs in Epictetus (Fragments, 42 ; see Westermarck, *Origin and Development of the Moral Ideas*, i. p. 693), and in Seneca (*de Beneficiis*, ii. 1). The question arises, Why did the great Church Fathers prefer the negative form to the positive form ? It seems that the negative form, which is said to confine us to the region of justice, is much more practical than the positive form, which takes us into the region of generosity. " Be just before you are generous " applies in this case. People must learn the lesson of strict justice before they aim at the higher principle of generosity. Dr. Emil G. Hirsch, in the *Jewish*

Encyclopedia (vi. p. 22), prefers the negative form, because, " What you would have others do unto you," makes self and possible advantages to self the central motive ; " what is hateful to you do not unto another " makes the effect upon others the regulating principle. It seems to me, however, that the *practical value* of the negative form was the determining factor in making this form of the Golden Rule so popular with both Jewish and Christian teachers. Most laws are given in the negative form, and the Golden Rule is no exception, although as we have seen, it was originally given in the positive form. Thomas Hobbes, no mean authority on political philosophy, sums up the various Laws of Nature in the one Universal Maxim, " Do not that to another which thou wouldst not have done to thyself " (*Leviathan* xv. and xvii. see Sidgwick, *History of Ethics*, 3rd ed. p. 167, and Graham, *English Political Philosophy*, p. 13). Many modern commentators regard the Golden Rule as identical with Kant's ethical maxim : " So act as to treat humanity, whether in thine own person or in that of any other, in every case as an end withal, never as a means only " (Hastings' *D.B.*, v., p. 42 and Bishop Gore, *Sermon on the Mount*, p. 182). In other words the positive Golden Rule is identical with the negative precept " do not exploit," which is used so often by modern teachers of ethics. We are not to have one standard for our neighbours and another for ourselves. As Bishop Gore says (op. cit. p. 182) : " We are to love our neighbour as ourselves. We are to remember that every one in God's sight counts for one ; and that nobody counts for more than one. This, I say, is the principle of all Christian social conduct." The Bishop would have been nearer the truth, if he had said that " this is the

236 SOURCES OF SERMON ON THE MOUNT

principle of all Jewish social conduct." His own words,
" we are to love our neighbour as ourselves," are taken
from the Jewish Law (Lev. xix. 18).

We have already seen that the Golden Rule is but a
Targum of this fundamental precept. " Love your
neighbour as yourself " means " do as you would be
done by." John Stuart Mill found in these words the
expression of the ideal perfection of utilitarian morality
(*Utilitarianism*, p. 323). Bishop Gore only credits the
Jews with the negative form of the Golden Rule. Dr.
Tasker in Hastings' *D.C.G.*, i. p. 653, and Professor
Votaw in *D.B.*, v. p. 42, hold the same view. Bishop
Gore adds : " But one great superiority of Jesus over
other teachers lies in the positive character of his teachings " (op. cit. p. 181). Professor Votaw (*D.B.*, v. p. 42)
sings the same song in another key : " Jesus, however,
so changed the wording of this principle as to give it a
new force and sphere, for he stated it—not negatively,
as it everywhere else appears, but *positively*, insisting
upon the loving service to others which is peculiar to the
Gospel." Professor Votaw has forgotten the pre-Christian positive forms in Ecclesiasticus xxxi. 15, and the
original positive precept in Leviticus xix. 18. Then we
are told by Professor Votaw : " Legalism says, ' Thou
shalt not ' do this and that— a system of repression ;
the Gospel of Life says, ' Thou shalt do countless good
and helpful things '—a system of development." The
Professor must be aware that the Gospel of Jesus, as
exemplified by the Sermon on the Mount, contains very
many negative precepts, e.g. " Swear not at all "
(Matt. v. 34) ; or " resist not evil " (ibid. 39) ; or " do
not do your righteousness before men " (vi. 1) ; or " lay
not up for yourselves treasures " (ibid. 19) and so on.

Repression or asceticism is not unknown in the Gospel (Matt. v. 29, 30).

By all means let us admit that the Golden Rule in the positive form, which is preserved in the Gospels, is of the greatest value. But let us be honest and acknowledge that it had been uttered in its *positive* form by Jewish teachers centuries before Jesus was born. Dr. Bischoff (op. cit. p. 93) lays the greatest stress on the fact that Philo, Tobit, and Hillel have the negative form of the Rule. He also makes no reference to the pre-Christian Jewish teaching of the Rule in its positive form. Further, he ignores the fact that the Didache and the Early Church Fathers as well as the New Testament use the negative form. To these Christian sources as well as to Tobit, Philo and Hillel, Bischoff must apply his criticism " that there is all the difference in the world between ' Neminem laede ' and ' Omnes jura.' " " Hillel's rule would be best fulfilled by the dead in the grave "— must apply to Paul and the other Christian authorities who have used Hillel's rule.

Seneca has the positive form : " The question remains, In what way should a deed of love (beneficium) be bestowed ? On this point I think I can show the readiest way ; let us give in the way in which we should wish to receive " (*de Beneficiis* ii. 1). I do not think that the Gospels were indebted to Seneca for this saying. There was no need to borrow from the Roman, when the Jews had the same teaching even in its positive form. If only one would pay a little more attention to the actual facts and let the Gospel tell its own story, we should hear less of the contrast between Jesus' teaching and that of the Rabbis, and instead of this, our attention would be drawn by Christian scholars to the common ground that unites the best teaching of the Gospel with the Pharisaic teaching current among the Jews when Jesus lived and taught. As we have already stated, the Golden Rule is declared by the First Gospel to be no new and strange principle, but " this *is* the law and the prophets." Jesus himself admits that this rule is not his own, but belongs to the teaching which he, in common with every Jew, received as the " heritage of the congregation of Jacob."

The old law of love of Leviticus xix. 18, which is paraphrased in the Golden Rule, occurs eight times in the New Testament, testifying to the imperishable value of this fundamental law of life and religion. We can understand that Rabbi Akiba considered the precept : " Love thy neighbour as thyself " as the all-inclusive summary of the Law. His contemporary, Simeon ben Azzai, agreed that this law of love was the summary of the Torah if read in conjunction with Genesis v. 1 : " This is the book of the history of *Man.*" This verse was the most important passage in the Bible, said Ben Azzai, showing that the Hebrew Scriptures are the charter of Humanity. What is in the Bible is for Man, especially the Royal Law, " Love thy neighbour as thyself " (Siphra Kedoshim c. 4, and see Jer. Nedarim x. 5., 41*c* and Genesis Rabba, xxiv. 7).

LITERATURE

For the influence of Seneca in the composition of the New Testament see Bauer, *Christus und die Cæsaren ;* Havet, *Le Christianisme et ses Origines.* On the Golden Rule see Dr. M. Güdemann's fine essay, *Die Nächstenliebe,* also Moritz Löwy, *Die Paulinische Lehre vom Gesetz* in *Monatsschrift für Geschichte und Wissenschaft des Judentums,* 1904, pp. 405 ff. ; J. Eschelbacher, *Das Judentum und das Wesen des Christentums,* p. 74 ; W. Bacher, *Agada der Tannaiten,* i., p. 4 ; Taylor's *Sayings of the Jewish Fathers,* pp. 142, 143 ; Bishop Westcott's *Two Empires,* p. 151, and Achad Ha'am in *Jewish Review,* i. 3.

CHAPTER XVIII

PREDESTINATION IN THE GOSPEL

THE epilogue to the Sermon on the Mount (vv. 13–27) contains three pairs of contrasts : the broad and the narrow ways, the good and the bad trees, and the well-built and the ill-built houses. The three sections are not connected with the preceding part of the Sermon. The first section in Matthew's recension is as follows :—
" Enter ye in by the narrow gate : for wide is the gate, and broad is the way, that leadeth to destruction, and many be they that enter in thereby. For narrow is the gate, and straitened the way, that leadeth unto life, and few be they that find it." In Luke (xiii. 23, 24) the saying occurs in a very different connexion, viz., in answer to the question, " Are they few that be saved ? "
" And (Jesus) said unto them, Strive to enter in by the narrow door : for many, I say unto you, shall seek to enter in and shall not be able." The First Evangelist has combined two totally distinct metaphors ; that of the two ways, and that of the two doors or gates. Then there is also a further implication which Luke emphasizes more strongly than Matthew, namely, that many are doomed to destruction whilst few are called to life eternal.

Let us first turn our attention to the well known metaphor of the *Two Ways*, which has been borrowed from the Old Testament and from pre-Christian writings of the Jews. This doctrine of the Two Ways is exceedingly interesting, and has played no small part in Jewish and Christian literature. We shall see that whilst in the Jewish writings, the doctrine of the Two Ways has implied Free Will ; in the Christian writings it has lost this colouring, and instead it has given place to the theory of Predestination.

The origin of the idea of the two ways of life is, I venture to suggest, to be sought in the Paradise story in Genesis. The tree of knowledge of good and evil was not to be touched by Adam and Eve (Gen. ii. 9, 17). Our first parents disobeyed and ate of this wonderful tree. Adam and Eve were then driven out of Paradise lest " he put forth his hand and take also of the tree of *life*, and eat, and live for ever ; therefore the Lord God . . . placed at the east of Paradise the Cherubim, with the flaming sword which turned every way to keep the *way of the tree of life* " (ibid. iii. 22–24). Here in Eden lay the way of life ; without was the way of death. Adam was doomed to die for his disobedience. Gunkel points out that it was reserved for the latest apocalyptic literature of the Jews to teach that even now Paradise is open to the righteous, and that in the future all good people will enjoy life eternal in Paradise (*Genesis*, 2nd ed. p. 21). True it is, that Judaism alone of all religions looks forward to a glorious future. Nevertheless it is possible for man even now to earn the right to enter Paradise. His birth as a Jew or Gentile affords no privilege or right. His life's conduct is the only standard whereby he is judged as worthy or not worthy of the future bliss. Some deserve eternal life by the work of a lifetime, and some obtain it by the merit of an hour's devotion to the service of God and man (Aboda Zara, 10*b*). Gunkel (op. cit. p. 6) gives several Old Testament references to the Tree of Life, namely (Prov. iii. 18 ; xi. 30 ; xiii. 12 ; and xv. 4). He also refers to the spring of eternal water that gives immortality (Prov. x. 11 ; xiii. 14 ; xiv. 27 ; xvi. 22 ; and Ps. xxxvi. 9).

Judaism teaches that righteousness, holiness, and goodness are some of the sources of eternal life, and are at the disposal of *all* the children of men (Siphra, Achrê Moth, xiii. 13). There is no question of privilege of birth, Jew and Gentile can inherit alike the future world on the same condition. " The pious (Chasidim) of all people will enjoy the bliss of the world to come " (Tosephta Synhedrin, xiii. 2, and Synhedrin, 105*a*). The heirs of the Kingdom of God are all who love truth and goodness. " I call heaven and earth to witness, whether one be a Gentile or an Israelite, a man or a woman, a slave (male or female)—that it is only in accordance with the deeds of his or her life that the Holy Spirit rests on him or her " (*Tana de bê Elijahu,* p. 48). Although the book, from which this quotation is taken, was finally written in 974 C.E. (*Zunz, Gottesdienstliche Vorträge,* 2nd ed., p. 119), there can be no doubt that Friedmann is right in recognizing in parts of this book, one of the oldest sources of ethics (Siphrê Hachasidim) used by the Talmud and Midrashim (see Introduction to *Tana de bê Elijahu,* p. 48).

But there is no need to turn to the admirable sayings of the Rabbis for the *universality* of the message of Judaism. The Scriptures speak of God as the *Lord of Hosts,* the God of *all* spirits. He is the Creator and God of humanity. Micah (vi. 8) cries : " He hath shewed thee, O *man,* what is good ; and what doth the Lord require of thee, but to do justly, and to love mercy, and to walk humbly with thy God." There is no reference to Israel or to any particular people. It is the universal appeal of God to humanity. The Psalmist speaks of the " Gate of the Lord " into which the righteous enter (cxviii. 20). The Siphra comments as follows :—" No mention is made here of Priest, or of Levite, or of Israelite ; but all the children of men (Jew and Gentile) can enter the Gate of God (i.e. eternal life in God's Kingdom) as it is written : " The *righteous* shall enter " (Achrê Moth, xiii. 13). This gate is unlike the narrow gate of the Gospel. It is exceedingly wide ; it is the gate of all the noble souls of humanity. The sin of Adam and Eve was not transmitted to their children. Judaism has again and again rejected the horrible doctrine of the heredity of sin, which is the kernel, the life-centre of New Testament theology and the justification of its soteriology. Most emphatically we assert that nowhere, in the whole of the Old Testament, do we find a single reference to the transmission of Adam's sin to his descendants. Just the opposite theory is expressly enunciated. Noah and all his descendants become a party to a new divine covenant of life. Abraham and his seed are chosen to become a blessing to humanity. Enoch and Elijah walk with God. There is no such thing, according to Jewish theology, as the actual necessary sinfulness of any man arising from the assumed generic guilt of mankind. Every man must answer for his own sin, and nobody else can be responsible for the guilt of his fellow. The eldest son of Adam and Eve was reminded by God that he had free will to choose between good and evil. There was no taint in his soul. The sin of his parents was not transmitted to him. God said, " Sin coucheth at the door ; and unto thee shall be its desire, *but thou shalt rule* over it " (Gen. iv. 7). Man can overcome temptation and sin. " Everything is in the hand of Heaven, except the fear of Heaven " (Berachoth, 33*b*). God rules all things, except the heart of man. The belief in inherited sin and the belief in the need of a Saviour, who had to die to save fallen humanity from the wrath of an offended deity are conceptions entirely un-Jewish and completely at variance with the teaching of the Law and Prophets. Paradise, the way of eternal life, is still open to all who seek to enter therein.

The next stage in the development of the idea of the " *Two Ways* " is to be found in Deuteronomy (xxx. 15, 16), where we read :—" See, I have set before thee this day life and good, and death and evil ; in that I have commanded thee this day to love the Lord thy God, to walk in his ways, and to keep his commandments and his judgments, that thou mayest live." Again, we find :—" I call heaven and earth to witness against you this day, that I have set before thee life and death, the blessing and the curse : *therefore choose life, that thou mayest live,* thou and thy seed : to love the Lord thy God, to obey his voice, and to cleave unto him, for he is thy life " (ibid. vv. 19, 20). In Jeremiah we have the metaphor in its most perfect form :—" Thus saith the Lord, behold, I set before you the way of life and the way of death " (xxi. 8). The first Psalm (v. 6) also speaks of the way of the righteous and the way of the wicked. " The path of life " and " the way of life " occur in Psalm xvi. 11, and Proverbs vi. 23 respectively.

The earliest reference to the " Two Ways " in post

Biblical Jewish literature is in the *Testaments of the Twelve Patriarchs* : " Two ways hath God given to the sons of men and two inclinations " (Test. Asher i. 3 ; cf. i. 5, and Aboth ii. 12, 13 ; cf. Taylor's ed., pp. 147 ff.). The two ways are of " good " and " evil." Philo also speaks of the Two Ways :—" The path of pleasure is well frequented by men." Opposed to this is " the path of prudence, and temperance, and the other virtues, even though they may not be utterly untravelled, are, at all events, not beaten much, for the number of those who proceed by those roads, and who form associations with virtue alone, disregarding, once for all, all other allurements, is very small " (*On the Tilling of the Earth by Noah*, § 23, M. i. p. 316).

When Rabban Jochanan ben Zakkai, a contemporary of Jesus, was on his death-bed, he was surrounded by his disciples. He began to weep, and his disciples said : " Why weepest thou ? " " Because I am about to appear before God, the Eternal Judge. Two ways are before me, one leading to Paradise and the other leading to Gehenna " (T. B. Berachoth, 28*b*, and see Aboth de Rabbi Nathan, xxv. p. 79 ; Tamid, 28*a*, and Aboth ii. 1).

A further proof of the Jewish origin of the metaphor of the " Two Ways " is furnished by the Didache, which is based on an earlier Jewish catechism for proselytes. The Didache has preserved this metaphor in the opening verse :—" Two ways there are, one of life and one of death, but there is a great difference between the two ways. The way of life is this : First, thou shalt love the God who made thee ; secondly, thy neighbour as thyself " (i. 1). The same metaphor occurs in the " Apostolic Constitutions " (vii. 1) and in the Epistle

of Barnabas (xviii.), where the ways are " light " and
" darkness " respectively. The Shepherd of Hermas
(Mandatum vi. 1) speaks of " the straight " or righteous
way, and the " crooked " or perverse way. The next
verse of the Shepherd has : " There are two angels with
a man, one of righteousness and the other of iniquity."
This is exactly paralleled by the Talmud, which speaks
of a man being accompanied on Friday evening by a
good angel and a bad angel (T. B. Sabbath, 119b, and
see Moreh Nebuchim iii. 22). The pseudo-Clementine
Homilies (v. 7) also refer to the two ways, the broad
way of the lost and the narrow way of the saved. The
Gospel teaching has been imitated here. Clement of
Alexandria adds that the Gospel (Matt. vii. 13, 14)
speaks of two ways, as do likewise the Apostles (should
this be the Didache ?) *and all the prophets*. Clement's
testimony confirms our contention that the doctrine of
the " Two Ways " has been borrowed by the Gospels
from Judaism. The Gospels speak of the " door " or
" gate " as well as of the " way " leading to life and
destruction. Parallels can be found in the Old Testament. Thus, Genesis (iv. 7) speaks of " sin couching
at the *door* " ; Job (xxxviii. 17) is asked :—" Have
the *gates* of death been revealed to thee or hast thou
seen the *doors* of the shadow of death ? " The term
" gates of death " is also found in Psalm ix. 13. Hosea
ii. 15, speaks of " the door of hope," and the Psalms
(cxviii. 19) mention " the gates of righteousness."

The remaining part of this section of the Sermon
(Matt. vii. 13, 14) reads :—" Many be they that enter in
(the way to destruction) . . . and few be they that
find (the way that leadeth unto life)." This doctrine
does not occur in the Old Testament. The Rabbis

urge that man has free will, even as Scripture teaches :
" and thou shalt *choose* life " (Deut. xxx. 19). There
is no doubt that Jesus believed that only a very small
number of people would be permitted to enter the coming Kingdom. This teaching is practically identical
with the theory of predestination. Throughout the
whole of the Old Testament there is never the least
doubt as to the absolute freedom or moral responsibility
of man. Man's freedom is part of the all-embracing
plan of God in his rule of the world. God desires that
the sinner should repent and live (see Ezek. xviii. 21).
It would have been impossible for an Old Testament
writer to have penned the words of the Gospel, " for
many shall seek to enter and shall not be able to enter "
(Luke xiii. 24). The *desire* " to enter " entitles a man
to find God's grace. " Return to Me and I will return
to you " (Mal. iii. 7), is the teaching of the Old Testament. The Gospel says, even if you return and seek
admission it will be in vain. The Gospels and the other
New Testament writings have not only enlarged the
domain of evil and sin, by making every man a sinner
at his birth ; but they have also rendered the possibility of obtaining the Grace of God more difficult than
under the Old Dispensation, by making it entirely depen-
dent on *belief* in Jesus as the only son of God. Mr.
Montefiore offers the following remarks in his commentary on Matthew vii. 13, 14 :—" The horrible doctrine that many go to ' destruction ' and few to ' life
eternal ' was not invented by Jesus, but it was accepted
by him. One wonders how any man could hold it and
yet believe in a loving God ; but the human mind is
capable of the oddest inconsistencies " (*S.G.*, p. 550).

Why does Mr. Montefiore forget to give the original

sources whence Jesus took this painful doctrine ?   I
unhesitatingly assert that it is only in the New Testament where the doctrine is accepted without a protest.
I entirely dissent from Mr. Montefiore's estimate of
the apocalyptic Fourth Book of Ezra.   In order to
defend Jesus, is it fair to burden the author of this
apocalyptic book with this horrible doctrine of the
" many doomed " ?

Mr. Montefiore adds " that the second thought " (in
this passage of the Sermon on the Mount) " is that the
way of life is narrow, because few are to find it, because
many are predestined to ' eternal death,' a few only
to eternal life.   This later, gloomier, pessimistic, and
irreligious view is prominent in this book " (of Ezra)
(*S.G.*, p. 551).

Now this is an extremely unfair way of representing
the attitude of the author of Ezra (or Esdras, as he is
commonly called).   He certainly speaks of the wretched
condition of his people.   He laments their misfortunes,
and like Job, questions the ways of God with man.   He
asks why " many have been created but few will be
saved " ? (viii. 3).   He refuses to admit the justice of
this view, which was probably advocated by some of
his contemporaries.   Like a true son of Abraham, he
pleads with God for those doomed and lost.   Nowhere
in the Gospels do we find this splendid religious and
moral standpoint.   Did Jesus regret the fact that many
would be refused admission to the life to come ?   Mr.
Montefiore has failed to appreciate the intense sympathy
for sinners which the author of Esdras shows (see *Grace
of God*, pp. 28, 29).

I am prepared to admit that Matthew's " many
are called but few are chosen " (xxii. 14), finds a good

parallel in Esdras' " many have been created, but few will be saved " (viii. 3). There is, however, this vital difference. Matthew and Luke *accept* this doctrine as a divine decree, whereas Esdras *combats* this doctrine, and appeals to the divine love and justice. If Esdras has compassion for the " many doomed," how much more should God have compassion ? This is finely expressed in God's reply to the noble appeal of Esdras :— " For thou comest far short that thou shouldst be able to love my creature more than I " (viii. 47). Where is the like to be found in the Gospels ? Let Mr. Montefiore be zealous for Jesus, but let him be at least just to Esdras.

According to the Gospel, the coming Kingdom of God is the heritage of those blessed ones only for whom it has been prepared from the foundations of the world (Matt. xxv. 34 ; cf. xx. 23). Many receive the invitation to enter, but only a few are allowed to enter (Matt. xxii. 2–14 ; Luke xiv. 16–24). The privilege depends on a certain " constraint " on God's part (ibid. v. 23) ; the author of the choice is God and not man (Mark xiii. 20). It is the Heavenly Father who has chosen his elect (Luke xviii. 7 ; Matt. xxiv. 22, 24, 31 ; Mark xiii. 20–22) before the world, in accordance with his own good pleasure, distributing as he will of what is his own (Matt. xx. 14, 15), so that the effect of the call to enter the Kingdom is already predetermined (Matthew xiii. 38, 43). Moreover, all providence is ordered for the benefit of the elect (ibid. xxiv. 22), and they are guarded from falling away (ibid. 24), and, at the last day, are separated to their inheritance prepared for them from all eternity (ibid. xxv. 34). The initiative is at every point taken by God, and no question can be entertained

of precedent merit on the part of the recipients of the
blessings.   Therefore, Jesus is said to bring this new
Gospel to the " lost " (Luke xix. 10), to " sinners "
(Mark ii. 17), to " babes " (Matt. xi. 25 ; Luke x. 21).
These " elect " are to receive the divine favour just
because they have no merit (Matt. xx. 1–16), and because they have been chosen by God (Mark xiii. 20).
The Pharisees who were not lost, not sinners whom
Jesus came to seek, not babes, are to be excluded ; and
therefore Jesus gives his teaching a special form, so
that it may be veiled from the Pharisees to whom it is
not directed (Mark iv. 11).   Only those who believe in
Jesus are of " God " (John viii. 47).   In John this
" new " doctrine is pressed still further.

The advent of Jesus in the world introduces a crisis,
a sifting by which those who, because they believe in
Jesus, are of God, are *in* the world, but not *of* it (ibid.
xv. 19 ; and xvii. 14).   They are separated from the
Pharisees who are *of* the world, that is, of their father
the devil (viii. 44), who is the Prince of this world (xii.
31 ; xiv. 30 ; xvi. 11).   This difference between men
is not due (according to the New Testament) to men's
conduct in the world, but to the will of Jesus and God.
Jesus gives eternal life or the life in the Kingdom to
come, to whom he will (v. 21).   As no one can come to
him out of the evil world, except it be given him by
the will of God (vi. 65, cf. vi. 44), so all that God gives
him (vi. 37, 39) and only such (vi. 35) come into the
Kingdom.   Jesus has " his own in the world " (xiii.
1) ; his " chosen ones " (xiii. 18 ; xv. 16, 19) whom by
his direct will he has taken out of the world (xv. 19 ;
xvii. 6, 14, 16), and for these only is his intercession at
the throne of grace offered (xvii. 9), and to them only

is eternal life communicated (xvii. 2 ; cf. iii. 15, 36 ; v. 24 ; vi. 40, 54 ; viii. 12). I have made use of Dr. War-field's article on Predestination (Hastings' *D.B.*, iv. pp. 47 ff.) for much of the matter in this paragraph. If the Pharisee of the first century rejected this teaching, he has earned a better title than " hypocrite." His belief in monotheism with its " measure for measure " morality could not become reconciled with any theory of predestination. " As we sow—so we reap " was true in heaven as well as on earth, but nevertheless the divine justice is ever outweighed by the divine love on which the world is established. The sinner is still a child of God, and the gates of tears are never shut. To gain Paradise by believing in the creeds of the Church is the way of salvation in modern Christianity which tries to forget the doctrine of predestination. Judaism teaches that " the *righteous* of all races inherit the future bliss " (Tosephta Synhedrin, xiii, 2).

The next verse of the Sermon says : " Beware of false prophets, who come to you in sheep's clothing, but inwardly are ravening wolves " (Matt. vii. 15). This is generally understood as a warning against untrust-worthy leaders in religion. Luke has no parallel. Does the verse express the experience of the primitive Church ? Might it not be a warning against Paul and his fol-lowers ? We know from the Didache (xi. 3–12) that the itinerant prophets were a menace to the early Church. There are several Old Testament references in this verse. The basis of this verse and the next five verses in the Sermon is Deuteronomy (xviii. 22), which deals with false prophets. The criterion of the true prophet, according to Deuteronomy, is accuracy in pre-diction. Jesus certainly cannot be regarded as a pro-

phet for this very reason.   His predictions as to his
Parousia (return) and as to the coming of the Messianic
Kingdom were both unfulfilled.   Matthew speaks of
" false " prophets.   Jeremiah warns against " lying "
prophets (xiv. 14 ff.).   " Ravening wolves " (Matt.
vii. 15) may be paralleled by Ezekiel's description of
the wicked leaders of the people—prophets, priests, and
" princes in the midst thereof are like wolves ravening
the prey " (xxii. 27).   Warning is also directed against
the false prophets who wear the prophetic dress, and by
their appearance easily deceive the people (see Zech.
xiii. 4 : " neither shall (the prophets) wear a hairy
mantle to deceive ").   The " false prophets," says Dr.
Plummer, " can hardly refer to any but Scribes and
Pharisees ; but the saying is of far wider application "
(op. cit. p. 116).   Dean Savage says that this title (of
" false prophets ") is, of course, applied not to the
Pharisees alone, but to the whole class of self-constituted
religious dictators, of which the Pharisees were the
existing representatives (op. cit. p. 237).   This interpretation is invalid by reason of the fact that the Sermon
speaks of false *prophets*, who prophesy in the name of
Jesus (Matt. vii. 22).   The false prophets are Christians,
who are workers of lawlessness (ibid. v. 23).

We have already pointed out that the commentators
tend to improve the text of the Gospels by reading into
it their own fancies.   If Jesus, or the Evangelist, was
referring to the Pharisees, they would have been mentioned by name ; as so frequently occurs in the Gospels.
The fact that they are not mentioned indicates that they
are not referred to in this connexion.

LITERATURE

On ' The Two Ways ' see Professor G. Klein, *Der Älteste*

Christliche Katechismus, pp. 163 ff. On 'Freewill,' see Kohler's *Theologie*, chapter 37, and *Bibliography*, p. 359, and *Jewish Encyclopedia*, article 'Freedom of Will'; Kaufmann's *Geschichte der Attributenlehre* deals with this subject. The Jewish philosophers discuss the problem of Freewill, cf. *Emunoth vedeoth* iv. 7; *Kuzari* v. 19 f.; *More Nebuchim*, i. 23 and iii. 16–20, *Ikkarim* iv. i ff. On 'Predestination' in John, see Schlatter, *Der Glaube im N.T.* pp. 217 ff. On the 'Spring of Eternal Water' (see above, p. 241) cf. Trumbull, *The Threshold Covenant*, p. 115.

NOTE

The 'Two Ways' (see above, pp. 239 ff.) occurs in non-Jewish literature, see Dietrich, *Nekyia* (1893) p. 191, and Hastings' *D.C.G.*, ii. p. 447; and Clemen (op. cit. pp. 37 f.).

CHAPTER XIX

THE WISE AND FOOLISH BUILDERS

I HAVE to consider now the concluding verses of the epilogue (16–27). The first section (vv. 16–20) begins and ends with the same verse. The text is : " By their fruits ye shall know them. Do men gather grapes of thorns, or figs of thistles ? Even so every good tree bringeth forth good fruit ; but the corrupt tree bringeth forth evil fruit. A good tree cannot bring forth evil fruit, neither can a corrupt tree bring forth good fruit. Every tree that bringeth not forth good fruit is hewn down, and cast into the fire. Therefore by their fruits ye shall know them " (16–20). It is hardly necessary to point out that many of the expressions in these verses are to be found in the Old Testament. Genesis iii. 18, speaks of " thorns and thistles " as the useless products of mother-earth. At the other extreme we have, as the most precious gifts of nature, the grape and fig. Thus Joel (ii. 22) sings : " for the tree beareth her fruit, the fig tree and the vine do yield their strength."

This section of the Sermon is probably a later form of Matthew xii. 33–37, which teaches that the character of a man may be known from his conduct. Both passages in Matthew (vii. 16–20, and xii. 33–37) may, with advantage, be compared with the following section from *The Testaments of the Twelve Patriarchs :*—" Therefore if the soul take pleasure in the good (inclination), all its actions are in righteousness; and if it sin, it straightway repenteth. For, having its thoughts set upon righteousness, and casting away wickedness, it straightway overthroweth the evil and uprooteth the sin. But if it incline to the evil inclination, all its actions are in wickedness, and it driveth away the good, and cleaveth to the evil, and is ruled by Beliar; even though it work what is good, he perverteth it to evil. For whenever it beginneth to do good, he forces the issue of the action into evil for him, seeing that the treasure of the inclination is filled with an evil spirit" (Asher i. 6–9). Dr. Charles, *in loc.*, compares this last passage with Matthew xii. 35: "The evil man from out of his evil treasure bringeth forth evil things." The illustration from good and worthless trees (Matt. vii. 16–20) was probably well known to Jesus, or the Evangelist, as a current proverb. An excellent parallel occurs in Ecclesiasticus: "The fruit of a tree declareth the husbandry thereof; so is the utterance of the thought of a man's heart" (xxvii. 6). The prophet or leader is known by his teaching. A good teacher produces good results, just like a good tree. The test of character is conduct. Another parallel occurs in Slavonic Enoch: "Blessed is he who understands every work of the Lord and glorifies the Lord God; for the works of the Lord are just; and of the works of man some are good and others evil, and *by their works* those who have wrought them *are known*" (xlii. 14). There can be little doubt that Matthew knew this passage.

We have already seen other verses in the Sermon which have a remarkable likeness to sentences in Enoch. The Bible employs the metaphor about the good tree and the good fruit (see Jer. xvii. 8, and Ps. i. 3). Philo has, " God judges by the fruit of a tree, not by the root " (*On Curses*, § 6, M. ii. p. 433). The Rabbis also say " our fruits testify against us " (Genesis Rabba, xvi. 3 ; Yalkut Isa. vii., 2) ; and " the fruit of a righteous man is his good conduct " (Genesis Rabba, xxx. 6). Even in the Bible the " fruits " of a life are mentioned, e.g. Proverbs (xi. 30).

In Luke, the proverb about the " beam and mote " is immediately followed by the metaphor about the trees :—" For there is no good tree that bringeth forth corrupt fruit ; nor again a corrupt tree that bringeth forth good fruit. For each tree is known by its own fruit. For of thorns men do not gather figs, nor of a bramble bush gather they grapes " (vi. 43–44). This context enables us to see that Matthew has probably used Luke or his source. The false prophets condemned are followers of Paul. Loisy says that the false prophets are the same persons mentioned in the next section (Matt. vii. 21–23). They are certainly not Jews, but people who work miracles in the *name of Jesus* (*E.S.*, i. p. 637). Of course there are endless commentaries which refer this section to the Pharisees. Thus Holtzmann quotes B. Weiss' opinion that the entire section (Matt. vii. 16–20) is directed against the Pharisees, whose hypocrisy is condemned by the Sermon generally (*Hand-Commentar*, p. 126). Jülicher (ii. p. 161) holds that Jesus was thinking of the dangerous teachers about him, such as the Pharisees. Matthew, however, has in mind the evil elements in the Christian community. It is hardly likely that this passage contains the least reference to the Pharisees. The Gospels invariably mention them by name when they are denounced. The many marked instances of the feeling of intense abhorrence for the Pharisees which runs through Matthew, form part of his controversial programme. This feature sufficiently proves that his Gospel is a party pamphlet. Not only were the Pharisees the " opposition," there was also Paul, whose rising influence threatened the power of the " original apostles." Jülicher (op. cit. p. 161) is undoubtedly right in describing Matthew's attitude as attacking the evil elements in the Christian community. In Matthew's famous eschatological discourse (xxiv. 4, 5, 24) a similar standpoint is adopted. The disciples are warned not to be led astray by false prophets who come in the name of Jesus. No Pharisee would come in the name of Jesus, nor would he claim to be a prophet. The late date of this eschatological discourse makes it impossible for Jesus to have uttered the warning about false prophets either here or in the Sermon on the Mount (see *Enc. Bib.* cols. 1,857 and 1,887). This will be made clear from the next section (vv. 21–23) :—" Not every one that saith unto me, Lord, Lord, shall enter into the Kingdom of heaven ; but he that doeth the will of my Father who is in heaven. Many will say to me in that day, Lord, Lord, did we not prophesy by thy name, and by thy name cast out devils, and by thy name do many mighty works ? And then will I profess unto them, I never knew you : depart from me, ye that work iniquity." The last words are a quotation from Psalm vi. 8.

Matthew here follows the Septuagint, and retains the word $\dot{a}\nu o\mu\acute{\iota}a$ (lawlessness), while Luke (xiii. 27) replaces this word by $\dot{a}\delta\iota\kappa\acute{\iota}a$ (iniquity). Matthew alone uses $\dot{a}\nu o\mu\acute{\iota}a$. From his standpoint, "iniquity" was identi-

cal with transgressing the Law. The Jewish-Christian
reverence for the Torah was undoubtedly more in accord with the teaching of Jesus, than with Paul's antinomian attitude.   Luke represents in this respect Paul's
standpoint, and therefore he speaks of " iniquity " and
not of " lawlessness " (see *Grace of God*, p. 19).   The
parallel to this part of the Sermon in Luke xiii. (25–27)
follows the section dealing with the " narrow door."
The passage in Matthew (vii. 21–23) which we are now
considering belongs to the eschatological element in
the Gospels.   This is proved by the reference in verse 22
to " that day."   It corresponds to Isaiah :—" And the
Lord alone shall be exalted in *that day* " (ii. 11 and 17).
The phrase " did we not prophesy by thy name " (Matt.
vii. 22) is taken from Jeremiah's description of the false
prophets :—" the prophets prophesy lies in my name :
I sent them not, neither have I commanded them,
neither spake I unto them " (xiv. 14).

  " Lord," which is addressed to Jesus, is used as a
divine title in this passage.   This is shown by the use of
" thy name " (v. 22) as a means of invocation in per-
forming the miracles (see also Matt. xv. 22 ; xx. 30, 31
and 1 Cor. xii. 3).   Both Luke and Matthew picture the
final scene of the Last Judgment.   Jesus is the Judge,
and his countrymen (i.e. the Jews) will be condemned to
hell, while the Gentiles from the four quarters of the
earth will be admitted to the Kingdom.   The last paragraph of the Sermon remains to be considered :—" Every
one therefore which heareth these words of mine, and
doeth them, shall be likened unto a wise man, which built
his house upon the rock : and the rain descended, and the
floods came, and the winds blew, and beat upon that
house ; and it fell not : for it was founded upon the

S

rock. And every one that heareth these words of mine, and doeth them not, shall be likened unto a foolish man, which built his house upon the sand : and the rain descended, and the floods came, and the winds blew, and smote upon that house ; and it fell : and great was the fall thereof " (24–27).

This final section of Matthew's recension of the Sermon is based on the following passage in Ezekiel : " Because, even because, they have seduced my people, saying, Peace ; and there is no peace ; and when one buildeth up a wall, behold, they daub it with untempered mortar : say unto them which daub it with untempered mortar, that it shall fall : there shall be an overflowing shower ; and ye, O great hailstones, shall fall ; and a stormy wind shall rend it. Lo, when the wall is fallen, shall it not be said unto you, Where is the daubing wherewith ye have daubed it ? Therefore, thus saith the Lord God ; I will even rend it with a stormy wind in my fury, and there shall be an overflowing shower in mine anger, and great hailstones in fury to consume it. So will I break down the wall that ye have daubed with untempered mortar, and bring it down to the ground, so that the foundation thereof shall be discovered ; and it shall fall, and ye shall be consumed in the midst thereof " (xiii. 10–14).

The Parable of the Wise and Foolish Builders has also been considered to be an expansion of Proverbs x. 25 :—" When the whirlwind passeth, the wicked is no more : But the righteous is an everlasting foundation " (see Prov. i. 26–33 ; xii. 7 ; and xiv. 11). The point in the parable is the folly of a man who " heareth these words of mine and doeth them not." The cry of Israel at Sinai :—" All that the Lord hath spoken, we will do "

and hear (Exod. xix. 8) has been the teaching of Judaism throughout the ages. It protests against the teaching of the Gospel that men should rather hear the words
of Jesus and do them. The Old Testament emphatically
repudiates the right of any new teacher to abrogate the
divine Torah and to replace its teaching by a new
message (Isa. lix. 21, and Deut. xviii. 22). The Parable
in the Sermon (vii. 24–27) is in harmony with the teaching of the Rabbis, in condemning religious profession
of those who know, but do not practise. Simeon, son
of Rabban Gamaliel, said :—" Not learning but *doing*
is the groundwork " (Aboth i. 17). Jülicher (ii. p. 260)
inclines to the view that the parallel in Luke (vi. 47–49)
is more original than Matthew.

The text in Luke is as follows :—" Every one that
cometh unto me, and heareth my words, and doeth
them, I will shew you to whom he is like : he is like a
man building a house, who digged and went deep, and
laid a foundation upon the rock : and when a flood
arose, the stream brake against that house, and could
not shake it : because it had been well builded. But
he that heareth, and doeth not, is like a man that built
a house upon the earth without a foundation, against
which the stream brake, and straightway it fell in ; and
the ruin of that house was great " (vi. 47–49).

Matthew seems to expand Luke's story. Whereas
Luke speaks merely of " a man that built a house,"
Matthew speaks of " a wise man " and " a foolish man."
Again Luke's " stream " is changed by Matthew into
" rain, floods, and winds." In both Gospels this parable
forms the conclusion of the Sermon. There is a good
parallel to this parable in Aboth de Rabbi Nathan.
Elisha ben Abujah said : A man who does good deeds

and diligently studies the Law, to whom is he like ?
He is like a man building a house with a stone foundation and with tiles (on the roof) : and when a flood
arises, and breaks against the walls, that house cannot
be moved from its place. But the man who lives an
evil life, in spite of having deeply studied the Law, to
whom is he like ? He is like a man building a house
with tiles for a foundation and with heavy stones (on
the roof) : and when a little rain comes, straightway
that house falls in (chapter xxiv., ed. Schechter, p. 77).
This parable is followed by another : A man who lives
righteously and studies the Law is to be compared to
cement spread over (large) stones, so that when a flood
comes the cement will still remain. But a man who
lives an evil life, in spite of having studied the Law, is
to be compared to cement spread over tiles, so that even
if a little rain should fall the cement would be immediately dissolved (ibid.).

The question of priority of these parables has been
discussed by Bischoff (op. cit. p. 96) and by Jülicher
(op. cit. p. 267). Bischoff acknowledges that Elisha
ben Abujah belongs to the end of the first century.
This seems to me sufficient evidence to permit his parable
being quoted as a contemporary parallel. It is earlier
than the Gospels. Jülicher argues that Elisha's parable
seems to be more developed than Luke's, and is therefore later. He fails to compare the Jewish parable with
Matthew's, which, as we saw, is an expansion of Luke's
parable, and is also more fully developed than the Rabbinic parallel. Jülicher, however, suggests another
solution. There may have been a proverb current
among the Jews of the first century c.e., which was
used by Jesus and Elisha, each in his own way. So let

it be. The Jew need not turn to the Gospel for this parable, and the Christian need not go to Aboth de Rabbi Nathan for the lesson that practice is better than theory.

The last two verses of the seventh chapter speak of the impression produced by the teaching of Jesus. We are told that " the people were astonished at his teaching " (vii. 28). This cannot be authentic, at least in its present connexion. The Sermon on the Mount was not delivered to the people at large, but only to the disciples. Mr. Montefiore thinks that the teaching of Jesus " is fresher and more instinct with genius than that of the Rabbis, of whose teachings we have records, in Talmud and Midrash. It is more inspired. It is grander. It is more prophetic. It seems to claim ' authority,' just as the prophets claimed it, because they were convinced that their words were from God. Such a consciousness of inspiration Jesus also must have possessed " (S.G., p. 555). Our study of the Sermon does not enable us to echo Mr. Montefiore's eulogy. Is the teaching of Jesus " fresher and more instinct with genius " than that of Philo or of *The Testaments of the Twelve Patriarchs* ? Is Jesus more inspired than Hillel ? We are forced to answer both questions in the negative. Did any of the Jewish teachers base their instruction on a false assumption, as Jesus is reported to have done, in enunciating the Law of Love (Matt. v. 43) ? Did any Rabbi say : " Every one who heareth these words of *mine* and doeth them " shall be saved (vii. 24) ? Did they not rather speak of *God's* words ? This was the attitude of the prophets, to whom Jesus bears no likeness.

" Looking back over the whole Sermon," says Mr. Montefiore, " one feels that one may not unjustly regard it as a meeting-ground and bond of union between Christian and Jew. For if the Sermon on the Mount be the charter of Christianity, if it contains the main principles of the religion of Jesus, it also contains nothing which is essentially antagonistic to Judaism " (ibid.) I am not prepared to accept this standpoint. Christianity ignores the Sermon on the Mount. It is not its accepted charter. It is, to an extent, based on Jewish teaching, but it has in some instances violated the Jewish spirit. " Ye have heard that it hath been said " —" but I say unto you " (v. 33, 38, 43) imply the abrogation of the old Law of God and the introduction of the new Law of Jesus. This can hardly be said to be " nothing which is essentially antagonistic to Judaism." The Christian as well as the Jew should bear in mind the criticism of Jerome :—" *The verily I say unto you* of the New Testament has replaced the *Thus saith the Lord* of the Old." In Dr. Schechter's *Studies in Judaism* (second series) we have a Rabbinic parallel to Matthew's phrase, " Ye have heard—but I say," which runs, " You might understand a given passage or law to mean, or to mean only, so and so, therefore there is a teaching to say that " (see also *Jewish Quarterly Review*, xii. p. 427). Mr. Montefiore rightly objects to this interpretation as being unsuitable for all the examples in the Sermon on the Mount (*S.G.*, p. 499).

I am inclined to admit that all the teaching in the Sermon, which is in harmony with the spirit of Judaism, is a possible charter for a world religion which is content to reckon Jesus of Nazareth as one of the many teachers of humanity—less inspired than the prophets of the Old Testament—whose vision was that of an apocalyptic dreamer, whose message was eschatological and therefore of little practical value for everyday life. When humanity has learned and practised Hillel's negative form of the Golden Rule, it will be time to speak of the positive form enshrined in Ecclesiasticus and in the Sermon on the Mount. Let us remember that it is quite impossible to say how much of the Sermon goes back to Jesus.

Mr. Montefiore points out a few passages which are the "original portions of the Sermon on the Mount—i.e. those which do not harmonize with, or are not easily paralleled by, Rabbinic teaching" (op. cit. p. 556). These original portions are v. 10–12, 32, 38–48 ; vi. 6, 18, 33. In all eighteen verses. The first reference (v. 10–12) speaks of the happiness of people persecuted for *Jesus'* sake. This is surely less beautiful and less religious than being persecuted for *God's* sake (Kiddush Ha-shem). There is also a statement in verse 12, which, as we have already seen, is prejudiced and unfair— " for so persecuted they the prophets who were before you." The next *original* passage is v. 32, which permits divorce only in the case of adultery. This text is contradicted by Mark (x. 2–12), which prohibits divorce for any cause. Again the text in Matthew was the standpoint of the School of Shammai, and therefore cannot be called " original." The third reference (38–48) deals with the *Lex talionis*, non-resistance and the Law of Love. We have already shown that all that is of practical value in this teaching was current among the Jews before the time of Jesus and the Gospels. Mr. Montefiore considers vi. 6, which deals with " secret prayer," as another original element. We have seen that the Rabbis also laid stress on private and secret prayer. The Church, and the Synagogue too, appreciate public prayer. The same criticism applies to fasting (v. 18). The last passage, which Mr. Montefiore considers to be original is (vi. 33) : " Seek ye first his Kingdom and his righteousness, and all these things shall be added unto you." Mr. Montefiore admits (op. cit. p. 544) the possibility of this verse having been modified by the editor. We saw that Luke's version is more original. We also noted that Pfleiderer considers Matthew's alteration of the original rigorism in Luke, as pointing in the direction of those " counsels of perfection " which meant a compromise between the new teaching and its practical working. Be this as it may, we cannot consider the saying, whether in Luke or in Matthew, as an original contribution to religious teaching. Amos and Philo have the same lesson. We do not deny that there are a few original sayings. Thus Matt. v. 22, makes a man liable to the Gehenna of fire if he call his brother a fool. Is it then permitted to call one's brother a hypocrite, or the child of the devil, or one of the brood of vipers ? Vituperation seems to be a marked characteristic of the Gospel teaching. Quite strange and un-Jewish is the use of " dog and swine " as terms of reproach applied to the heathens (vii. 6). The *acceptance* of the doctrine of the " narrow gate " is also original (vii. 13, 14.)

Quite contrary to the spirit of Judaism is the principle of non-resistance, inculcated by the Sermon (v. 39). Equally un-Jewish is the asceticism demanded by Jesus (v. 29, 30). The principle of having no care for worldly things (vi. 25–34) is also original. In all these cases Judaism prefers to adhere to her old paths, and for this reason the Sermon on the Mount cannot be regarded as the ideal meeting-ground and bond of union between

Jew and Christian. This is not to condemn the teaching of the Sermon. It has its part to play in the religious training of the world. The Gentiles have not displayed any desire to accept the heavy yoke of God's Kingdom (i.e. the Torah). Instead, they have gladly exchanged this old Law for the new Law of the Gospel that offers an easy yoke to all who are willing to *believe* in the claims of Jesus. No Jew could possibly admit these claims, which involve (1) his right to abrogate the Divine law, (2) his power to forgive sins, (3) the efficacy of his vicarious atonement, and (4) his ability to reveal God the Father of man to whomsoever he will. Underlying these stupendous claims is the belief in the divinity of Jesus and his unique divine sonship. There was nothing to be urged against all these claims on the part of a heathen in the year 33 C.E. Then, as now, the Jew has refused to admit the validity of these claims. They are contrary to the specific teaching of the Old Testament, and are therefore rejected by Israel. Nevertheless, the Jew admits that Jesus, the Gospels and Christianity have been of the greatest benefit to non-Jewish people. The same applies to Mohammed, the Koran and Islam. According to Maimonides, both of these daughter-religions have been providentially sent into the world to prepare the way for the coming Messianic age (Hilchoth Melachim xi. 4 ; cf. Kuzari iv. 23 and Nachmanides, Derasha, ed. Jellinek, p. 5). We do not fail to recognize that there is a very large common ground that brings Jew and Christian together. If the Gospels divide the Jew from the Christian, the Old Testament unites them. God the Father of all is also admitted by Christians to be the God of Israel, as well as the God to whom Jesus cried : " My God, My God, why hast thou forsaken me ? " (Matt. xxvii. 46). We have seen that even in the Gospels there is a considerable Jewish element. Four-fifths of the Sermon on the Mount is exclusively Jewish. These facts have been recognized by the Rabbis, who in the early Middle Ages proclaimed the Christians to be Gerê Toshab (i.e. proselytes of the Gate ; see Isaac b. Sheschet, Response 119). Judaism has repeatedly declared that Christians are not to be identified with *Nochrim* or *Goyim* (heathens ; cf. Chulin, 13*b*, and Tosaphot, Aboda Zara, 2*a*, and Tosaphot, Bechoroth, 2*b*). Israel has not forgotten that his mission is to cause all the families of the earth to be blessed through his medium. Israel is the hedge guarding the garden of humanity (Exodus Rabba, ii. § 5). Israel gave the world the belief in one Heavenly Father, the precious word of God enshrined in the Hebrew Scriptures and the belief in the coming Messianic age, when universal peace will unite all men in the universal brotherhood, and Jew and Christian will forget their differences in the great joy that each will have found in the other his brother and friend. Shall *we* see the dawn of this day of true religion ? Then shall God return to Zion, and the Redeemer will come to lead men to the everlasting light of truth and love.

LITERATURE

On ' Relation of Jew to Christian,' see Zunz, *Gesammelte Schriften* i. pp. 65–67 ; Kohler, *Theologie*, pp. 313 ff. ; Hermann Cohen, *Die Nächstenliebe im Talmud ;* E. Grünebaum, *Die Sittenlehre des Judenthums* (Mannheim, 1867), pp. 230 ff. and L. Philippson, *Die Entwickelung der religiösen Idee im Judenthume, Christenthume und Islam.*

INDEX OF SUBJECTS AND NAMES

T

U

INDEX OF PASSAGES

J. INDEX OF HEBREW WORDS